Party On!

Party On!

*Political Parties from Hamilton and
Jefferson to Today's Networked Age*

John Kenneth White
Matthew R. Kerbel

OXFORD
UNIVERSITY PRESS

OXFORD
UNIVERSITY PRESS

Oxford University Press, Inc., publishes works that further
Oxford University's objective of excellence in research, scholarship,
and education.

Oxford New York
Auckland Cape Town Dar es Salaam Hong Kong Karachi
Kuala Lumpur Madrid Melbourne Mexico City Nairobi
New Delhi Shanghai Taipei Toronto

With offices in
Argentina Austria Brazil Chile Czech Republic France Greece
Guatemala Hungary Italy Japan Poland Portugal Singapore
South Korea Switzerland Thailand Turkey Ukraine Vietnam

Library of Congress Cataloging-in-Publication Data available

ISBN 978-0-19-994610-5

For our daughters, Jeannette White and Gabrielle Kerbel

Contents

Preface

A s the United States heads into the 2012 presidential election cycle, an outside observer might be forgiven for believing that the vaunted American two-party system is in trouble. Divided government, hyper-polarized factionalism, a total lack of bipartisanship, considerable public dissatisfaction with the Democratic and Republican parties, and an insurgent Tea Party and Occupy Wall Street "movements"—all bespeak challenges to the traditional party politics that distinguish American government.

This book builds its premise on a foundation of bedrock principles essential to understanding the nature of American political parties. First, parties arose out of the practice of politics, not out of Constitutional decree. Parties have been contentious and controversial from the beginning—going all the way back to philosophical debates between Alexander Hamilton and Thomas Jefferson at the founding of the nation and persisting up to today. We bring these debates alive throughout this book and show how they play out in contemporary political contexts.

We also show how party politics in America have developed over time, from the Federalists and Anti-Federalists to the Democrats and Republicans of today. Parties have not remained stagnant or monolithic, and they continue to demonstrate flexibility and adaptability—especially when it comes to the media and mechanisms they employ to mobilize voters and conduct the business of government.

From the penny press to the Internet, parties have exercised new technologies throughout history and, in some cases, have been instrumental in spurring or recreating them. This book focuses on the ways in which political parties have engaged with information and outreach and continue to expand their influence in ingenious new ways.

The premise of this book is that, despite superficial appearances and popular misconceptions, political parties are not only alive and well in American politics—they are virtually (and actually) indestructible. So, love them or hate them, you are invited to the party of American government: neither Democratic nor Republican but an indomitable competitive system emulated the world over even as it is challenged on the home front with every electoral season. *Party on!*

Acknowledgments

Writing a book incurs more than the usual number of obligations, and this work is no exception. Both of us have many people to thank. We are indebted to Dean James J. Greene of the Catholic University of America for approving our requests from the Catholic University of America Research Foundation. These requests enabled us to hire Anne Roan Thomas to assist with the preparation of the manuscript, which she did with her usual expert care. We are deeply indebted to Jennifer Knerr, the executive editor at Paradigm Publishers, for sharing our vision of making the story of American political parties accessible to students and readers alike. We appreciate her persistent prodding and careful editing that helped make this book a better one. We are also indebted to the staff at Paradigm for their constant support and encouragement. We are especially beholden to the journalists and the many participants from both major parties who have freely given their time to speak to our students and, in the process, have helped us gain valuable insights into today's politics.

As always, we remain beholden to our families who have patiently tolerated the countless hours we have put into the book. Our wives, Yvonne and Adrienne, remain a constant source of love and support—and we could not have done this without them. We dedicate this book to our children, Jeannette White and Gabrielle Kerbel, who share their parents' affection for our political system and its rich history. We are confident that they will continue to follow the story of American politics long after our work here is done.

We complete this book at a moment when many Americans are disillusioned with our politics. Following the tragic wounding of Congresswoman Gabrielle Giffords, and the killing of several others in Tucson, Arizona in January 2011, President Barack Obama spoke at a memorial service. There, he reminded his listeners of a nine-year-old child, Christina Taylor Green, who perished in the attack. President Obama said, "I want to live up to her expectations. I want our democracy to be as good as Christina imagined it. I want America to be as good as she imagined it. All of us—we should do everything we can to make sure this country lives up to our children's expectations."[1]

We share President Obama's desire to live up to our children's expectations. The history of American parties is one of constant adaptation and renewal. Today, both parties need to reinvent themselves so that they can live up to our (and our children's) expectations. This book is the story of how we arrived at the present moment. The rest, as they say, is up to us.

Introduction

Of Elephants and Donkeys, Candidates and Institutions, Patriots and Progressives

I t was Election Eve and the presidential candidate was going home to cast his ballot. After months of campaign events and countless miles in the air, this would be his last campaign flight. Accompanied by his wife, immediate staff, and a pool of journalists, the weary candidate wondered aloud about his fate. The mood was tense but hopeful as the flight crew served champagne and shrimp cocktail, and the candidate's entourage ate pensively as the airplane worked its way west. Finally, the candidate's wife broke the ice and asked the campaign's traveling pollster, "Are we *really* going to win tomorrow?" The reply was a simple, yet understated, "Yes, we are really going to win."[1]

So it was aboard Ronald Reagan's campaign plane on November 3, 1980. A day later Reagan received 51 percent of the votes cast, compared to incumbent president Jimmy Carter's 41 percent, and independent candidate John Anderson's 6.6 percent. In the all-important Electoral College, Reagan's victory was even bigger: 489 votes to Carter's 49. Reagan's coattails stretched to nearly every other contest. Republicans won every close U.S. Senate race, giving them control of that body for the first time since 1952. In the House of Representatives, Republicans gained 35 seats, leaving the Democrats with a paper majority, but one tempered by Reagan's ability to woo conservative Southern Democrats to his cause. Surrounded by all this good news, Republicans broke open their champagne corks while morose Democrats drank to forget.

But Reagan's victory wasn't necessarily a Republican one. Eight years earlier, a leading Washington journalist, reflecting the conventional wisdom of the time, declared that political parties were officially dead. In *The Party's Over*, David S. Broder set forth an unsparing diagnosis of the many ailments afflicting what remained of the once grand old parties: "My view is that American politics is at an impasse, that we have been spinning our wheels for a long, long time; and that we are going to dig ourselves ever deeper into trouble, unless we find a way to develop some political traction and move again."[2] Broder was hardly alone in his downbeat diagnosis. Around the time Reagan was flying on his campaign plane, political scientist Everett C. Ladd expressed the prevailing consensus that "all the anchors are being raised at the same moment in American politics, and the electoral ship is drifting as never before."[3]

With the electoral ship adrift, Reagan's victory seemed like a personal, not a partisan, triumph. Thus, when political scientist Wilson Carey McWilliams was asked to describe the meaning of the election, his succinct answer was, "It didn't mean much."[4] Even Reagan's own pollster, Richard B. Wirthlin, was cautious: "I don't believe that this is a realigning election. Partisan identification remained relatively stable. However, the size of the margin [for Reagan] and the issues that are raised concerning leadership may condition the possibility of a future realignment, if the Reagan administration is successful in achieving some of its objectives."[5]

The returns seemed to bolster the argument that Reagan's charismatic persona had won the presidency for him: One in four Democrats deserted their party for Reagan; partisan control of the executive and congressional branches was divided, as congressional candidates seemed to win on their own merits. As one Republican famously put it before the Reagan era began, the GOP was akin to "a Hertz car we all rent around election time."[6] Once Election Day was past, the party was discarded for another two or four years. Democrats comforted themselves into thinking they could still win their share of contests, even if they could not penetrate Reagan's Teflon-coated presidency. Shortly after losing the presidency in the 1984 Reagan landslide, Democratic presidential nominee Walter Mondale blamed his loss on Reagan's charming persona and ability to communicate. "Modern politics," Mr. Mondale said, "requires television," adding,

"I think you know I've never really warmed up to television, and in fairness to television, it's never really warmed up to me."[7]

The creation of a more personal, imperial-like presidency posed a unique threat to the American party system.[8] Some 50 years before, the American Political Science Association issued a stern warning should the parties find themselves in such a weakened position that a president could easily overpower them:

> When the President's program actually is the sole program ... , either his party becomes a flock of sheep or the party falls apart. In effect, this concept of the presidency disperses the party system by making the President reach directly for the support of a majority of the voters. It favors a President who exploits skillfully the arts of demagoguery, who sees the whole country as his political backyard, and who does not mind turning into the embodiment of personal government.[9]

Twenty-eight years to the day that Ronald Reagan captured the presidency, a similar scene played itself out on another candidate's campaign plane. As the aircraft hurtled to a last-minute Election Day rally in a toss-up state, the candidate and his entourage were focused on the same question that Nancy Reagan posed to her campaign's pollster decades before: "Are we *really* going to win tomorrow?" The answer was the same as it was in 1980, but still the tension lingered. The candidate confided to his chief political strategist, "I think we're going to win, but if we don't I'll be at peace. We've run as good a campaign as you can run, and if it isn't there, it isn't there."[10] At a final rally, the candidate's supporters sensed victory and exuded hope. Said one, "We are one day, one moment, from the rebirth of our very nation."[11]

Wandering amidst the throngs of reporters and campaign workers, Barack Obama would make no official predictions, except to say, "You know, whatever happens, it's extraordinary you guys have shared this process with us, and I just want to say thank you and I appreciate you." Obama gave a birthday kiss to a young photographer, shook hands with the aircrew, and said, "OK, guys, let's go home," adding, "It will be fun to see how the story ends."[12] With that, the aircrew handed out bottles of red wine to those onboard, and the plane carrying the future president was on its way homeward.[13] Meanwhile, the mood on the John McCain campaign plane was gloomy. When the candidate asked, "How many are we down by?" a dispirited senior advisor responded, "Let's not talk about that tonight."[14]

And as Barack Obama's victory became clear, the 2008 election began to assume a deep significance. In his concession speech, John McCain stated the obvious: "This is an historic election, and I recognize the special significance it has for African Americans and for the special pride that must be theirs tonight."[15] Obama agreed, noting that the results of the election ratified the essence of the American Dream: "If there is anyone out there who still doubts that America is a place where all things are possible, who still wonders if the dream of our founders is alive in our time, who still questions the power of our democracy, tonight is your answer."[16] In the glow of the moment, both candidates sought to set the outcome of the 2008 race above partisan interests.

Many agreed with the notion that the election of the first African American president put the election of 2008 into a different category: one that eschewed partisanship and focused on the country's aspirations of equality of opportunity for all. John Lewis, a civil rights hero of the 1960s who had been badly beaten by the Alabama state police in a civil rights march, said of Obama's victory, "We have witnessed tonight in America a revolution of values, a revolution of ideals. There's been a transformation of America, and it will have unbelievable influence on the world."[17] Jesse Jackson, another civil rights leader from the same era, remarked, "I'd like for those nameless, faceless martyrs [of the 1960s] to show up for just one night, to know they were redeemed tonight."[18] When Obama's victory was made official by the television networks, Michelle Obama turned to her husband and declared, "You are the forty-fourth president of the United States. Wow. What a country we live in."[19]

Obama's victory was not just a ratification of American ideals. It was a decisive political win. Obama won 53 percent of the ballots cast—the highest percentage for a Democrat since Lyndon B. Johnson in 1964—and he beat Republican John McCain by more than 10 million votes. In the Electoral College, Obama captured 365 electoral votes to McCain's 173. Democrats padded their congressional majorities, adding 20 more House seats to the 31 they had already accumulated just two years before. And, after a long recount in Minnesota, the Democratic Party secured a filibuster-proof 60-vote majority in the Senate.

But Obama's sweep was very different from Ronald Reagan's 28 years before. While Reagan had amassed considerable support from Democrats and independents, Obama's victory was a thoroughly partisan one. For all his talk of bipartisanship and joining Republican Red States with Democratic Blue States in a common enterprise,

Obama won only 9 percent support from Republicans, while gathering an overwhelming 89 percent support from Democrats. And for all the conservative carping about John McCain's maverick tendencies, he still won 90 percent of Republican ballots, while only 1 in 10 Democrats bolted their party to support him.[20] Far from being declared dead, partisanship had been resuscitated. Many came to heed Ronald Reagan's thinking about partisanship: "A political party isn't a fraternity. It isn't something like the old school tie you wear. You band together in a political party because of certain beliefs of what government should be."[21] The result was more partisan voting, more money being contributed to aspiring office seekers, stronger party organizations (especially at the national level), and more party-line voting in the halls of Congress and elsewhere.

There were many reasons for the partisan revival. One of them was the Internet. A dozen years before Obama's 2008 victory, the Internet was a campaign curiosity. In an infamous lapse during a 1996 presidential debate, Republican Bob Dole implored voters to visit his website, but, inexplicably, gave the wrong address. Now organizing on the Internet has given rise to a "netroots" phenomenon that was indispensable to Obama's success. Just as the party machines of yesteryear had organized urban precincts, the Internet has become a social tool for bringing together voters of like-minded persuasions. Put another way, in just a few short years, the Internet has moved politics from a one-way conversation from candidates to voters (in which candidates implored backers for money) into a two-way conversation where Americans can answer back using blogs and bucks.

The latter was especially important in 2008, as Obama raised an unprecedented $745 million, mostly via Internet donations.[22] Obama's unprecedented success in raising more money than ever before in U.S. history left the public financing rubric of presidential elections in tatters—an era that began in the 1970s when everyone was sure that partisanship was over and that the parties would be dependent on federal regulation and protections provided in the laws for their survival. Steve Schmidt, who served as John McCain's chief strategist in 2008, believes that any successful Republican presidential candidate in 2012 must raise close to $1 billion. The consequence of that fact, he adds, is that "public financing is over."[23]

Other aspects of the 2008 election also had echoes in a partisan past. Back in 1800, when the nation had its first truly contested presidential election, the two parties of the day—the Federalists and the Democratic-Republicans—controlled the major newspapers, particularly in Philadelphia where citizens could choose either *The Gazette of the United States* (Federalist) or the *Aurora* (Democratic-Republican). These newspapers did not just tell the story of major events, they gave an undeniably partisan cast as to how voters should think about them. Today, newspaper readership has declined considerably, as fewer Americans turn the news pages with their ink-stained hands. Internet blogs have become the partisan papers of our time, as readers turn to their favorite websites—not always to seek new ideas, but to ratify opinions and biases they already possess. Partisan websites—whether they are sympathetic to the Democratic or Republican parties—have become the means by which ever-larger numbers of Americans participate in an electronic public square.

In the wake of the 2008 election, we have also seen the emergence of "Tea Party" voters. Not a political party in a formal sense, the Tea Party has come to define the opposition to President Obama and his agenda, as Tea Party enthusiasts advocate—sometimes very vocally—for a program of less government involvement in everyday life, which they believe is essential to maintaining personal liberty. Evoking Revolutionary-era patriots, the Tea Party is the functional expression of a conservative agenda that finds itself most at home in the Republican Party, and the ability of the Tea Party to mobilize successfully against Republicans who deviate from their agenda has made them a potent force in Republican politics. Partly a grassroots movement and partly organized by elites, the Tea Party now shares the public square with netroots activists on the progressive Left, who operate within but at times in opposition to the Democratic Party, which, like their counterparts on the Right, is at times perceived as deviating from movement goals. Greater partisanship, and at times paralysis, is the consequence of these core groups constraining the parties from engaging each other on terms their respective base supporters do not accept.

How did this happen? How did we go from the early days of the Reagan era, where parties were declared all but dead, to the Obama era, where both academics and partisans alike acknowledge a revival of sometimes uncompromising partisanship? One reason is the perpetual arguments of U.S. politics, conversations begun by Alexander Hamilton and Thomas Jefferson two centuries ago. Back then, Hamilton and Jefferson asked and answered very differently questions that persist to this day:

◆ How do we limit our freedoms and still possess them?
◆ How much government should we have, and when is it too excessive?

♦ When do we need a national government to act in the interests of all of our citizens?

♦ When is it appropriate to leave matters to local customs and practices?

For two centuries, Democrats and Republicans have battled over Alexander Hamilton's concept of a national family of Americans who are inextricably tied to one another (which means a strong role for the federal government) and Thomas Jefferson's preference for lightly governed local communities (which necessitates a more modest role for the federal government). Our varied responses to this ongoing dispute between these two conceptions of America say much about who we are and what kind of government (and society) we want at any given moment.

This book tells the roller-coaster story of political parties, once iron-clad institutions that eroded over time to the point where they were counted out, only to revive and adapt to new and different challenges. Chapter 1 describes the emergence of the arguments developed by Thomas Jefferson and Alexander Hamilton about the appropriate scope and nature of the federal government, which, as we will see, reverberated through the long history of political parties in America, and which provide the backdrop for the discussion in this book. Chapter 2 details the first century of that history, and explores how parties developed a uniquely American character while adapting to new times and technologies. Chapter 3 takes this history into the twentieth and twenty-first centuries, focusing on forces that molded party organizations into powerful institutions at the turn of the former century and on forces that eroded and then helped rebuild them at the turn of the latter. Chapter 4 describes the evolution in how parties choose their presidential candidates, with an emphasis on nomination politics in today's interconnected age. Chapter 5 notes how party loyalties strengthen during periods of realignment (when a particular party can claim an enduring majority) and erode during periods of dealignment (when independent voters become decisive in elections). Chapter 6 explores the way parties have been challenged by the emergence of social media. Chapter 7 notes the importance of money in politics, explores the state of campaign finance laws, and examines how the social networking tools of the Internet are revolutionizing fundraising. Chapter 8 examines the role of the party in government, including the newly strengthened congressional campaign committees. Chapter 9 looks at the role of third parties in U.S. history and notes that at key junctures they have helped the major parties adjust to changing public demands. Chapter 10 notes that the cumulative effect of these trends is a strengthening of national parties—a triumph for Alexander Hamilton in his eternal argument for a binding national force that could override Thomas Jefferson's preference for a more localized partisanship.

Individual presidential elections, like those of 1980 and 2008, may stand out because their results endure over time. But the saga of the U.S. party system remains a fascinating story for more than these moments, because parties are always evolving as institutions. With each election we learn not only about how the two major parties address the eternal questions of politics, but how we, as Americans, give different answers to them at key moments in our history. The story of this evolution is the story of this book.

1

Political Parties in an American Setting

The Framers of the U.S. Constitution were well versed in the writings of Aristotle, Locke, Montesquieu, and other democratic thinkers. From their extensive reading of history, they understood the dangers of unchecked ambition and the necessities of free speech and minority protections so vital in creating a representative democracy. The tripartite system of government they created—consisting of a president, Congress, and judiciary—has endured with only modest revisions to their original work. In the two centuries since the U.S. Constitution was ratified, those who have inhabited the presidential offices have sung its praises. For example, upon leaving the presidency in 1796, George Washington urged that the Constitution "be sacredly maintained—that its administration in every department may be stamped with wisdom and virtue."[1] Forty-two years later, Abraham Lincoln told the Springfield, Illinois, Young Men's Lyceum that the Constitution should become "the political religion of the nation."[2]

However, while the Framers realized great success in establishing political institutions, they struggled with how to organize elections. Popular, democratic elections were a novel experiment that many believed could not happen without widespread turmoil and violence.

One Massachusetts delegate to the Constitutional Convention in Philadelphia contended that the "evils we experience flow from the excess of democracy."[3] Alexander Hamilton agreed: "The people are turbulent and changing; they seldom judge or determine right."[4] By the late twentieth century, however, the "excess of democracy" had become universal. The last time the U.S. Census Bureau counted, there were 511,039 popularly elected officials. Of these, 491,669 held local positions; 18,828 were state officeholders, with half of them serving as administrative officials and judges.

The Constitution's Framers were skeptical of political parties, thinking of them as factions to be avoided. So it was to their great astonishment that political parties proved to be the agents that made the document's provisions and the complex system of elections work. Parties afforded a way of organizing elections, legitimizing opposition, and guaranteeing peaceful transitions of power. Once in office, they helped elected officials work together and bridged some of the differences between and among government institutions. One might assume, therefore, that political parties would be welcome instruments of governance. Quite the contrary. For more than 200 years, Americans have steadfastly refused to embrace party-led government—preferring instead that their leaders act in a nonpartisan manner. In 1956, John F. Kennedy wrote a Pulitzer Prize–winning book, *Profiles in Courage,* which extolled those who placed conscience above party.[5] In 2002, Kennedy's daughter, Caroline, published a sequel to her late father's work titled *Profiles in Courage for Our Time.*[6] Both of these books captured a widespread public desire to put policymaking above partisanship. In one poll conducted prior to the 2010 midterm elections, 84 percent of respondents said they would cast their congressional ballots based on a candidate's issue positions, character, and resume. Only 11 percent said that a candidate's political party would determine their vote.[7]

Given the widespread public ambivalence directed at all political parties since the country's founding, it should come as no surprise that American parties have struggled to find their rightful place. The "solutions" to this dilemma have varied from place to place and time to time. For example, parties acquired a degree of public approval at the end of the nineteenth century as America entered the Industrial Age. After the first decade of the twenty-first century, parties have had to search for a place in a new, postindustrial, computer-centric era.

This book explores the evolution and role of political parties in America, and the remainder of this chapter sets the foundation for that discussion. We start by looking at the love-hate relationship

Americans have with parties and how this has influenced party development. Next, we address what roles parties play and how they differ from other players in the political system. The chapter ends with a discussion of the disparate perspectives on political parties held by Hamilton and Jefferson, which will help to structure much of the discussion in this book.

POLITICAL PARTIES: INSTITUTIONS AMERICANS LOVE TO HATE

The Founding Fathers were elitists who wanted to minimize the role citizens would play in choosing their officeholders. They were especially fearful of political parties, arguing that it was necessary, in Madison's words, to "break and control the violence of faction [meaning parties and other special interest groups]."[8] James Madison, George Washington, Alexander Hamilton, John Adams, and Thomas Jefferson all believed that an enlightened citizenry would have no use for parties. Instead of parties, Madison hoped that other mediating institutions would "refine and enlarge the public views by passing them through the medium of the chosen body of citizens, whose wisdom may best discern the true interest of their country and whose patriotism and love of justice will be least likely to sacrifice it to temporary or partial conditions."[9] Madison believed that a multitude of interests would proliferate through continental expansion, thus making the development of large, mass-based parties virtually inconceivable: "You make it less probable that a majority of the whole will have a common motive to invade the rights of other citizens; or if such a common motive exists, it will be more difficult for all who feel it to discover their own strength and to act in unison with each other."[10]

Madison's belief that parties were unsuited filters for mass expressions of public opinion was based on his reading of history. He thought that human beings were emotional creatures, embracing different religions and political leaders with a zealotry that usually resulted in chaos and violence. Most of Madison's contemporaries agreed, and they scorned political parties as vehicles that would, inevitably, ignite uncontrollable political passions. George Washington, for example, was especially critical of partisan demagogues whose objective, he claimed, was not to give people the facts from which they could make up their own minds, but to make them followers instead of thinkers. In an early draft of a 1792 speech renouncing a second term (it was never delivered when he had a change of heart), Washington maintained that "we are all children of the same country ... [and] that our interest, however diversified in local and smaller matters, is the same in all the great and essential concerns of the nation."[11] Determined to make good on his intention to leave office in 1796, Washington issued his famous farewell address, in which he admonished his fellow citizens to avoid partisanship at any cost:

> Let me ... warn you in the most solemn manner against the baneful effects of the spirit of party.... It exists under different shapes in all governments, more or less stifled, controlled, or repressed; but, in those of the popular form, it is seen in its greatest rankness and is truly their worst enemy. The alternate domination of one faction over another, sharpened by the spirit of revenge natural to party dissension, which in different ages and countries has perpetrated the most horrid enormities, is itself a frightful despotism.... [The spirit of party] agitates the community with ill-founded jealousies and false alarms; kindles the animosity of one part against another; ferments occasional riot and insurrection. It opens the door to foreign influence and corruption, which finds a facilitated access to the government through the channels of party passions.[12]

Washington was hardly alone in admonishing partisanship. Six years before Washington's famous farewell and prior to the end of the Revolutionary War, John Adams bemoaned the drift of the country's elites toward party politics: "There is nothing I dread so much as a division of the Republic into two great parties, each arranged under its leader and converting measures in opposition to each other."[13] Abigail Adams, observing the effects of partisan attacks on her husband during his presidency, wrote, "Party spirit is blind, malevolent, un-candid, ungenerous, unjust, and unforgiving."[14] James Monroe, the nation's fifth chief executive, urged his backers to obliterate all party divisions. When Abraham Lincoln sought reelection in 1864 under the newly created National Union banner, half a million pamphlets were published bearing titles such as "No Party Now but All for Our Country."[15]

The danger of faction against which the Framers warned still resonates with most Americans. During the 1992 presidential campaign, when a small group of registered voters was asked what the two parties meant to them, two shouted "corruption!" Others used words like "rich," "self-serving," "good-old-boy networks," "special interests," "bunch of lost causes," "lost sheep," "immorality," "going whatever way is on top," and "liars."[16] Other polls confirm the public scorn for party politics. When asked in 2006 to describe the nature of corruption in Washington, D.C., 39 percent said it was caused by bad apples in both parties enriching themselves; 23 percent blamed big corporations; 19 percent identified corporate lobbyists and bribes as the problem; 16 percent said it was caused by one party having too much power and becoming arrogant and overreaching.[17]

Even party leaders seem skeptical about a place for parties in the American setting. In the keynote address that launched Barack Obama's national career at the 2004 Democratic National Convention, the future president spoke of the ills that stem from dividing the country into partisan groups:

> The pundits like to slice and dice our country into Red States and Blue States; Red States for Republicans, Blue States for Democrats. But I've got news for them. We worship an awesome God in the Blue States, and we don't like federal agents poking around our libraries in the Red States. We coach Little League in the Blue States and have gay friends in the Red States. There are patriots who opposed the war in Iraq and patriots who supported it. We are one people, all of us pledging allegiance to the stars and stripes, all of us defending the United States of America.[18]

Because this message resonates with so many people, political figures often find it advantageous to downplay political labels. Seeking reelection in 1972, Richard Nixon instructed his staff not to include the word Republican in any of his television advertisements or campaign brochures. Four years later, Gerald R. Ford was bluntly told by his advisors not to campaign for Republican candidates lest his support erode among independents and ticket splitters.[19] Campaigning for the presidency in 2000, George W. Bush mentioned the Republican Party just twice in accepting its nomination.[20] Democratic candidate Al Gore never mentioned his party in his acceptance speech.[21]

Students of political parties, however, have a much higher regard for them than do politicians and the public. In his book *The American Commonwealth*, published in 1888, James Bryce began a tradition of scholarly investigation of political parties by devoting more than 200 pages to the subject. His treatment was laudatory: "Parties are inevitable. No free large country has been without them. No one has shown how representative government could be worked without them. They bring order out of chaos to a multitude of voters."[22] More than a century later, scores of other academicians agree with Bryce. In a 1996 amicus curiae (friend-of-the-court) brief filed with the U.S. Supreme Court, the Committee for Party Renewal, a bipartisan group of political scientists, summarized the views held by most party scholars:

> Political parties play a unique and crucial role in our democratic system of government. Parties enable citizens to participate coherently in a system of government allowing for a substantial number of popularly elected offices. They bring fractured and diverse groups together as a unified force, provide a necessary link between the distinct branches and levels of government, and provide continuity that lasts beyond terms of office. Parties also play an important role in encouraging active participation in politics, holding politicians accountable for their actions, and encouraging debate and discussion of important issues.[23]

Without parties, the Committee for Party Renewal claimed that civic life would be reduced to "a politics of celebrities, of excessive media influence, of political fad-of-the-month clubs, of massive private financing by various 'fat cats' of state and congressional campaigns, of gun-for-hire campaign managers, of heightened interest in 'personalities' and lowered concern for policy, of manipulation and maneuver and management by self-chosen political elites."[24] Such statements buttressed the consensus that strong, vital parties are a prerequisite for a healthy democracy. Thus, political scientists measure the march toward democracy in such diverse nations as Iraq, Afghanistan, and Haiti in terms of those countries' capacities to develop strong party organizations that are the foundations for free, democratic elections—even as average Americans deplore what they see as the scourge of parties in their own country.

THREE IMPORTANT PARTY DISTINCTIONS

One topic that bedevils any examination of parties in America is how one goes about defining them. What is a political party? What makes one organization more "party-like" than another? What are the differences among interest groups, campaign consulting firms, political action committees, and political parties? What are the various components of political parties? Are parties member oriented, or are they simply tools for an office-seeking elite?

Scholars have wrestled with these and other related questions for some time. Many of these topics are discussed in the chapters that follow, but a few clarifications are in order. They center around three questions:

1. How do political parties differ from other organizations, particularly those concerned with the outcome of government activity?
2. What are the various elements that comprise American political parties?
3. What do parties seek to accomplish and how are their activities related to these goals?

These three questions have occupied the attention of scholars since the formal study of U.S. political parties began in earnest after World War II. But they have a renewed urgency in today's interconnected world. Even though the Internet allows individuals to access thousands of web pages dealing with politics—with the national and state Democratic and Republican parties occupying only a handful of sites—the major parties still retain their importance. Democrats and Republicans hold positions on a variety of issues, and identification with a particular political party provides vital cues to voters. For example, according to an August 2010 USA *Today*/Gallup poll, Democrats and Republicans held widely different opinions on major issues considered by Congress during the first two years of the Obama administration (see Figure 1.1). On every item, the gap between the two major parties ranged from a cool 24 points to a frigid 56 points! Simply put, on nearly every major issue confronting the United States today, Democrats and Republicans have two very different worldviews. In this environment, the strategic objectives of the two major parties matter a great deal because their partisans ascribe great weight to them.

HOW PARTIES DIFFER FROM OTHER ORGANIZATIONS

At first glance, strangers to the American party system might find little distinction between parties and interest groups. Indeed, Madison's own discussion of "faction" is vague, and scholars have tangled with this issue for nearly two centuries. In the 1940s, for example, one

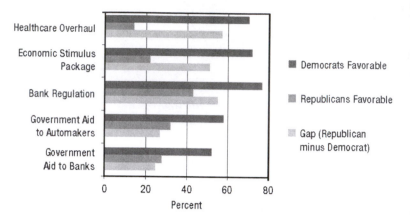

FIGURE 1.1   Democrats and Republicans on Major Issues Addressed by Congress in the First Two Years of Obama Administration

Source: Lydia Saad, "Among Recent Bills, Financial Reform a Lone Plus for Congress," Gallup Press Release, September 13, 2010.

student of political parties suggested that parties differ from special interest groups in that the latter "promote their interests by attempting to influence the government rather than by nominating candidates and seeking the responsibility for the management of government [as political parties do]."[25] Others disagreed, noting that interest groups do influence nominations, elect favorite candidates, and manage the government by influencing the appointment of officials and actual decisions being made. So what, if anything, distinguishes a political party from, say, the American Association of Retired Persons, the Environmental Defense Fund, the National Rifle Association, or the National Association of Manufacturers? We would point to three important distinctions:

1. Parties run candidates for office under their own label. Although interest groups may consistently back candidates of one party, such as the AFL-CIO's support of Democrats or the National Association of Manufacturers' support of Republicans, they do not have a party label and they do not officially nominate candidates for office.

2. When it comes to determining policy, parties have a broad range of concerns. A cursory reading of the 2008 Democratic and Republican Party platforms shows that both had something to say about every imaginable political issue. Democrats addressed the issues of economic growth, health care, retirement security, terrorism, energy, the environment, and government

reform, among others. Republicans promoted free trade, border security, health savings accounts, education vouchers, market solutions to environmental problems, small business growth, and an economic safety net for farmers. Interest groups have a much narrower set of concerns. The American Association of Retired Persons, for example, is keenly interested in policies affecting older Americans but pays scant attention to environmental legislation. The Environmental Defense Fund makes its views plain on modifications to the Endangered Species Act but offers little input on how to combat terrorism. Likewise, the National Rifle Association offers its unadulterated opposition to gun control but has little to say on other issues such as reforming Social Security.

3. Political parties are subject to state and local laws, and the relationship between parties and the state is an intimate one. Interest groups, on the other hand, are private organizations operating under minimal state or federal regulations and with the aid of constitutional protections of free speech, assembly, and petition.

Interest groups and parties have worked together on numerous occasions. The merging of business interests with the Republican Party during the Industrial Revolution is one example. The close ties forged by Franklin D. Roosevelt between the Democratic Party and organized labor to win important backing for the New Deal are another. Today, there are so many overlapping activities between political parties and interest groups that the competition between the two has become especially intense—a development that is discussed in greater detail in Chapter 2.

THE COMPONENTS OF AMERICAN POLITICAL PARTIES

In ancient Greece, when the priestess of Apollo at Delphi made ready to deliver a prophecy, she positioned herself on a special seat supported by three legs, the tripod.[26] The tripod gave the priestess a clear view of the past, present, and future. Political scientists in the early 1950s likened political parties to the famous tripod of so long ago, contending that parties are supported by three legs: party in the electorate, party organization, and party in government.[27]

Party in the electorate (PIE) refers to those who identify with a particular party. In some countries, party organizations require active participation in order to be considered a member, which often means paying a membership fee. In the United States, however, party membership is not nearly as well defined. Here, the "party in the electorate" denotes a person's psychological attachment to a particular party. Some root for a political party the way others might cheer on their favorite baseball team. Attaching oneself to a political party in this fashion can manifest itself in a range of activities, although party identification may be weak and does not automatically translate into partisan behavior. Some people will vote exclusively or primarily for candidates of their party, although it is possible to identify with a party and still vote for the opposition or not vote at all. Some people choose to register as a Republican or Democrat when they register to vote, but formal registration is not a requirement for being included in the party in the electorate. Other formalized party activities may include participation in a party primary, raising money at a party fundraiser, or making telephone calls to help get out the vote for a party's candidate.

Party organization (PO) refers to the formal apparatus of the party or the party bureaucracy. It encompasses physical assets like the party headquarters, collective activities like quadrennial national conventions, leaders and rank-and-file workers, and regulations governing how activities are structured and how leaders and workers are to behave. When party meetings are held, members of the organization show up. When partisans pass out literature during a campaign, the party organization is responsible for delivering the pamphlets. The Republican National Committee (RNC) and the Democratic National Committee (DNC) each have headquarters in Washington, D.C., and Democratic and Republican state party committees can be found in every state capital.

Party in government (PIG) refers to those who have captured office under a party label. For example, Democrats in the Senate comprise one segment of the Democratic Party in government led by majority leader Harry Reid (D-Nevada). His counterpart, Senator Mitch McConnell (R-Kentucky), leads the Republican Party in government in the U.S. Senate, in his capacity as minority leader. As president, Barack Obama is the overall head of the Democratic Party in government. When George W. Bush was in office, he functioned in the same capacity for Republicans. Branches of the party in government may be found in any legislative, executive, or judicial body that organizes itself along partisan lines, from the president and Congress down to states, counties, cities, and towns.

In the 1950s, the tripod model of political parties seemed both accurate and parsimonious. Partisanship was broad and fixed as tightly as one's religion. The public was divided between Democrats and Republicans, and they voted accordingly. What few "independents" there were generally did not vote and therefore placed themselves outside the political system. Legislative leaders were important figures. Party organizations were fixtures in nearly every community and controlled nominations for most elective offices. Citizens were active in party organizations, either for ideological reasons or for the sense of belonging to the larger community that partisan activity engendered. Elected officials carried the party banner openly. In an age of black-and-white television, the tripod model nicely captured how the three party components neatly fit together.

DOES THE TRIPOD MODEL WORK IN A NETWORKED AGE?

Near the close of the twentieth century, the tripod model no longer described political parties as crisply as it had in previous years, in large part because of the withering of the party in the electorate. Voters had turned away from both the Democratic and Republican parties, as evidenced by a steady increase in self-described independents. Party-centered campaigns had given way to candidates making their case to individual voters on broadcast and cable television. But whereas the party in the electorate had diminished, party organizations have demonstrated a surprising resilience and are more powerful than they were at any time in the last century—even as the technological revolution has changed how party organizations operate, how issues are communicated, and what citizens think about when they contemplate "politics." As for the party in government, contradictory trends exist. Party-line voting in Congress and state legislatures is much more prevalent than it was a half-century ago, but divided government—that is, split partisan control of the executive and the legislative branches of government—is commonplace. Moreover, even though elected officials are prone to adhere to the party line while in office, they seem increasingly willing to abandon their party when seeking office. Thus, questions abound. Are parties doing well, or are they withering away? Do parties remain an important part of our political system? The lack of consistent answers has undermined the explanatory power of the tripod model.

The rise in the importance and availability of information has changed the way parties operate. During the agricultural era, the key to production was land; in the Industrial Era, human labor; today, it is trained intelligence. In the early 1970s, sociologist Daniel Bell heralded the coming of a new postindustrial society that placed a premium on the gathering and dissemination of information.[28] In the subsequent four decades, American life has been transformed by several interrelated developments:

♦ Society has become wealthier and more affluent compared to earlier eras. Most workers are salaried professionals, whereas in the Industrial Era most employees were blue collar and were paid by the hour. Today, there are nearly 40 million who hold management, professional, and related occupations, while another 14 million workers are listed in service occupations. These numbers exclude the nearly 24 million Americans who hold sales and office jobs.[29]

♦ Brainpower has replaced manual labor as a key tool of productivity. A college degree, often followed by a postgraduate degree, has become the "union card" for employment in the Information Age.

♦ Technology that revolutionized mass communication has reshaped the way we interact with each other and diminished the once restrictive boundaries of time and space.

♦ New occupational structures, and with them new lifestyles and social classes, are creating new elites, including a self-selected political elite that works to influence political outcomes online through blogs and social networking.

♦ Modes of recreation have changed. More people find recreational outlets in their living rooms via television and the Internet. Social networking sites like Facebook are what coffee socials were in a bygone era.

Even something as ubiquitous as email is a relatively new and transformational technology. In the years since 1971, when the first email was sent to a computer at the Pentagon,[30] an email revolution has changed the nature and form of voter contact. Today, both parties maintain an extensive email database they can access with a click of a mouse. In 2008, Barack Obama's presidential campaign was able to build an email list of *13 million* supporters who voluntarily joined his campaign through his website.[31]

WHAT DO POLITICAL PARTIES SEEK TO ACCOMPLISH?

In one respect, the answer to this question is simple: Parties seek to win elections. Winning means that parties seize power and can control one or more branches of federal, state, or local governments. Seizing power can also have material benefits, as parties collect the so-called spoils of office. Several notable political party definitions follow this logic:

♦ A political party is a group organized to gain control of government in the name of the group by winning election to public office (Joseph Schlesinger).[32]

♦ A political party [is] any group, however loosely organized, seeking to elect government officeholders under a given label (Leon Epstein).[33]

♦ Political parties can be seen as coalitions of elites to capture and use political office. [But] a political party is more than a coalition. A political party is an institutionalized coalition, one that has adopted rules, norms, and procedures (John Aldrich).[34]

Others argue that a party's true purpose is to implement its ideology by adopting a particular set of policies. Winning elections and controlling the government are means to larger ends—changing the course of government. Some definitions of party capture this objective:

♦ [A] party is a body of men [sic] united, for promoting by their joint endeavors, the national interest, upon some particular principle in which they are all agreed (Edmund Burke).[35]

♦ [A] political party [is] an organization that seeks to achieve political power by electing members to public office so that their political philosophies can be reflected in public policies (Jay M. Shafritz).[36]

The foremost problems with using the election-policy dimension to capture the essence of parties are that it is static and incomplete and it discounts the diversity of party structures in the United States. The history of parties is continually evolving as new conditions arise. Suggestions that U.S. parties are "election driven," "policy oriented," or searching for the "vital center" assume that it has always been so, and that all party organizations scattered throughout the nation follow a similar pattern. A close reading of U.S. history suggests that party goals and activities have varied over time. As we will see shortly, sometimes parties have leaned toward the election-centered definition; at other times they have been closer to the policy-driven perspective. Therefore, instead of defining party goals in any sort of concrete way, conceivably the best approach is to remain mindful of the dichotomy between winning elections or remaining true to one's principles, then trying to discern when each perspective best fits a given moment in history.

ORIGINS: HAMILTON VERSUS JEFFERSON

After traveling what was then the breadth of the United States in 1831 and 1832, Alexis de Tocqueville remarked, "All the domestic controversies of the Americans at first appear to a stranger to be incomprehensible or puerile, and he is at a loss whether to pity a people who take such arrant trifles in good earnest or to envy that happiness which enables a community to discuss them."[37] More recently, de Tocqueville's complaint was echoed in the oft-heard line: "There's not a dime's worth of difference between the Democratic and Republican parties."

Such ideological homogeneity has given rise to a belief that the United States is a special country set apart from its European origins. Speaking before a joint session of Congress in the wake of the September 11 attacks, George W. Bush described Osama bin Laden as a loathsome harbinger of fear, whereas the United States was a special place that cultivated freedom. Bush asked his listeners to "uphold the values of America and remember why so many came here."[38] Such expressions constitute what some have called American Exceptionalism.[39] The ideological consensus in the United States remains so pervasive that it even influences how Americans speak. Expressions such as "the American Dream" and "the American Way of Life" (along with the damning phrase "un-American") reflect the extraordinary self-confidence most Americans have in the experiment devised by the Framers. Historians have been struck by the rigidity of the American mind. As one has observed, "Who would think of using the word 'un-Italian' or 'un-French' as we use the word 'un-American?'"[40]

But such ideological rigidity does not mean that disagreements are lacking either in the history books or in contemporary news accounts about politics. After the Constitution was ratified and George Washington took his place as the nation's first president, Alexander Hamilton and Thomas Jefferson began to act, as Jefferson recalled, "like two cocks."[41] The raging battle between these two stubborn and forceful men was personal and political. Both were staunchly committed to individualism, freedom, and equality of opportunity, yet they differed strongly on how these values could be translated into an effective form of governance.

Those disagreements came from the vastly different solutions each man devised to a vexing problem—namely, how liberty could be restrained such that it could be enjoyed. For his part, Hamilton preferred that liberty be coupled with authority: "In every civil society, there must be a supreme power, to which all members of that society are subject; for, otherwise, there could be no supremacy, or subordination, that is no government at all."[42] Jefferson, meanwhile, preferred that liberty be paired with local civic responsibility. It was on that basis that the enduring struggle between Hamiltonian nationalism and Jeffersonian localism began.

Hamiltonian nationalism envisions the United States as one "family," with a strong central government and an energetic president acting on its behalf. Addressing the delegates to the New York State convention called to ratify the Constitution, Hamilton noted, "The confidence of the people will easily be gained by good administration. This is the true touchstone." To him, good administration meant a strong central government acting on behalf of the national—or family—interest. Thus, any expression of a special interest was, to use Hamilton's word, "mischievous."[43] But Hamilton had his own partialities, favoring the development of the nation's urban centers and an unfettered capitalism. His espousal of a strong central government aroused considerable controversy.

Unlike Hamilton, Jefferson had a nearly limitless faith in the ordinary citizen. To a nation largely composed of farmers, he declared, "Those who labor in the earth are the chosen people of God, if ever He had a chosen people."[44] Jefferson's devotion to liberty made him distrust most attempts to restrain it, particularly those of the federal government: "Were we directed from Washington when to sow, and when to reap, we should soon want bread."[45] In 1825, Jefferson warned of the expanding power of government and wrote that the "salvation of the republic" rested on the regeneration and spread of the New England town meeting.[46] The best guarantee of liberty in Jefferson's view was to restrain the mighty hand of government. Table 1.1 highlights several additional differences between Hamilton's and

Jefferson's views of government, with a special focus on how these differences might relate to the party system.

This debate between the political descendants of Alexander Hamilton and Thomas Jefferson is the touchstone for partisan conflict and party politics in America that continues to this day. Martin Van Buren, among many others, traces the evolution of parties to the factional disputes between Hamilton and Jefferson. According to Van Buren,

> The two great parties of this country, with occasional changes in name only, have for the principal part of a century, occupied antagonistic positions upon all important political questions. They have maintained an unbroken succession, and have, throughout, been composed respectively of men agreeing in their party passion, and preferences, and entertaining, with rare exceptions, similar views on the subject of government and its administration.[47]

Over time the two parties, with changing names and roles, recast Hamiltonian nationalism and Jeffersonian localism to suit their

Table 1.1 The Hamiltonian and Jeffersonian Models of American Governance

Hamiltonian Nationalism	Jeffersonian Localism
Views the United States as one national "family."	Sees the United States as a series of diverse communities.
Prefers a concentration of power in the federal government so that it may act in the interest of the national family.	Prefers to give power to state and local governments so that they can act in deference to local customs.
Inclined to constrain liberty for the sake of national unity by marrying liberty with a strong central authority.	More inclined to favor liberty and wary of national authority. Prefers to concentrate governmental power at the state and local levels.
Trusts in elites to run the government.	Trusts in the common sense of average Americans to run their government.
Prefers a hierarchical party structure populated by "professional" party politicians.	Prefers a decentralized party structure populated by so-called amateur politicians, who often are local party activists.
Sees parties as vehicles whose primary purpose is to win elections and control the government.	Views parties as more ideologically based. Commitment to principles is viewed as even more important than winning elections.

evolving interests. During the Civil War and the Industrial Era that followed, Republicans stood with Hamilton, whereas Democrats claimed Jefferson as one of their own and promoted states' rights. Since the days of Franklin D. Roosevelt's New Deal, Democrats have consistently aligned themselves with Hamilton, likening the nation to a family. In a 2010 commencement address at the University of Michigan, Barack Obama channeled Hamilton by calling for a larger role for government to meet the challenges of the twenty-first century:

> There are some things we can only do together, as one nation—and our government must keep pace with the times. When America expanded from a few colonies to an entire continent, and we needed a way to reach the Pacific, our government helped build the railroads. When we transitioned from an economy based on farms to one based on factories, and workers needed new skills and training, our nation set up a system of public high schools. When the markets crashed during the Depression and people lost their life savings, our government put in place a set of rules and safeguards to make sure that such a crisis never happened again, and then put a safety net in place to make sure that our elders would never be impoverished the way they had been. And because our markets and financial systems have evolved since then, we're now putting in place new rules and safeguards to protect the American people ....
>
> Government is the police officers who are protecting our communities, and the servicemen and women who are defending us abroad. Government is the roads you drove on and the speed limits that kept you safe. Government is what ensures that mines adhere to safety standards and that oil spills are cleaned up by the companies that caused them. Government is this extraordinary public university—a place that's doing lifesaving research, and catalyzing economic growth, and graduating students who will change the world around them in ways big and small ....
> Government shouldn't try to dictate your lives. But it should give you the tools you need to succeed. Government shouldn't try to guarantee results, but it should guarantee a shot at opportunity for every American who's willing to work hard.[48]

Whereas Obama and his fellow Democrats espouse Hamiltonian nationalism, the Republican Party since the birth of the New Deal has immersed itself in the values cherished by Jeffersonian localism. Campaigning for the presidency in 1936, Alf Landon assailed the "folly" of Franklin Roosevelt's New Deal and denounced the "vast multitude of new offices" and the "centralized bureaucracy" from which "swarms of inspectors" swooped over the countryside "to harass our people."[49] Landon promised that his restrained and prudent management of the federal bureaucracy would result in an outpouring of freedom by a simple adherence to the following dictum: "I want the Secretary of the Treasury to be obliged to say to committees of Congress every time a new appropriation is proposed, 'Gentlemen, you will have to provide some new taxes if you do this.'"[50] Today's Republicans strike a similar theme. In their *Pledge to America* document released in advance of the 2010 congressional election, Republican candidates accused Obama and the Democrats of threatening personal liberty by enlarging the powers of the federal government:

> In a self-governing society, the only bulwark against the power of the state is the consent of the governed, and regarding the policies of the current government, the governed do not consent.
>
> An unchecked executive, a compliant legislature, and an overreaching judiciary have combined to thwart the will of the people and overturn their votes and their values, striking down longstanding laws and institutions and scorning the deepest beliefs of the American people.
>
> An arrogant and out-of-touch government of self-appointed elites makes decisions, issues mandates, and enacts laws without accepting or requesting the input of the many.[51]

In 2010, Republicans promised to restore the powers of state and local governments and limit the powers of the federal government to those reserved to it in the U.S. Constitution. Virginia Republican Governor Bob McDonnell captured the essence of the party's thinking: "Top-down, one-size-fits-all decision making should not replace the personal choices of free people in a free market, nor undermine the proper role of state and local governments in our system of federalism."[52]

Many historians believe that since the nation's founding the character of the American people has not changed greatly. Though our values may be constant, the circumstances in which they are applied are not. The whiff of civil war, the onset of a depression, or the ravages of inflation inevitably cause Americans to take stock of their situation, alter their expectations of government, and choose a political party and a course of action in a manner consistent with the enduring values of freedom, individualism, and equality of opportu-

PARTIES IN A NETWORKED AGE

Fox News and the Constitution

Cable news media are becoming ever more focused and narrow in their audience targeting. "Code words" and themes are merging as cable channel identifiers. From July 2009 through the midterm elections of 2010, Fox News stepped up its already prominent trumpeting of the Constitution, the Founding Fathers, and the virtues of free market capitalism. References to these touchstones of democracy were found in more than 620 news stories, an average of over 50 per month. Fox News pundits including Glenn Beck, Sean Hannity, and Bill O'Reilly regularly tied their Constitutional advocacy to an attack on what they termed the Obama Administration's socialism, communism, and Marxism. Cries to "take our country back" resounded from Sarah Palin's proclamation on Sean Hannity's program throughout the conservative and Tea Party protests of the spring and fall of 2010. Many of these protests were focused on objections to Obama's health care reform—"Obamacare"—which the Tea Party in particular has targeted as unconstitutional.

Source: Street, Paul, and Anthony DiMaggio. 2011. *Crashing the Tea Party: Mass Media and the Campaign to Remake American Politics.* Boulder, CO: Paradigm Publishers.

nity. At critical junctures, Americans have shifted from Hamiltonian nationalism to Jeffersonian localism. Such shifts in public attitudes have usually been influenced by a dominant personality. Abraham Lincoln reasserted Hamilton's vision of a national family in order to save the Union; Franklin Roosevelt redefined Hamiltonian nationalism to meet the challenges of the Great Depression. At other times, Jeffersonian localism has thrived, as when Ronald Reagan cited the federal government as the problem, not the solution to our problems. George W. Bush rhetorically echoed Reagan and Jefferson. Barack Obama has tilted back toward Hamilton, FDR, and Lincoln.

Sometimes, Americans do not want to choose between Hamiltonian nationalism and Jeffersonian localism. Instead, they want to enjoy the fruits of both. So, for instance, "netroots" activists—people engaged in online-driven efforts to reform the Democratic Party, whom we will discuss elsewhere in this book—align themselves with the first three Hamiltonian positions and the last three Jeffersonian positions in Table 1.1 without feeling any sense of contradiction. Thus, they view the United States as a national "family" (albeit made of up diverse communities), believe concentrated federal power is necessary to bringing about a progressive agenda, and are willing to trade off a degree of liberty in exchange for greater government safety-net protections. At the same time, they trust the wisdom of average Americans—such as those who have chosen to engage in online political activism—over elite decision making, oppose Democratic Party professionals, and chafe when they perceive elected Democrats abandoning principle in order to win elections.

This melding of Hamiltonian nationalism and Jeffersonian localism is not unusual in American history. It reasserts itself during periodic swings from one faction to the other, when the parties test their ideas and battle for dominance amidst changing political and social problems. Over time, this enduring battle has produced surprising results. Hamilton would be astonished to learn that his concept of a national family is being used to promote the interests of have-nots, especially women and minorities, or as the basis for universal health insurance. But as this book suggests, political parties cannot escape the vineyards tilled by Hamilton and Jefferson, whose ideas give expression to American ideological impulses and serve as instruments to implement the constitutional designs of the Framers in a world they never could have envisioned.

After a period in the late twentieth century when it appeared political parties were dying, they remain alive and well at the start of the twenty-first century and make a considerable contribution to the democratic process. For all their deficiencies, parties still afford average Americans the best avenue for speaking their minds and being heard; this remains true in today's networked age. As you read the chapters to follow, you are invited to assess for yourself the role and consequence of political parties in our system. You will find that despite the changes political parties have experienced through the centuries, it is still possible to find Hamilton's and Jefferson's fingerprints on the parties that dominate today's networked politics. Culturally, economically, geographically, and demographically, the United States has been a fluid work in progress since those two men fashioned organizations that would formalize the political divisions of post–Revolutionary War America. That these organizations would somehow evolve into the groups that now institutionalize the red state–blue state divisions of twenty-first-century politics, and that they would continue to function in a world networked at the speed of light, is a testament to the enduring nature of a set of institutions that were not even imagined by the Constitution's authors. As they face each other across a steepening ideological divide, Republicans and Democrats, today's conservatives and liberals, party on, continuing a dialogue with deep historical and institutional roots.

2

The Rise, Fall, and Rebirth of Party Politics

The most frequently quoted lines in the study of political parties were penned in 1942: "It should be flatly stated," wrote political scientist E. E. Schattschneider, "that the political parties created democracy and that modern democracy is unthinkable save in terms of parties."[1] Schattschneider's proclamation is found in nearly every text on political parties written since the 1940s (you just read it here), and most political scientists still accept his assertion as a fact. Yet, to the average citizen, political parties are synonymous with corruption, gridlock, and elitism. Americans relish bashing parties and confounding the experts by splitting their votes among them. Concentrating power in one party has become so suspect that some voters have taken an odd pleasure in choosing presidents of one party and Congresses of another. This process of "cohabitation" (the French term for divided government) is often an uneasy one for party leaders, but voters don't care much about how it makes elites feel. Questioned immediately after the 2010 elections, 43 percent of Americans said it was good for the country for control of the White House and Congress to be split between Democrats and Republicans, an identical figure to what pollsters found during the 2008 and 2006 political cycles. Only 21 percent said divided government was a bad thing.[2]

Given such cavalier treatment by voters, it should come as no surprise that political parties have had a tortured and tormented history. Although Americans, along with the British, can claim to have invented the modern political party, few take pride in this accomplishment. For more than 200 years, political parties have searched for their rightful place in the American polity without ever quite finding it.

THE COLONIAL EXPERIENCE

Contemporary political parties have their roots in colonial America, where pre–Revolutionary War parties were little more than extensions of rival family clans such as the Wards and Hopkins in Rhode Island and the DeLanceys and Livingstons in New York. The contests between these clans invariably centered on an ideological dispute over the reach of royal authority in the colonies, which began almost as soon as the British ships carrying settlers to Jamestown left port in 1607. On one side were those loyal to the Crown and the appointed royal governors; those opposed were faithful to the elected colonial assemblies. Those supporting the Crown were often wealthy, having received immense land grants from the king, whereas those who did not share these special privileges were tradesmen, small shop owners, and those who tilled the soil and had become accustomed to the hardships of the New World. These poor, adventurous outcasts were suspicious of authority figures, especially the king, and their political cynicism was deep-seated.

Although these divisions structured colonial politics, localism and diversity prevented mature parties from forming. In pre-Revolutionary America, each colony had its own customs, history, and political identity. Moreover, there was a great diversity of individual interests among small-freehold farmers, plantation slaveholders, merchants, shipowners and builders, emerging manufacturers, and others. In addition, there were numerous ethnic and religious groups, divided between those who desired an aristocratic and consolidated republic and those who preferred a more democratic regime with power concentrated in the states.

The American Revolution forged these cleavages into a debate about self-governance. Tradesmen and laborers despised King George III and favored severing ties with Britain. Dubbed patriots, many advocated violence to end what they saw as British subjugation.

PARTIES IN A NETWORKED AGE

New Media and Politics from the Founding Forward

The parties have not always been Republicans and Democrats, and "new media" have taken several forms before the Internet. Here are some examples to explore more fully:

Paul Revere	"One if by land; two if by sea."
Thomas Paine	Common Sense
Ben Franklin	Poor Richard's Almanack
Alexander Hamilton	The Federalist Papers

It's a long leap from these early precursors to the world of blogging, tweeting, meet-ups, and apps, but people pushing politics using every medium possible is nothing new.

Increased taxation, coupled with Royal disregard of their interests, prompted a number of high-profile protests, such as the Boston Tea Party of 1773 and the sinking of the *Gaspee* off the Rhode Island coast one year earlier. Edmund Burke, a member of the British House of Commons at the time, noted that "the state of America has been kept in continual agitation. Everything administered as [a] remedy to the public complaint, if it did not produce, was at least followed by, a heightening of the distemper."[3]

Colonial loyalists remained faithful to the British Crown, and they regarded the patriots as rabble-rousers. With the uprisings at Lexington and Concord in 1775, the contest between the patriots and loyalists became an outright civil war, with well-organized patriots winning control of state governments throughout the colonies. Through societies like the Sons of Liberty, they held rallies, sponsored "committees of correspondence" to spread their views, and recruited important community leaders to their cause. Patriot leader Thomas Paine espoused the virtues of self-rule in his 1776 pamphlet *Common Sense*, and John Adams organized his fellow Bostonians to fight against "foreign" influence in colonial affairs. Their activities were less focused on winning elections (there were few voters at the time) than on shaping public opinion.

Even before the Revolutionary War ended, Adams wrote to a correspondent, "There is nothing I dread so much as a division of the Republic into two great parties, each arranged under its leader and converting measures in opposition to each other."[4] But, enduring conflict over the structure and scope of post-Revolutionary governing institutions moved the new nation inexorably in the direction of opposing camps. Differences that turned violent precipitated the collapse of the Articles of Confederation, the young republic's first governing document. For a brief time after the Revolution, a short-lived boom in imports from England pushed the cost of agricultural and manufactured goods downward. Money became scarce, resulting in a severe economic depression that began in the late 1770s and lasted nearly a decade. Working-class citizens and small farmers were hardest hit. Bank foreclosures skyrocketed. Most states levied heavy taxes in a largely unsuccessful attempt to eliminate their wartime debts. By the mid-1780s, the demands for action grew louder.

To avoid bloodshed, some states passed laws to postpone foreclosures and allow farmers to use agricultural products to help pay loans. But none of these actions eased the governing crisis, which came to a head when former army captain Daniel Shays led a mob of farmers against the state government of Massachusetts in 1787. Their purpose was to prevent foreclosures on their debt-ridden land by keeping the country courts of western Massachusetts from sitting until the next election. The state militia eventually dispersed the mob, but the uprising, which became known as Shays's Rebellion, galvanized the states to convene delegates in Philadelphia for the purpose of drafting a new governing document.

The differences underlying Shays's Rebellion persisted during and after the Constitutional Convention. The Constitution's supporters, who became known as Federalists, and those who opposed its ratification, dubbed Anti-Federalists, carried their disputes from Independence Hall in Philadelphia to the various state capitals. Anti-Federalists contended that representatives in any national government must reflect a true picture of the people, possessing an intimate knowledge of their circumstances and needs. This could only be achieved, they argued, through small, relatively homogeneous republics such as those already constructed in the existing states. One prominent Anti-Federalist spokesperson asked, "Is it practicable for a country so large and so numerous . . . to elect a representation that will speak their sentiments? . . . It certainly is not."[5] Federalists believed that a representative republic was possible and desirable—especially if populated by those "who possess [the] most wisdom to discern, and [the] most virtue to pursue, the common good of society."[6]

FEDERALISTS VERSUS REPUBLICANS

George Washington assumed the presidency in 1789 believing that parties were unnecessary and that he could bypass them by creating an "enlightened administration." To that end, Washington took into his Cabinet the leading political antagonists of his time: Alexander Hamilton as treasury secretary and Thomas Jefferson as secretary of state. Less than a year after becoming president, Washington's experiment of having a government without parties faltered. Hamilton and Jefferson vehemently disagreed in the Cabinet councils over how to manage the growing economic crisis.

Hamilton offered a sweeping plan to revive the sagging economy—the most controversial portion of which involved the complete assumption of debts incurred by the states during the Revolutionary War. To Hamilton and his Federalist followers, this policy was not only sound economics but good politics: By helping those who backed the revolt against King George III, confidence in the national government would be restored and nearly $80 million would be put in the pockets of those most likely to reinvest in the nation's tiny infrastructure. The result would be an increase in the flow of goods and services accompanied by a general rise in living standards.

To pay for full assumption, Hamilton proposed an excise tax on distilled spirits that became known as the Whiskey Tax. Because most whiskey producers were farmers in the South and West, this measure shifted the tax burden from northeastern business owners to small farmers—in effect, punishing those most likely to support Jefferson's Republicans. Additionally, to ensure that enough money would fill the federal coffers, Hamilton advocated establishing a Bank of the United States that would make loans and collect interest payments while it curbed the diverse practices of state-chartered banks. The idea of a national bank, not one of the powers specifically given to the Congress in the Constitution, created enormous animosity between advocates of states' rights and those seeking a more powerful national government—a dispute that would not be resolved until 1819 by the Supreme Court in the case of *McCulloch v. Maryland*.

Jefferson and the Republicans believed that federal assumption of state debts would create a windfall for the monied class, especially those living in New England. Opposition to Hamilton's scheme was led in the House of Representatives by James Madison. He agreed with Hamilton that the economy needed strengthening, but he fretted about the shift of capital from the agricultural states (including his native Virginia) to a few northeastern manufacturing states. Moreover, Madison thought that the Whiskey Tax would be a financial disaster for small farmers. His prediction came true in 1794 when farmers in western Pennsylvania caused an uprising that became popularly known as the Whiskey Insurrection. Madison corralled 17 House members to his side—about one-quarter of the chamber. About the same number of legislators opposed him. At the conclusion of the First Congress, an exasperated Hamilton exclaimed, "It was not till the last session that I became unequivocally convinced that Mr. Madison, cooperating with Mr. Jefferson, is at the head of a faction decidedly hostile to me and my administration; and actuated by views, in my judgment, subversive to the principles of good government and dangerous to the union, peace, and happiness of the country."[7] Vice President John Adams likewise bemoaned the "turbulent maneuvers" of factions that could "tie the hands and destroy the influence" of those who desired to promote the public interest. Adams told his son-in-law that the partisan battles between Hamilton and Jefferson had created a "division of sentiments over everything."[8]

The battle between Hamilton and Madison extended beyond the halls of Congress to the newspapers. In a move that foreshadowed the inextricable link that would develop between political parties and the mass media, Hamilton forged a close alliance with John Ward Fenno, publisher of the *Gazette of the United States*. Madison, not willing to let Fenno's editorials go unanswered, persuaded Philip Freneau to edit a rival newspaper, the *National Gazette*. These party-controlled newspapers, although having a small number of subscribers (the *Gazette of the United States* had only 1,500), quickly became the most popular method of communicating with the party faithful.[9] Together, they helped clarify this first battle between Hamiltonian nationalism and Jeffersonian localism, even as they exacerbated the animosity between these two leaders. The battle of epithets that played out in the country's young newspapers ensured that partisanship would overflow the Washington administration to capture much of American society.

Despite intense congressional opposition, Hamilton's economic plan won approval after some wily backroom maneuvering. Jefferson played a key behind-the-scenes role, endorsing the bill in exchange for assurances that the federal capital would be moved south from New York City to a new District of Columbia. But Jefferson's role in advancing Hamilton's initiative alienated his agrarian constituents. Seeking to mend political fences, Jefferson embarked on a tour with his ally James Madison during the spring of 1791 that was to have profound consequences for party development. Ostensibly, the duo set out on a nature tour to "observe the vegetation and wildlife in the region," but their real purpose was to sample public opinion. In effect, they were testing the waters for the formation of a new political party. In New York City, Jefferson and Madison met with Robert Livingston and George Clinton—two longtime rivals of Hamilton—as well as Senator Aaron Burr, who was attempting to broaden his political influence.

Two years later, in 1793, Jefferson and Hamilton renewed their struggle. This time, the issue was how to respond to the French Revolution. To Jefferson and his followers, the French cry for "liberty, equality, and fraternity" was an extension of the American Revolution. Thomas Paine was so moved by the French revolutionaries that he journeyed to France to help the cause. At the same time, the German Republican Society was formed in Philadelphia. Its members sympathized with the French revolutionaries and believed that the American Revolution was losing momentum because of Hamilton, who, they claimed, was endangering the promise of democracy contained in the Declaration of Independence. By 1798, there were 43 of these popular societies, organized in every state except New Hampshire and Georgia.

To Hamilton and his Federalist backers, the French Revolution signaled the emergence of anarchy and a rejection of traditional Christian values. They were horrified by the mob violence and feared that the emerging republican movement could lead America down the same path. Jefferson remarked that these different reactions to the French Revolution "kindled and brought forth the two [political] parties with an ardor which our own interests merely could never incite."[10] Jefferson dubbed Hamilton's party the "monocrats." For his part, Jefferson never referred to his party as the "Democrats," because the term conjured visions of mob rule; he preferred the name "Republicans" to describe his emerging political organization.

When the bloody beheadings of the Terror of 1793 became known, reservations about the French experiment became widespread. Seeking to cool the growing political passions in his own country, President Washington sent James Monroe to Paris and John Jay to London to obtain treaties that would protect American shipping interests and keep the United States out of the European political thicket. But when Jay returned with an agreement that many believed was partial to the British, a political firestorm erupted. The treaty was so controversial that Washington waited six months before submitting it to the Senate for ratification in 1795, where it barely received the two-thirds majority required for passage.

By 1796, Hamilton's controversial economic policies and the Jay Treaty divided public opinion and led to the creation of the nation's first official political parties. The Federalists took their name to signal their intention to create a strong, centralized government. (Note that this group of Federalists does not refer to the defenders of the Constitution crafted in Philadelphia in 1787.) The opposing Republicans wished to make clear that they were devoted to the people and "the republican principle" of representative governance. (This group later changed its name to the Democratic Party and continues to function under that label today.) Most Federalists were affluent businessmen from the northeastern states, whereas Republicans won backing from small farmers in the mid-Atlantic and southern states. The division proved so powerful that in 1796 a presidential election was hotly contested for the first time. Thomas Jefferson was so opposed to the Jay Treaty that he accepted the Republican call to lend his name as a presidential candidate. The battle between Federalist John Adams and Republican Jefferson was a close one, with Adams winning 71 electoral votes to Jefferson's 68. Under the peculiar constitutional arrangements of the time—which did not anticipate or account for political party competition—runner-up Jefferson became vice president.

The 1796 Adams-Jefferson contest was more than a struggle between two men—it was a battle between two political organizations. Although there were scores of local groups, some even using the term *parties* before 1796, the election of 1800 saw the emergence of political organizations as we know them today. Propelled by a strong conviction that the Federalist-controlled U.S. government was abandoning sacred "republican principles," Jefferson and the Republicans formed a party replete with grassroots supporters, which ran slates of candidates for numerous offices on a platform of issues that appealed to the American sense of limited government and a prevailing fear of placing too much authority in one individual.

In what proved to be a futile attempt to stem the growing Republican tide, John Adams and his Federalist followers in Congress sought to emulate Jefferson's organizational skills. Because they had less grassroots support—there were no Federalist clubs to speak of—organizing proved difficult. Yet, by virtue of the fact that they ran the government, they could use their positions to press their advantage, in the process confirming some of the Founders' fears about the factional dangers of partisanship. Thus, the Federalist-controlled Congress passed the 1798 Sedition Act, which made it a misdemeanor to publish false or malicious information and provided that anyone convicted of conspiring to hinder the operations of the federal government would be subject to heavy fines and possible imprisonment. The Alien Acts, which became law in the same year, made it easier to deport political adversaries who were not citizens—especially the growing Irish population, which was pro-Republican, as well as any migrating French revolutionaries. Fourteen indictments were issued between 1798 and 1800. One Republican was jailed because he carried a placard protesting the acts; another was sentenced to six months for attempting, in the words of a Federalist-appointed judge, to "mislead the ignorant and inflame their minds against the President."[11]

Jefferson worried that these new laws might make it possible for the Federalists to install one of their own as a president-for-life. Thus, the organizing efforts of Jefferson and Madison became a whirlwind of activity as the election of 1800 approached. Republican members of Congress met in Philadelphia and formally endorsed Jefferson for president and Aaron Burr for vice president. The Federalists responded by nominating a ticket consisting of John Adams of Massachusetts and Thomas Pinckney of South Carolina—the first of many North-South pairings.

As in 1796, the Adams-Jefferson contest was hard fought. Hamilton warned his Federalist followers that no defections would be tolerated in the Electoral College. But Hamilton's admonition notwithstanding, Jefferson prevailed. As in the first Adams-Jefferson race, the southern states backed Jefferson while most of the Northeast sided with Adams. But the switch of New York from Adams to Jefferson—the culmination of Jefferson's courting of New Yorkers that began with his 1791 "nature tour"—paid off. Clinton and Livingston, together with Burr's New York City organization, rallied the troops on Jefferson's behalf. New York's electoral votes gave Jefferson an eight-vote plurality in the Electoral College. The Republican victory, which had to be ratified in the House of Representatives, extended to both houses of Congress. As Jefferson later recalled, "The Revolution of 1800 was as real a revolution in the principles of our government as that of 1776 was in its forms."[12] That revolution, as John Adams later observed, was the rejection of what Adams called "the monarchial principle"—a reference to his belief that those in power would do what is right for the country regardless of partisanship. After Jefferson's victory, future presidents would be party leaders. Adams himself blamed his lack of party standing for his defeat: "Jefferson had a party; Hamilton had a party; but the commonwealth [a reference to Adams] had none."[13] Jefferson replied that political parties had become an inevitable part of public life that had separated the two founding brothers.

JACKSON AND MASS-BASED PARTIES

In the two decades following Thomas Jefferson's election, Republicans strengthened their hold on the government and overcame an abortive attempt by the Federalists to lengthen their stay. But this did not stop the partisan bickering between Jeffersonian localists and Hamiltonian nationalists and their successors. One of the very first, and most bitter, partisan battles Jefferson faced involved the "midnight appointments" of loyal Federalists to the federal judiciary made by John Adams upon leaving the presidency in March 1801. The Federalists hoped that by making these appointments they could limit the damage done by the Republicans until the next election in 1804. One of those appointed by Adams was William Marbury, who was slated to become a justice of the peace. The incoming Republican secretary of state, James Madison, refused to deliver Marbury's nominating papers after the outgoing Federalist secretary of state, John Marshall, failed to deliver them in time. In response, Marbury and seven others sued the government, claiming that Madison had defaulted on his duty to serve his appointment papers. The Supreme Court heard the case of *Marbury v. Madison* in 1803. In a landmark ruling, Chief Justice John Marshall (the same former secretary of state who had been appointed to the Court by John Adams) wrote that Marbury was entitled to his appointment, but Congress had exceeded its authority when it gave the Court the power to order Madison to surrender the papers, which it had done in a provision of the Judiciary Act of 1789. Marshall thus wormed his way out of a certain confrontation with President Jefferson while expanding the Federalist principle of strong central government by claiming for the Court the authority to declare acts of the other branches unconstitutional, an authority known as judicial review.[14]

The next 20 years saw what historians sometimes call the Era of Good Feelings because of the apparent lack of political disagreement. In truth, the Republicans were so powerful and organized that for the only time in American history there was essentially a one-party government with no serious electoral competition. The trio of Jefferson, Madison, and Monroe established a Virginia dynasty that controlled the White House; in the five elections held between 1804 and 1820, Republicans won between 53 and 92 percent of the Electoral College votes and held between 61 and 85 percent of the seats in Congress.

Meanwhile, the Federalists had started down a path to political obscurity, sealed by their reaction to the War of 1812. Federalists, who retained a strong base of support in the New England states, vehemently opposed the war, believing that it would seriously impede vital trade with England. They dubbed the conflict "Mr. Madison's War," and New Englanders continued to illicitly trade with the British, sometimes even withholding money and militia from the war effort. Republicans, in turn, stoked popular outrage at the British impressment of American sailors—the removal of British-born sailors from American vessels and forced entry into the British navy—and believed that the rampant nationalism would unify their diverse party. Partisan passions escalated after Congress declared war on Great Britain in 1812. When the *Federal Republican,* a Federalist newspaper located in Baltimore, editorialized against the war, an angry mob razed the building where it was printed. Elsewhere, Federalist sympathizers were beaten, stabbed, and even tarred and feathered. Two years later the Federalists met in Hartford, Connecticut, and proposed generous peace terms. Rumors persisted that the Federalists favored the secession of the New England states from the Union, and the party, already weakened by its antiwar stance, fell into disrepute. By 1820, the Federalists had become political dinosaurs, not even bothering to nominate a token candidate to oppose James Monroe in that year's presidential contest. Hamilton's party faded into the history books; however, Hamilton's ideas did not.

The strength of the Republicans ultimately was their undoing. By 1810, the House of Representatives was filled with a variety of Republicans. Some were traditional states' rights advocates; others wanted an enlarged role for the federal government to enhance westward expansion. Thus, even though most elected officials were Republicans, the label became increasingly ambiguous. By 1824, the divisions within the party had widened into a chasm. Five candidates, each representing a different Republican faction, aggressively sought the presidency: Henry Clay, the powerful Speaker of the House and champion of westward expansion; John C. Calhoun, secretary of war and supporter of states' rights; Andrew Jackson, the hero of the Battle of New Orleans; John Quincy Adams, son of the former president and secretary of state under Monroe; and William Crawford, former treasury secretary and, like Calhoun, a doctrinaire states' rights advocate. The Congressional Caucus (the means by which Republican nominees had been chosen since 1800) convened in Washington, D.C., in February and selected Crawford to be the party's standardbearer with Calhoun as his running mate. The remaining three candidates boycotted the caucus and persuaded their respective state legislatures to place their names in contention.

On election day, Jackson led in the popular votes cast, winning 153,000 more than the combined votes cast for Adams and Crawford.

But Jackson failed to win an electoral majority. The all-important Electoral College vote split, with Jackson receiving 99 votes; Adams, 84; Crawford, 41; and Clay, 37. Under such conditions, the Constitution turns the matter over to the House of Representatives for a final decision among the top three contenders. Clay, excluded from consideration, backed Adams, who reciprocated by promising to make Clay secretary of state in the new administration. Because he was the powerful Speaker of the House, Clay was able to clinch the House vote, and the presidency, for Adams.

Jackson's supporters were outraged by what they believed was a corrupt quid pro quo between Adams and Clay. They considered Adams a usurper in the White House, and in several state capitals they plotted a comeback, with New York senator Martin Van Buren providing the organizational muscle. Van Buren correctly suspected that his home state could be decisive in the 1828 election and formed an alliance with Jackson that would help put "Old Hickory" over the top and avenge his 1824 defeat.

By 1826, several states had changed their laws allowing voters to choose delegates to the Electoral College rather than leaving the task to the various state legislatures. A general loosening of voter qualifications also greatly enlarged the size of the potential electorate. Meanwhile, the Republican Party continued fracturing. On one side were the Adams-Clay followers who were determined to implement internal improvements to the nation's infrastructure. Like the Federalists of two decades earlier, they were convinced that national prosperity necessitated an active government. On the other side were the so-called traditional Republicans whose ranks included Van Buren. They opposed internal improvements, including road and canal construction, because they believed such projects would violate state sovereignty. Jackson had managed to keep his distance from both factions, remaining a popular figure without an official party organization—until Van Buren took charge of his campaign.

Van Buren's first step toward involvement in national politics was to solidify his following in Congress. He quickly became leader of the Democratic-Republicans, a name chosen to express solidarity with the more egalitarian agrarian wing of the Republican Party. Van Buren undertook scores of trips around the country, campaigning for Jackson wherever he went. His goals were to arouse public indignation against the Adams-Clay deal, conduct door-to-door canvasses in every town, and make sure that Jackson supporters went to the polls on election day. Adams's forces derided Jackson as a military butcher and even called the chastity of his wife into question. Nonetheless, Jackson handily beat Adams, winning all of the south, the new western states, and Van Buren's New York. Just as significant, voter turnout doubled from 25 percent in 1824 to 50 percent in 1828. Jackson and Van Buren were the first to understand the power of mass-based party politics. Political parties were now firmly established as a primary vehicle for translating public sentiments into governing policies. Henceforth, parties became a mainstay of American political life.

With his victory, Jackson's Democratic-Republican Party, which shortened its name to the Democratic Party, had overtaken Jefferson's Republican Party. Henry Clay, John C. Calhoun, and others banded together as the opposition Whigs. Their name was intended to summon up the spirits of those who composed the patriot party during the heyday of the American Revolution and the British Whigs of the eighteenth century. Whigs stood for restrained executive powers, westward expansion, and protective tariffs. Thus, by the mid-1830s, a two-party system had taken root on American soil. But unlike the earlier political skirmishes between Hamilton and Jefferson, ideological differences were gradually supplanted by a "politics of personality," as people decided they either loved or hated Jackson. In addition, by raiding the federal treasury Van Buren purchased an additional degree of party unity. The bargain was straightforward: State and local Democrats would be given dollars from the national treasury as long as they called themselves Democrats, supported Jackson on most matters, and took no controversial policy stands. As for issues of local concerns, they were free to do as they saw fit. This move established a pattern of reciprocal deference characterized by both linkages and autonomy between levels of the party system. In this case, local party organizations would be linked to the state and national organizations, but they were also free to run their own shows.

By forming a political machine capable of winning elections, Van Buren won the grudging admiration of his opponents. Parties had moved beyond a collection of like-minded followers to organizations seeking the control of government. Indeed, organization has been a watchword in party politics ever since. As we will see in subsequent chapters, the resource-driven nature of party organizations and policy independence defines much of contemporary politics and is determining the role parties play in the twenty-first century.

During Jackson's presidency, power shifted from the affluent to the common citizen. Jacksonian Democracy had a number of consequences—the most significant of which was an immense increase in both the number of officials chosen by election and the number of people allowed to participate in electoral politics. Between 1824 and

1848, voter turnout increased from 25 percent to 79 percent—and in some states was as high as 92 percent. State and national party conventions emerged as important decision-making bodies in selecting candidates for office. A partisan press flourished, as parties used newspapers to communicate with their expanding ranks of followers—a low-tech precursor to the partisan weblogs of the twenty-first century.

To Van Buren, this new political environment posed both challenges and opportunities. Could the ever-increasing range of political voices be harmonized into consistently supporting one political party? Could issues attract new backers, or would appealing personalities be the key to winning new supporters? Van Buren maintained that the answers to these questions lay in building a party organization that was committed to principles even as it dispensed political favors. But jobs, not principles, formed the basis of politics in the 1830s and 1840s. The emergence of the spoils system (as in, "to the victor belong the spoils of the enemy"[15]) had a single purpose: to fill government jobs with loyal party workers. Even the mailman was a party loyalist. The spoils system meant that those filling these so-called patronage jobs would work diligently for the party or risk being bounced from the payroll. Because a job was based on one's party activity, giving time and money to the party became a means of ensuring economic security.

Over time, the spoils system changed the essence of politics. Elections were no longer solitary affairs confined to the affluent. Instead, they were community events, as issues and candidates were debated over the "cider barrel." Party organizations sponsored picnics, socials, and dinners and held rallies, demonstrations, and conventions. By immersing themselves in the social fabric of civic life, parties kept citizens involved and inspired their loyalty on election day. Many voters proudly displayed their party affiliation by wearing political buttons on their lapels. Indeed, party devotion affected more people and reached more deeply than ever considered possible. The result was a stable pattern of voting; true independents and vote-switching between elections were rarities.

Parties reached their zenith by the late nineteenth century. They organized politics by affording social outlets, presenting tickets of candidates, drafting platforms, and initiating meaningful cues and symbols to voters. In short, American politics was party politics. Parties provided coherence to political thought, even as they created new social organizations and, on occasion, divided families—creating a politics of "us versus them," which reached its height during and immediately following the Civil War.

Although sectionalism had been a factor in American politics since 1796, the growing economic disparities between north and south during the first decades of the nineteenth century heightened those regional differences. The North was increasingly urban and ethnically pluralistic as it developed a strong industrial-based economy, whereas the South remained mostly agricultural. This economic gulf led each region to see its political interests differently.

The politics of the two regions became increasingly irreconcilable. In 1846, Democratic congressman David Wilmot from Pennsylvania introduced legislation prohibiting slavery in any territory acquired from the Mexican War. The Wilmot Proviso passed in the House, where representatives from states prohibiting slavery were in the majority, but proslavery Southerners blocked it in the Senate. Bitter animosities ensued, splitting the Democrats and Whigs in half. Northern Democrats moved toward establishing a new abolitionist party while Southern Democrats defended slavery. The Whig Party split into two factions: Conscience Whigs supported the Wilmot Proviso while Cotton Whigs believed that the federal government had no business outlawing slavery. When the Whig Party refused to consider the Wilmot Proviso during the 1848 election, many Conscience Whigs left the party in disgust.

By 1854, any remnant of party unity was shattered when the Kansas-Nebraska Bill became law and annulled the Missouri Compromise of 1820 by permitting slavery if voters in these two states approved. The Kansas-Nebraska Bill created a political firestorm and ignited violence between supporters and opponents in the two states. Proslavery Democrats backed the new law and excluded abolitionist Democrats from party councils. Opposition to the new law was widespread in the North, resulting in protests that led to the creation of the Republican Party. After an 1854 Republican gathering in Ripon, Wisconsin, one participant observed, "We came into the little meeting held in a schoolhouse Whigs, Free Soilers, and Democrats. We came out of it Republicans."[16] Four years later, the Republicans attained major party status when Democrats lost 40 percent of their northern seats in the House of Representatives, enabling the Republicans to win control—an extraordinary achievement. In 1860, Republicans nominated Abraham Lincoln for president; in a four-way race, he won every free state except New Jersey. Democrats had become the party of the South, and Republicans the party of the North; the Whigs collapsed from their inability to reconcile the incompatible demands of their Conscience and Cotton factions.

Slavery sealed the Whigs' fate, but the question of immigration also contributed to their demise. Powerful nativist, anti-Catholic sentiments buffeted northern Whigs following a huge influx of Irish immigrants. The failure of the Irish potato crop in 1840 and the death from famine of over a million people prompted more than 750,000 Irish to emigrate to the United States from 1841 to 1850, eroding Anglo-Saxon Protestant domination of many northern cities. Anti-Catholic riots erupted in Boston, Philadelphia, and New York.

As anti-immigrant fervor spread, an organization called the Know-Nothings gained influence. Their name derived from members' statements that they "kn[e]w nothing" about this secret society's existence. Adopting the name American Party, the Know-Nothings believed that "foreigners ha[d] no right to dictate our laws, and therefore ha[d] no just ground to complain if Americans see proper to exclude them from offices of trust."[17] Their contempt for the foreign-born was directed at Roman Catholics, who, they believed, owed their primary allegiance to the pope rather than the Constitution—a prejudice that was not fully expunged until John F. Kennedy became the first Catholic president in 1961. The Know-Nothings enjoyed their greatest success in 1854 when they successfully competed in Massachusetts, New York, Maryland, Kentucky, and California. In Massachusetts, where Irish Catholic immigrants had been pouring into the state at a rate of more than 100,000 per year, the Know-Nothings won all but 3 seats in the more than 350-seat state House of Representatives, every congressional seat, and all statewide offices including the governorship. One despondent Whig declared, "This election has demonstrated that, by a majority, Roman Catholicism is feared more than American slavery."[18]

In 1856, the Know-Nothings attempted to capitalize on their victories by selecting former president Millard Fillmore to be their presidential candidate. Fillmore and Republican candidate John C. Fremont split the antislavery vote, resulting in Democrat James Buchanan's victory. The schism was eventually repaired as the Know-Nothings became subsumed into the ranks of an insurgent Republican Party, which retained its popular majority from its inception until the Great Depression of the 1930s. Republicans benefitted from having been the party that saved the Union and emancipated the slaves. Civil War veterans were reminded by GOP leaders to "vote as you shot," and their partisan loyalties were reinforced by generous benefits allocated by Republican-controlled Congresses. Later, Republicans became associated with industrialism and economic prosperity. They appealed to farmers by supporting the Homestead Act, which offered cheap land in the West, and won support from business and labor by advocating high protective tariffs and land grants designed to develop transcontinental railroads. Only when the Republicans were divided, or nominated weak candidates, were Democrats able to win the presidency—as happened with Grover Cleveland in 1884 and 1892 and with Woodrow Wilson in 1912 and 1916.

POLITICAL MACHINES

European immigration exploded between 1890 and 1930, when more than 15 million left Europe—roughly the same number who had emigrated to the United States from all countries during the period 1820 to 1890. For those stepping from the steerage ships, confusion about where to stay and find employment predominated. The Industrial Revolution provided jobs, but at low wages and under insufferable conditions. Few services existed to help the downtrodden. In this make-it-on-your-own atmosphere, political party machines helped ease the transition for many immigrants and in the process cemented one-party rule in large American cities. By 1900, robust party machines ruled in New York, Chicago, St. Louis, Boston, Pittsburgh, Philadelphia, Kansas City, and Minneapolis. At the state level, machines controlled Pennsylvania, New York, Ohio, Illinois, Michigan, and Wisconsin.

In exchange for a job, food, and occasional help with the law, party "bosses" asked for votes on election day. George Washington Plunkitt, one-time head of New York's Tammany Hall machine, was infamous for his candid portrayal of how the machine worked, and he won the undying loyalty of those who benefitted from it. The more people the machine helped, the greater was its grasp of the reins of power. State political bosses, mayors, and other ward leaders doled out thousands of patronage jobs to loyal party workers. Awarding jobs after a campaign was a top priority. One party leader reputedly met with his director of patronage every week to pursue every application for every city job down to the lowliest ditch digger's. In fact, patronage was an important party tool that continued to be widely used until the dawn of today's Networked Age.

The machines were also aided by local election laws that ensured that voting was not a private matter, permitting party machines to exercise a corrupt hold on power. Prior to 1888, each party printed its own ballot, usually in a distinctive color. Voters chose a party ballot and placed it in the ballot box. Split-ticket voting was not possible under this system, and the public selection of a ballot made it no se-cret whom the voter preferred. Moreover, election "inspectors" were appointed by the party machine to view the proceedings, sometimes even getting their supporters to vote more than once or to vote under the name of a deceased person. Characteristically, the bosses required firms doing government business to pay a kickback fee. The same held true to secure favorable health and safety inspections and zoning regulations. Overt corruption was tolerated because party leaders had such a devoted following. If someone's house burned, a child was ar-rested, or there was no food in the pantry, it was the boss who came to the rescue. As Chicago resident Jane Anderson wrote in 1898,

> If the Boss's friend gets drunk, he takes care of him; if he is evicted for rent, arrested for crime, loses wife or child, the Boss stands by him and helps him out .... The Boss gives presents at weddings and christenings; buys tickets wholesale for benefits; provides a helping hand at funerals, furnishing carriages for the poor and a decent burial for the destitute when they are dead, keeping his account with the undertaker and never allows a county burial. To ask where the money comes from which the Boss uses this way would be sinister.[19]

The period from the 1830s to the 1890s can be described as America's true party period; parties shaped the government and the way average citizens thought about politics. Some have even described this period as the "cult of parties," meaning that voters felt a lifelong commit-ment to a particular party. During the twentieth century, however, the party tale took a number of interesting twists and turns—once again, peculiarly American ones. Starting with the progressive era at the turn of the twentieth century, parties began to lose their strength and entered into a long period of decline, only to emerge, reinvented and revived, as something quite different than they were during the era of the party machine. We'll consider that part of the story in Chapter 3.

Throughout their history, however, the rivalry between Alexander Hamilton and Thomas Jefferson persisted, as party leaders split over how much influence the federal government located in Washington, D.C., should have in local affairs. In the nineteenth century, Demo-crats supported Jeffersonian limits on the national government; in the twentieth century, this would become the Republican Party's position. But so deeply embedded is the ongoing debate between Hamilton and Jefferson that it persists in the twenty-first century. In an era defined by instantaneous communication, debates about the role of government persist on the major parties' websites, on ideological blogs, and on Facebook and Twitter. These debates echo the Hamilton-Jefferson divide and, far from making old divisions obsolete, strengthen age-old philosophical differences. It is not uncommon to find, on the pages of conservative and progressive blogs, Hamilton and Jefferson used to justify or explain current political divisions. For instance, this entry appeared on the conservative blog RedState in 2010:

> If Mr. Jefferson were alive today, he would no doubt approve greatly of the great American spirit that remains alive and well, while simultaneously fearing that Americans have so allowed government to dominate their lives as risking extinguishment of that flame .... As we work to stop the explosive growth of government and the corrosion of our deeply held American values, we must remember what the founders sacrificed and risked to give this gift to us. We furthermore must remember, and not run away from, the righteousness of our cause, ... as Mr. Jefferson wrote.[20]

This entry, in turn, appeared on the progressive blog Daily Kos:

> What provokes me to write this is the Tea Party idea that they represent the vision of the founders. They wear t-shirts that read "Jefferson, Madison, Hamilton: Right-Wing Extremists." Poppycock! Balderdash! Liberals represent the vision of the founders far more than conservatives do, and we need to let Americans know it.[21]

Thus, remnants of nineteenth-century partisan habits have been revived in the very partisan and highly networked twenty-first century, manifesting themselves not just in the wearing of political buttons or attending party functions, but in the 24/7 world of online communication.

3

Party Organizations in the Twenty-First Century

One hundred years ago, had you walked up to someone and asked whether the two-party system was necessary, you likely would have received a puzzled expression—and not just because you were talking to a stranger. Americans had forged connections to public officials through parties, and they spent much of their leisure time involved in party-related activities. To paraphrase James Madison, "Eliminating parties from politics would be like separating air from fire; how could the latter exist without the former?"

Indeed, shortly after the presidential race of 1840, where some 80 percent of eligible voters came to the polls, Charles Dickens traveled to the United States. While riding on a train he made the following observation:

> Quiet people avoid the question of the presidency, for there will be a new election in three and one-half years, and party feelings run very high: the great constitutional feature of this institution being, that [as soon as] the acrimony of the last election is over, the acrimony of the next begins; which is an unspeakable comfort to all strong politicians and true lovers of their country: that is to say, to ninety-nine men and boys out of every ninety-nine and a quarter.[1]

That was then. By the dawn of the twenty-first century, the fervor for elections and party politics was all but gone, the victim of dramatic changes in the relationship between parties and citizens that we will detail in this chapter. In a 2000 poll, the American National Election Study found that just 34 percent of respondents talked to others about why they should vote for a particular candidate. The study also found that only 3 percent of Americans worked for a party or candidate in the 2000 election, only 10 percent wore a button or put a bumper sticker on their car, and only 26 percent were "very much interested" in the campaign that year. These figures are even more revealing when subgroups of the population are considered, such as younger Americans.[2]

It was a low tide for party politics. Then, less than 10 years later, America witnessed an election that, if not entirely reminiscent of the heyday of partisan engagement, at least temporarily reversed the trends toward disengagement. Spurred by a captivating battle between Hillary Clinton and Barack Obama, then by the historic possibility of Obama's election, millions of new voters, many young and nonwhite, flooded the electoral process and ensured Obama's election. Obama's skillful use of Internet-based social networking techniques reached many of these voters in an unconventional campaign that spurred many Americans to work for the candidate, helping to enlarge his base and turn out the vote. More than one in four Americans reported having had some contact with the Obama campaign.[3] It may not have looked like the near-unanimous level of interest Dickens observed in 1840, but it didn't look like anything from the recent past either. Were the parties back? We will consider the possibility in this chapter.

As we conclude our saga of parties in U.S. history, we'll confront a number of issues related to the decline and possible resurgence of parties in America. What caused parties, once vital players in politics at the close of the nineteenth century, to decline in influence by the close of the twentieth? When and why did these changes occur? Were they intentional or the by-products of other developments unrelated to politics? And, have these transformations shifted what remains of the party system in a Jeffersonian or Hamiltonian direction?

THE PROGRESSIVE ERA

Party machines reigned in an America that, by the turn of the twentieth century, had become a place of great inequalities brought about by the Industrial Revolution. Colossal fortunes were made by the likes of John D. Rockefeller, Cornelius Vanderbilt, and J. P. Morgan, industrial giants who controlled the production and delivery of everything from oil to sugar, copper to beef, tobacco to rubber, and candy to locomotives. But many urban residents huddled in tiny tenements after working long hours in unsightly factories and sweatshops. Farmers suffered from falling prices for their goods, low inflation, and the private ownership of railroads. Appalachian coal miners were forced to accept insufferable working conditions because the government did little to help and there was no other work available. Poverty-stricken 12- and 13-year-old children were often pressed into work because their small bodies could fit more easily into the tiny mine shafts.

Calls for reform abounded but went largely unheeded, as the U.S. government and most states pursued a laissez-faire policy on economic matters. Many Republicans, who were the majority party at the time, believed the federal government should confine itself to those explicit powers given the president and the Congress in the Constitution. That meant virtually no government intervention in ending child labor, alleviating horrendous working conditions, and improving the poverty-level wages paid by the industrial giants. Frustrated by government inaction and gridlock, the working class mobilized. Labor unions, such as the Federation of Labor and the Knights of Labor, quickly expanded. But they were no match for a government aligned with corporate interests. When the unions decided to strike, government injunctions were issued to summon workers back to the factories. Union leaders were jailed for conspiracy and contempt for not obeying the injunctions. Labor riots ensued—notably the Pullman Car Strike in May 1894 following a cut in workers' wages. The American Railway Union, led by Eugene Debs, authorized a sympathy strike that spread from Chicago to the Northwest. After several outbursts of violence, President Grover Cleveland sent thousands of federal troops and marshals into Chicago in August 1894 under the pretense of protecting mail deliveries. With that, the strike came to a screeching halt.

It was of no small consequence that many upper-class citizens felt the corruption of party machines. Gas, water, and electric companies faced little competition and gouged customers at every turn. Residents could either pay the prices set by the company or go without lights, heat, or fresh water. By the early 1880s, the reformers banded together, calling themselves mugwumps—a name that became synonymous with independent or nonpartisan voters. They were less concerned with the substance of public policy than with the allegedly corrupt manner in which it was made. The winds of change were blowing, and the party machines were about to confront a storm.

But ending corruption was easier said than done, as legions of workers continued to owe their livelihoods to the city jobs and contracts provided them by party machines through the spoils system. By the second decade of the twentieth century, reformers had organized as progressives, forming a third party aimed at upending corrupt Democratic and Republican Party bosses. The Progressive Party platform of 1912 described how the party machines controlled by both the Democrats and the Republicans had become a threat to liberty:

> Political parties exist to secure responsible government and to execute the will of the people. From these great tasks both of the old parties have turned aside. Instead of instruments to promote the general welfare, they have become the tools of corrupt interests which use them impartially to serve their selfish purposes. Behind the ostensible government sits enthroned an invisible government owing no allegiance and acknowledging no responsibility to the people. To destroy this invisible government, to dissolve the unholy alliance between corrupt business and corrupt politics is the first task of the statesmanship of the day.[4]

Former President Teddy Roosevelt carried the Progressive Party banner that year, despite his early association with the Republican Party establishment. Roosevelt began his political career after returning as a hero from the Spanish-American War in 1898. He was elected governor of New York, thanks to the backing of GOP boss Senator Thomas C. Platt, but was quickly sickened by the graft that characterized New York politics. Rather than abandoning party politics, however, Roosevelt attempted to remake the Republican Party into an agent of reform. His efforts did not sit well with the party chiefs, and they vowed to get rid of their nemesis. Platt engineered Roosevelt's nomination as the Republican vice presidential candidate in 1900, believing the obscurity of the vice presidency would surely bury Roosevelt. That plan backfired when, within a few months of his inauguration, McKinley was assassinated and Roosevelt became the twenty-sixth president of the United States. Almost overnight, Vice President Roosevelt was catapulted from obscurity to prominence.

Roosevelt's reform agenda was relatively modest. Besieged by conservative, business-minded congressional Republicans on the one hand, and reform-minded Progressives on the other, Roosevelt chose a middle-of-the-road course. He declined to seek reelection in 1908, opting to support his longtime friend, Secretary of War William Howard Taft, who easily defeated Democrat William Jennings

Bryan. Frustrated by Taft's lackluster performance as president and by his failure to espouse Progressive reforms, Roosevelt once again sought the presidency in 1912. But wresting the Republican nomination from an incumbent president whom he had virtually anointed proved impossible, so Roosevelt accepted an invitation to join with like-minded renegade Republicans who had organized as progressives. This new party adopted the nickname "Bull Moose" (following Roosevelt's declaration that he was "as strong as a bull moose"), and the name stuck. The Bull Moose platform called for the direct election of U.S. senators, women's suffrage, restricting the president to a single six-year term, a constitutional amendment allowing an income tax, the institution of a minimum wage, the prohibition of child labor, the creation of a Department of Labor, and even the overturning of some judicial decisions.

Roosevelt finished second, winning more votes than the Republican Taft—the best performance for a third-party presidential candidate in the twentieth century. But, the Republican split enabled Democrat Woodrow Wilson to enter the White House. These results proved to be a high-water mark for the Progressives and marked only an interlude in GOP control of the White House. The Progressive Party faded from the scene in 1916 after Roosevelt refused its nomination, and most of its followers returned to the Republican ranks. Robert M. LaFollette Sr. was the Progressive Party's presidential nominee in 1924 and attracted 16 percent of the popular vote, but he won only his home state of Wisconsin. In retrospect, though, the 1912 election had a decisive impact on the progressive struggle. Democrats, as well as conservative Republicans, could no longer withstand the power of the reform wave, as both parties were vulnerable to insurgent candidacies. President Wilson won enactment of several Progressive planks, as did most state and local governments. By attacking political parties so vehemently and scoring so solidly with the voters, the Progressives ensured that the remainder of the twentieth century would be an antiparty age.

However, it had taken decades of gradual and persistent reform efforts for Progressives to change how political parties operated. Reform initiatives began in 1870, shifted into high gear during the 1890s, and finally slowed after the 1912 elections. One reason why the Progressive movement was successful was this slow forward movement. Once a state or city was "cleaned up," residents elsewhere took notice and demanded reform in their own communities. Almost like an avalanche, the Progressive movement gathered more followers as it pushed ahead, until nearly all in its path were engulfed.

The media also aided the Progressive cause. Facing an entrenched party structure fueled by patronage, progressives turned to the press to expose some of the conditions made possible by government neglect. Journalists called "muckrakers" (a term attributed to Teddy Roosevelt) graphically exposed the inhuman conditions permitted to flourish in sweatshops and on farms by a government that turned a blind eye to the suffering of the working classes. Newspapers and magazines found an audience for these lurid and disturbing accounts, and over time, with the assistance of charismatic leadership, Progressives were able to chip away at machine control by successfully promoting a set of legal reforms, eventually changing not only the character of party politics but the nature of government itself. Key Progressive reforms included the introduction of the Australian ballot, direct primary elections, a merit system to replace the spoils system, municipal ownership of utilities, ballot initiatives, nonpartisan municipal elections, direct election of U.S. senators, and women's suffrage.

The Australian Ballot. When each party was allowed to print its own ballot on distinctly colored paper, machine politicians could keep track of how people voted and take retribution against anyone who voted against them. Bribery in the form of vote buying was also easy. The Australian ballot, named after its country of origin, curbed these abuses. It required that election ballots be prepared by the states, not party organizations. Ballots were to be identical and include the names of all candidates seeking office, thereby enabling voters to cast a secret ballot. It did not eliminate intimidation and bribery, but party henchmen could now lose an election and never know whom to blame. The new ballot also enabled citizens to split their tickets—that is, to vote for candidates of opposing parties running in the same election. The Australian ballot was first introduced in Kentucky in 1880; by 1896 most states had followed suit.

Direct Primary Elections. Existing election laws made it easy for party bosses to keep reform-minded candidates off the ballot by controlling the nominating process. To qualify for the ballot, candidates had to receive the party's nomination, which was cleared by party leaders in private and subsequently ratified at local or state party conventions. A civic-minded reformer might consider running for office under a third-party label, but most state election laws were written with the consent of both Democrats and Republicans, thereby prohibiting insurgent candidates and parties from participating in the election process. Direct primary elections provided a solution to this dilemma. Instead of a small group of party leaders choosing a nominee, all party supporters would be given the opportunity. Nominations would be made through elections, called primaries, where the entire party membership had a say.

The Merit System. Supported by generally well-to-do urban mug-wumps, the idea of filling government posts on the basis of merit rather than favoritism posed a direct threat to the patronage relationships at the heart of political machines. Attacking the patronage system de-nied party machines the ability to provide government jobs to faith-ful subordinates, while assuring that government positions would be filled with qualified people—a novel idea at the time. Thus, the merit system (later termed the civil service) became a pillar of the Progres-sive platform, favored by reformers weary of lackluster government services. The idea was not initially well received by party leaders, but following the assassination of President Garfield by a disappointed job seeker in 1881, Congress established the Civil Service Commission to set standards for employment by the federal government and create thousands of permanent federal jobs that would continue regardless of which party controlled the White House. By the turn of the twentieth century, most states followed the federal government's example, dealing a decisive blow to party machines.

Municipal Ownership of Utilities. At the turn of the twentieth century, utility companies that had been awarded their franchises by the party machines charged exorbitant rates even as they continued to provide poor service. The companies were guaranteed huge profits, raising the cost to customers who had no choice but to pay. Party leaders kept profits high because they were receiving huge kickbacks from the companies in exchange for franchise rights. Reformers realized that breaking this cozy relationship meant that public regulation of utility companies was necessary, and they pushed measures to do so through state and local governments. Many of these businesses remained pri-vately owned, but in exchange for the franchise they agreed to allow a public board or commission to set rates. Other services, such as garbage collection, sewage removal, and transportation, would be assumed by government under new agencies administered by employees who got their jobs through the merit system.

Ballot Initiative, Referendum, and Recall. One way to link voters to their government is to give average citizens a direct say in what government does. Another is to dismiss elected officials should they lose voter confidence. In an era of partisan corruption, Progressives championed these reforms. The ballot initiative requires a legislature to consider specific measures. The referendum gives voters a voice on policy matters by gathering enough signatures to place a measure on a ballot. The recall allows voters to remove elected officials in a special election before their term of office is over. South Dakota was first to authorize ballot initiatives in 1898; Oregon was first with referenda in 1902 and with recalls in 1908. After California instituted ballot initiatives in 1910 under outspoken Progressive Republican Governor Hiram Johnson, these measures earned national attention, and by the 1920s about three-fourths of the states allowed initiatives, referenda, and recalls. Today, these forms of direct popular participation are commonplace. In 2003, California voters recalled unpopular Governor Gray Davis and replaced him with Arnold Schwarzenegger, and in 2011, Wisconsin voters were contemplating the recall of controversial Governor Scott Walker and several of his Republican state senate allies. In recent years voters in various states have been permitted to voice their preferences on a host of policy questions including gay rights, campaign finance reform, gambling, and the legal use of marijuana.

Nonpartisan Municipal Elections. Progressives generally believed that the problems facing most municipalities were technical and could be solved by a combination of professional administration and scientific principles. Following this logic, Progressives pushed for nonpartisan city elections, where candidates were not identified by party label. Boston was the first to implement this reform in 1909; two decades later, 26 of the nation's largest cities had followed suit. Like the direct primary, however, this reform has been only modestly successful. Although the party labels of these mayoral candidates may not be printed on the ballot, it is generally no mystery which candidates are sponsored by a particular political party.

Direct Election of U.S. Senators and Women's Suffrage. Two additional Progressive measures helped reduce the influence of party machines: the direct election of U.S. senators and extending the vote to women. Under Article I of the Constitution, the election of senators was left to state legislatures. Progressives argued that this provision, combined with a six-year term and staggered elections, insulated the upper chamber from public opinion. They provided the impetus for the Seventeenth Amendment (ratified in 1913) that allowed citizens to cast a ballot for individual senatorial candidates. Women's suffrage was another Progressive cause. In 1890, Wyoming was the first state to grant women the right to vote, followed by Utah and Idaho in 1896. Even though the women's suffrage movement was centered in the East (primarily New York and Massachusetts), change did not come to that region until 1919—the year the Nineteenth Amendment to the Constitution was ratified, giving women everywhere the right to vote. Credit for passage of the amendment lies with the grit and determination of women demanding equality, especially Susan B. Anthony and Elizabeth Cady Stanton. But Progressive reformers also lent their voices to the cause because they believed that once women were enfranchised, corrupt party machines would suffer at the polls.

Over a long period of time, Progressives fundamentally altered the party system by changing politics from a private affair to a public concern. During the 1800s, parties conducted their business free from government interference, operating as private organizations. Progressives demanded public oversight and regulation of most party activities, transforming the parties into quasi-public agencies subject to legislative control. This meant eliminating most "mediating institutions," especially the party machines. The direct primary stripped party leaders of their ability to completely control nominations; the secret ballot reduced voter intimidation and election fraud; the merit system lessened patronage opportunities; and public control of utility companies drained party coffers. The direct election of U.S. senators and women's suffrage were the icing on the cake.

Placed on the defensive by disclosures of corruption and a growing sense of public outrage, party bosses yielded to the inevitable and accepted reform. But this did not mean that they were willing to commit suicide. In fact, many reform measures that reduced corruption inadvertently worked to strengthen the two-party system. Although the direct primary precluded complete control over nominations by party leaders, a candidate's ability to get on a state primary ballot required a massive number of signatures. This labor-intensive process was something parties were well suited to accomplish. Senators were subject to direct popular election, but they needed a party nomination to win a place on the ballot and initially relied on party organizations to run their campaigns. The merit system reduced patronage, yet there remained scores of "exempt" and "temporary" positions to be filled. Utilities might be controlled by boards and commissions, but the city government–corporate nexus was far from broken. Party war chests continued to overflow with contributions from businesses.

Some Progressive reforms ironically strengthened the major parties' legal standing. The new laws curtailed the worst abuses of the machine era but also made independent and minor-party candidacies more difficult. Instead of adhering to the Australian practice of omitting party designation on the ballot, most states adopted a general election ballot that required party labels to be placed alongside a candidate's name. It was easy for the two major parties to keep this official ballot recognition because state law reserved a place for whichever two parties received the most votes in the last election. Any remaining parties would have to circulate petitions before the next election to gain ballot access—a difficult and extremely time-consuming chore.

Another change during the Progressive movement that has come under scrutiny is voter registration. In a provocative book, entitled *Why Americans Still Don't Vote, and Why Politicians Want It That Way,* scholars Frances Piven and Richard Cloward argue that voter registration requirements, implemented around the turn of the twentieth century, were designed to shrink the size of the electorate. For leaders of both parties, demobilization created a more manageable and controlled system. They write,

A system of registering voters seems at first glance a reasonable development. It was, after all, simply a means of compiling a list of those who were eligible to vote, a procedure that became more necessary as the population grew, and as the vote fraud perpetrated by the clientelist political parties became more common. In practice, however, the way the lists were compiled had a great deal to do with who was likely to be on them, and who was likely to be omitted.[5]

Nonetheless, Progressive reforms directly attacked the Jeffersonian style of local governance by shifting governing responsibilities to nonpartisan administrative agencies in order to fight corruption at the local level. Jeffersonian localism was then dealt a second blow one generation later, when Franklin D. Roosevelt's New Deal politics called on the national government to take an unprecedented role in protecting its citizens.

THE NEW DEAL AND PARTY POLITICS

Other than Wilson's upset victory in 1912 and his narrow reelection victory four years later, Republicans controlled the federal government during the first third of the twentieth century. By decisive margins, Warren Harding won in 1920, Calvin Coolidge in 1924, and Herbert Hoover in 1928. This Republican trifecta profited from a strong national economy, and as long as the economy prospered,

Republicans would retain their natural majority. But everything changed on October 24, 1929, when the stock market crashed and the Great Depression began. Stock values dropped nearly 75 percent overnight, and two years later unemployment reached 25 percent. Farmers were especially hard hit, seeing prices for commodities drop to their lowest levels since 1910. Thousands of children were unable to attend school due to a lack of shoes.

In 1932, Franklin Delano Roosevelt, the popular governor of New York and cousin to Teddy, won the presidency in a landslide. Roosevelt won 42 states to President Hoover's 6, and Democrats carried both houses of Congress by overwhelming margins. In the Senate, Democrats won 59 seats to the Republicans' 37; in the House, Democrats had 312 members to the Republicans' 123. Roosevelt moved rapidly to take advantage of these majorities, proposing a flurry of legislation designed to provide immediate relief to those he described as "ill-nourished, ill-clad, and ill-housed." During his first term, Congress approved the Tennessee Valley Authority (TVA), the National Recovery Administration (NRA), the Works Progress Administration (WPA), the Public Works Administration (PWA), the Civilian Conservation Corps (CCC), and the Social Security Act. The first hundred days of Roosevelt's administration, which saw the creation of so much of what came to be known as the New Deal, set a standard against which Roosevelt's successors have been measured ever since.

Roosevelt's New Deal drastically transformed both the national government and the political parties. Abandoning its laissez-faire posture, the federal government became an active player whose primary responsibility was to ensure the economic well-being of the people. The New Deal signaled the emergence of a system whereby the federal government regulated some elements of the economy; elevated the cause of organized labor, farmers, and the elderly; and redistributed wealth through a progressive income tax. It also transformed the relationship between citizens and government. Prior to Roosevelt, a rugged individualism prevailed. But the Great Depression made it possible for Roosevelt to construct a foundation for economic security. The inalienable rights secured by the Constitution—speech, press, worship, due process—were supplemented by a new bill of rights "under which a new basis of security and prosperity can be established for all—regardless of station, race, or creed."[6]

The president became the center of the governing process—in effect, a guarantor of economic rights granted by the New Deal. To ensure a more efficient and enlightened administration, Roosevelt proposed the 1939 Executive Reorganization Act, which gave the president extraordinary powers and created a personalized White House bureaucracy known as the Executive Office of the President—an agency that has epitomized the personalization of presidential power.

The rise of executive-centered government was a serious blow to local party organizations. Local and state powers diminished as Americans looked to the federal government, especially the president, for leadership. Surprisingly, the two parties had not established ongoing national party organizations until the late 1920s. Under Roosevelt, Democrats established a permanent national headquarters in 1932, and Republicans quickly followed suit. Since then, the Democratic National Committee and the Republican National Committee (and their congressional counterparts) have vastly expanded their money-gathering abilities even as local party organizations have withered. Together, they constitute the focal points of the two-party system.

The cumulative effects of the Progressive and New Deal reforms on political parties were apparent by the 1950s. The rise of nonpartisan administration was so complete, and the concentration of power at the federal level so entrenched, that the last vestiges of the spoils system had been removed and party-centered politics had begun to disappear. By 1964, Jeffersonian localism—which concentrated power at the state and local level, instead of the federal government and especially the presidency—was viewed as a radical departure from the norm. Presidential nominee Barry Goldwater acknowledged but sought to combat this new reality, telling the Republican Convention, "Extremism in the defense of liberty is no vice. Moderation in the pursuit of justice is no virtue."[7] He lost 44 states to Lyndon B. Johnson.

TELEVISION AND CANDIDATE-
CENTERED POLITICS

Aside from Progressivism and the New Deal, the cold war deeply affected party politics. Initially, the rise of communism was a boon to Republicans, who had been shut out of the White House in five consecutive elections from 1932 through 1948. From 1952 to 1988, Republican presidential candidates benefitted from increased cold war tensions between the United States and the Soviet Union. Promising America "peace through strength," Dwight D. Eisenhower, Richard M. Nixon, Ronald Reagan, and George H. W. Bush won the presidency because they projected the right combination of steadiness and toughness. In the 10 presidential elections held between 1952 and 1988, Republicans won 7.

But as a party, Republicans paid a high price for their presidential victories. Eisenhower, Nixon, Reagan, and the first President Bush were "plebiscitary presidents"—winning personal victories without increasing the number of people who called themselves Republicans. Thus, although the cold war served the interests of Republican presidential candidates, the growing personalization of political campaigns weakened the Republican Party. Democrats also grew weaker, as their congressional incumbents ran increasingly personal campaigns, often emphasizing their own local accomplishments rather than broad party themes. Accordingly, voters came to view politics in terms of individual rather than party competition.

Party activists, who had conducted campaigns throughout most of U.S. history, were pushed aside by professional campaign consultants who used mass-based voter contact techniques to reach large numbers of voters through television and direct mail. These people learned their craft in marketing firms rather than in the trenches of partisan political warfare, and turned electioneering into a professional contest between strategists and handlers. Today, nearly every congressional candidate, most state legislators, and a growing number of municipal officials hire campaign consulting firms, who provide a breathtaking range of services necessary to waging mass campaigns: polling, conducting focus groups, fundraising, direct mail, radio and television production, event planning, demographic research, and message development. Volunteer-based and party-run campaigns are a rarity, as candidates prefer to let hired professionals run things.

More than any other factor, television turned campaigns into exercises in consumer marketing and candidates into clay to be molded and sold to the public as reflections of what people tell pollsters they want in their politicians. As an entertainment medium that plays directly to people's emotions, television is an ideal vehicle for reaching voters at a gut level, and smart candidates managed by savvy handlers have used it to great effect to connect with voters on a large scale—without actually forming the direct associations characteristic of the era of patronage politics. In the television age, politics became an exercise in manipulating mass public opinion.

PARTIES IN A NETWORKED AGE

The Advent of the Television Era and Party Politics

Roosevelt had his fireside chats; Kennedy mastered the art of television—or so the mythology goes. But television came of age during the Eisenhower era, and Ike was the first president to realize that television allowed him to circumvent the press and go directly to the American public with his message. He built the first television studio in the White House, staged press conferences and photo opportunities, and seized every chance to use television to project and enhance his image around the world. Kennedy was a TV natural—suave, telegenic, charismatic—but it was his debate partner and political antagonist, Richard Nixon, who ultimately showed the transformational power of television. Nixon learned many lessons from losing the first televised presidential debates to Kennedy—not the least how to control the beast and recreate himself using television in ways that would hoodwink a nation. Ironically, even as Nixon used the new medium of television to overcome his old political problems, it would be the older technology of sound recording that would help to bring his presidency down.

Source: Kerbel, Matthew R. 2009. *Netroots: Online Progressives and the Transformation of American Politics*. Boulder, CO: Paradigm Publishers.

Acquiring a party's nomination by abandoning the party in favor of personalized voter outreach dates back to when television was an infant medium in the 1950s. Dwight D. Eisenhower was the first presidential candidate to employ television advertising, and, not coincidentally, he was the first of several "citizen politicians" to seek and win the presidency on the strength of their personal biographies and with the help of a carefully calibrated television campaign. On February 2, 1952, Citizens for Eisenhower opened its doors, managed not by Republican partisans, but by a mortgage banker and the president of the Ford Foundation, and propelled by advertising executives who had run successful television campaigns for consumer products like aspirin.[8] They presented Eisenhower to the voters as a nonpartisan office seeker who was simply renting the top slot on the Republican ticket, selling the public on the idea that the likable World War II hero with humble Midwestern roots was a natural for the presidency. For their part, voters could support Eisenhower without making a partisan commitment. It was a marriage of convenience.

Richard M. Nixon emulated Eisenhower's approach in 1968, but took it a giant step further by using television to reinvent himself after his failed 1960 presidential campaign and an unsuccessful run for governor of California in 1962. In the parlance of hired image consultants, Nixon suffered from "high negatives" among voters who didn't trust him after a checkered career clouded by ethical questions. In an age of candidate-centered campaigns, it was unlikely that Nixon could have been elected without an image makeover; however, in the previous era of strong party organizations it would have been equally unlikely that party leaders would have given him their blessing to try. At least in the age of candidate-centered politics, Nixon was free to try to transform his image, and he found in television the perfect vehicle for creating what his consultants cleverly called the "New Nixon": honest, open, sympathetic, and accessible.

However, Nixon's efforts were at their core quite cynical, because in order to project an image of openness, his handlers understood that they had to run a closed campaign from inside a television studio, limiting access to reporters and calibrating the candidate's every move in order to avoid spontaneous exchanges that might undermine the campaign's carefully crafted message. And, they recognized that resuscitating the candidate's image didn't mean really changing anything about Nixon, who remained aloof and enigmatic to the people around him.[9] As long as they could get enough people to *believe* Nixon to be more embraceable, they could solve his electability problem, so they staged a performance for voters using a medium known foremost for its ability to tell a story.

INSTITUTIONAL RETRENCHMENT

Just as presidential campaigns were becoming candidate-centered affairs, the national political parties engaged in efforts to reinvent themselves so as to become relevant in changing political times. The Republican Party went first. Even though Richard Nixon won the presidency in 1968, Democrats maintained their control of both houses of Congress and most state and local offices. By 1973, the GOP was in serious trouble as the economy soured; then, in 1974, the Watergate scandal forced Nixon's resignation. The 1974 midterm elections proved disastrous for Republicans, when a large class of Democratic freshmen, dubbed "Watergate babies," was elected in heretofore safe Republican districts. Following Jimmy Carter's 1976 victory, some prognosticators predicted that the GOP was headed for extinction.

Given the prevailing pessimism, leaders in the Republican National Committee (RNC) decided to reconfigure the party. The task fell to the newly appointed chair, William Brock, a former U.S. senator from Tennessee. To enhance the party's electoral prospects, Brock opted to centralize power within the RNC. He initiated a four-part strategy to accomplish this goal: (1) aggressive fundraising, (2) organizational improvements, (3) better candidate recruitment, and (4) changing the party's image.

Fundraising. Believing that Republicans needed more money to win more elections, Brock decided to solicit it from ordinary voters, using some of the same techniques for party building that campaign consultants used on behalf of electing candidates. Large computerized lists of potential prospects were sent letters asking for small contributions. Although the response rate to these direct mail solicitations was low, those who gave were placed on a donor list and asked every six months or so to contribute more money. Brock argued that direct mail had two advantages: (a) By seeking small individual contributions, the party could shatter its image of catering to the rich; and (b) if successful, direct mail could raise large sums. Brock's bet paid off. In 1977, the RNC expanded its base of contributors from 250,000 to 350,000. Three years later, a phenomenal 1.2 million Republicans were sending in checks payable to the RNC. Even though the average contribution was small—just $25—total receipts grew from $12.7 million in 1976 to more than $26 million in 1980.[10]

Organizational Improvements. Brock revamped the organizational structure of the national committee by installing 15 regional directors to help plan strategy and bolster the state parties; establishing task forces to encourage states to develop long-range plans; providing regional finance directors to help raise money; and sending one organizational expert to help each state committee. Brock also initiated a program whereby state and local party organizations could use RNC-owned equipment and sophisticated technologies at a minimal cost. A massive computer network enabled the state and local Republican parties to download a variety of software programs to expedite accounting, word processing, direct mail, get-out-the-vote drives, mailing list maintenance, and political targeting. Finally, the RNC provided GOP candidates with low-cost polling services. In 1980, it supplied 130 campaigns with discounted polling, sometimes for as little as $250.[11] Thus, Brock reconfigured the RNC to meet the demands of modern-day political organizations where high technology, survey research, computer-driven targeting, television advertisements, and direct mail are all essential tools.

Candidate Recruitment. Brock also realized that these tools meant nothing without good candidates. He instituted a "farm team" approach to candidate development by recruiting prospective Republicans to seek lesser offices. Once these rising stars got a taste for public life, Brock reasoned, they would seek higher office, and thanks to their previous political experience, they would win. Toward that end, the RNC created the Concord Conferences that permitted young professionals, party leaders, and prospective candidates to discuss strategy, tactics, and the importance of political involvement. In 1980, more than 600 men and women attended these events. Brock also developed other forums for would-be candidates that included training seminars on issue development, public speaking, managing the inevitable stresses of a campaign, and media relations. Between 1977 and 1980, more than 10,000 Republicans, mostly state and local candidates, attended these sessions.[12]

Image Repair. Finally, Brock sought to refurbish the Republican Party's tattered image. Prior to his tenure, the Republican Party was likened to a country club inhabited by older, white, well-to-do men. Brock wanted these "country club Republicans" to make way for more women and minorities. To accomplish this, he spent $640,000 in 1977 to attract more African Americans to the Republican ranks, largely without success. A few years later, Brock organized a similar effort to recruit women. To help these efforts along, he began publication of a lively opinion journal. Entitled *Commonsense,* it included articles from prominent conservative Democrats, independents, and Republicans—providing an intellectual breath of fresh air to replace what had become stale party doctrine. By 1980, new ideas had become the hallmark of the GOP.

The Democratic Party's reaction to the Brock reforms was to say, in effect, "Stop until we can catch up!" Disgruntled Democrats pointed to Brock's success at fundraising and wondered how they could match it. In 1978, for example, the RNC disbursed more than $2.7 million to state and local candidates, whereas the Democratic National Committee (DNC) contributed just $107,000.[13] After Democrats took a drubbing at the polls in 1978 and 1980, the grumbling grew louder. The head of the Association of State Democratic Chairs complained, "The 1980 election was a referendum on national party structure. We were outspent, out-targeted, and out-polled. The RNC did a superlative job. The Democratic Party should hang its head in shame."[14]

But the Democratic Party found itself unable to match the organizational sophistication of the Republican National Committee during a time when Republicans were regularly winning presidential elections and, eventually, would take control of Congress while making deep inroads at the state and local level. Under the leadership of Charles Manatt, who was chosen in 1981 to serve as chair of the Democratic National Committee, the DNC was reorganized to provide stronger managerial leadership and fundraising prowess. Manatt tripled the number of DNC staffers, began a series of training seminars for state and local candidates, organized a State Party Works program that allowed state parties access to state-of-the-art campaign techniques and strategies, devised a massive voter registration program, and copied the RNC's successful direct mail efforts.[15] Although these changes resulted in more prolific fundraising, that didn't translate into success at the ballot box. In 1984, Democratic presidential nominee Walter F. Mondale lost 49 states against incumbent President Ronald Reagan.

Institutional retrenchment also involved greater institutional specialization, notably the development of branch organizations designed to finance and manage legislative contests. At the national level, these organizations are called the Hill committees because of their origins within the halls of Congress. There are four units, one for each party in each house of Congress: the Democratic Congressional Campaign Committee (DCCC), the Democratic Senatorial Campaign Committee (DSCC), the National Republican Congressional Committee (NRCC), and the National Republican Senatorial Committee (NRSC).

In one respect, campaign committees are a very old invention. The NRCC was established in 1866 by Radical Republicans from the Northeast to protect against political retaliation from their rival Andrew Johnson of Tennessee, who had become president after Abraham Lincoln's assassination and controlled the RNC by virtue of his holding the presidency. Not to be outdone, a group of pro-Johnson Democrats created the DCCC. Senators had little need for these legislative party organizations until the Seventeenth Amendment was passed in 1913, instituting direct election of senators. Senate campaign committees were established by both parties shortly thereafter.

However, these committees were unimportant players until the 1970s, serving as little more than fundraising apparatuses for incumbents to collect money in Washington and channel it back to local districts. No professional staff or permanent headquarters existed for these "poor sisters" in the party hierarchy. All that began to change in the 1960s, as the cost of campaigning began to escalate, television became an integral part of political campaigns, partisan loyalties weakened, and progressive reformers stripped local parties of much of their patronage, resulting in fewer volunteers showing up at party headquarters. Accordingly, members of Congress turned to the congressional campaign committees for help. Once again, Republicans were the first innovators. Taking their lead from Bill Brock, the Senate and House Republican campaign committees devised extensive direct mail programs. Other "inside the Beltway" fundraising schemes were pursued, including holding extravagant dinner parties in Washington, D.C. The result was an avalanche of cash: NRCC receipts quintupled from nearly $12 million in 1978 to $58 million in 1984, while NRSC receipts ballooned from $2 million in 1978 to $82 million in 1984. During the 2010 election cycle, the combined receipts for both GOP committees totaled more than $194 million.[16]

Democrats followed a similar path. Under the aggressive leadership of California congressman Tony Coelho, the DCCC implemented scores of new fundraising programs. Coelho made it a practice to visit hundreds of business and trade associations asking for contributions. According to Representative Barney Frank, "Tony Coelho was very good at explaining the facts of life to PACs: if you want to talk to us later, you had better help us now."[17] Similarly, Hill committees began playing a brokerage role, serving as intermediaries between special interest groups and needy candidates. At meet-and-greet events, candidates and PAC representatives commingle as if on a blind date, to help candidates hit it off with the PAC representatives and convince would-be donors that the candidates stand a good chance of winning and will not forget their friends after Election Day. Time only made the Democratic campaign committees more powerful. In 2010, the Democratic congressional committees raised more than $230 million to help their party's congressional candidates.[18] Although vastly different in form and capacity from their earlier incarnation, political party organizations found a way to reinvent themselves and reestablish their relevance in the political process.

PARTIES AND THE ADVENT OF THE INTERNET

Richard Nixon's success at reinventing himself became the template for how to run a campaign in the television era, and it was emulated

by other successful candidates who, with the help of media professionals, crafted biographical appeals that resonated with iconic American
lore: Jimmy Carter as the Lincolnesque figure who would never lie to
you; Ronald Reagan as the cowboy who came to town to clean up
the mess made by others; Bill Clinton as the everyman from a small
town with a name that could have been created by a screenwriter—
Hope, Arkansas. That Clinton spent most of his formative years in
Hot Springs was conveniently overlooked because it conflicted with
the campaign narrative (no media consultant would have a candidate
say, "I still believe in a place called Hot Springs"). But omissions
small and large became regular components of television campaigns
built around carefully constructed imagery, to the detriment of our
political discourse. It is not a coincidence that the era of television's
ascendancy coincides with declining participation and rising levels
of mistrust toward political figures.[19]

The advent of the Internet as a political tool suggests we are moving into a new age when politics will not be driven exclusively by
television. As we will discuss in Chapter 6, this may herald public
reengagement in politics comparable to what we saw prior to the
ascendancy of television. There is already widespread evidence that
this is happening. Since the turn of the century, Internet activism
has infiltrated the mainstream. Sizable "blogospheres" have emerged
on the left and right of the political spectrum, where the voluntary
endeavors of politically engaged citizens fuel serious efforts to influence elections, policy outcomes, and media narratives.[20] In the 2004
presidential campaign, former Vermont governor Howard Dean
shocked the political world by taking an obscure, long-shot candidacy to the verge of the Democratic nomination on the strength
of hundreds of thousands of supporters who self-organized on the
Internet. Four years later, Internet supporters made the difference in
Barack Obama's unlikely run against Senator Hillary Clinton for the
Democratic nomination and the presidency.

This leads us to the question we posed at the start of the chapter:
Is the increased involvement and excitement surrounding the 2008
Obama campaign a sign of party resurgence in the emerging Internet
era? The evidence is not at all clear. The Obama–Clinton contest
played out during the Democratic Party primaries, it's true, but the
Obama campaign was candidate-centered rather than party-centered,
continuing a key twentieth-century trend. Obama's election brought
with it large Democratic congressional majorities, but how many of
the new voters who also pulled the lever for down-ballot Democrats
were Obama loyalists first and Democrats second? Many of them did

not turn out two years later to vote in congressional elections where Obama was not on the ballot.

These observations suggest that while Internet politics may revitalize participation, it may not have the same effect on parties. Instead, the Internet promises to create more customized relationships between candidates and supporters that could strengthen their political bonds. The success of Obama's Internet campaign rested in part on a web presence that users could tailor to suit their needs and wishes so that they could take the initiative, if so inclined, to organize events, write testimonials, give money, volunteer, or persuade friends and neighbors about the strengths of the candidate. We will discuss this operation in more detail in Chapter 6. Unlike television, Internet communication is individualized and personalized, and candidates who know how to use it can do so to create a loyal following. It is an open question whether the social networking tools made possible by technological advances and effectively employed by an Internet-savvy Obama campaign will continue to engage voters when other candidates try to use them, or whether 2008 will be seen as a one-time phenomenon involving a charismatic candidate running during a moment of great dissatisfaction with the status quo. It is an equally open question as to how the success or failure of future Internet efforts will shape the political parties.

Consider also that the 2010 election restored divided government only two years after a Democratic sweep, brought about in part by a segment of the electorate that continues to swing between Republicans and Democrats—sometimes with such rapidity that it can almost cause whiplash. This result also continues a trend from the weak-party television era. And divided government in recent years has facilitated polarization and paralysis, in part through the emergence of Tea Party voters who largely identify with the Republican Party and have mobilized to vote in Republican primaries, successfully moving Republicans to assume a hard-core antigovernment Jeffersonian position. This, too, could be a sign of the weakening of parties, as members of the party in government are hamstrung by the intense wishes of their base in the electorate. On the other hand, it could be evidence of a partisan revival, as Tea Party supporters thrust themselves into political discourse in a manner reminiscent of nineteenth-century party politics, using the Republican Party as their vehicle.

Simultaneously, on the left, progressives have been organizing online in an attempt to move Democratic Party elites to embrace their positions on wealth inequity, prodding Democrats to challenge rather than acquiesce to the demands of large banking and corporate interests in such policy areas as health care, energy, taxes, and economic stimulus. Philosophically aligned with the Progressive movement of the early twentieth century, online progressive organizations and blogs affiliate with the Democratic Party but are also among the party's harshest critics. Like the Tea Party movement, the emergence of online progressives may signal a weakening of party influence if their efforts make bipartisan compromise more difficult. Or their push to reshape the Democratic Party, if successful, may prove to be evidence of a revival in the importance of party organizations.

Then there are questions about what happens to the relationship between new media campaign operations and the political parties when campaigns are successful. Upon taking office, President Obama fine-tuned his campaign web presence, rechristened it Organizing For America, and folded it into the everyday operations of the Democratic National Committee—effectively remaking the national party in the image of his successful Internet campaign. With that, the relationship between party and politician had completed a 180-degree shift from the turn of the twentieth century, even as party activity returned to the community level. Whereas the party of 100 years earlier had aided candidates by organizing campaigns and government, recruiting grassroots workers, and providing a social outlet for community activities, now an Internet campaign run by a candidate was performing these functions in the name of the party.

Americans have never fully embraced political parties. As we have seen, public distaste for parties lingered throughout the nineteenth and twentieth centuries, even as they became more deeply rooted in the political system. Parties were tolerated because they helped create an efficient means of organizing mass-based politics. Just when they reached their zenith, a reform wave swept the nation and systematically dismantled much of the leverage party machines held on the system. Progressives stripped party organizations of their institutional strengths and helped change public attitudes toward them. Direct primaries reduced the capacity of party leaders to control who got on the ballot. Referenda allowed average citizens to go over the heads of elected officials to change public policy. Franklin D. Roosevelt continued the movement away from parties by nationalizing governance. The cold war, television, and the emergence of candidate-centered campaigning accelerated the personalized presidency, which shows no signs of subsiding even as the Internet becomes more prevalent in our politics.

Through it all, though, political parties have proved to be resilient. The principal difference between the major parties at the onset of the twenty-first century from their predecessors lies not in their relative standing but in their characters as players in the process. The Progressive movement and other phenomena that have contributed to party decline might best be described as a shift from Jeffersonian-style local parties to more nationally based parties in the Hamiltonian tradition. Now the Internet promises to engage Hamiltonian mass parties in the business of Jeffersonian–style local politics, while planting the locus of control over political operations more firmly in the hands of politicians. We will consider the possibilities in Chapter 6.

After decades of change, candidates still seek office using a party label, elected officials of the same party still caucus together, and voters still rely heavily on party identification when voting. But as the centuries change, these Hamiltonian–style organizations continue to meet with widespread skepticism as they did a hundred years before; they remain an integral but often unwelcome part of the family of American politics.

4

Nominating Presidents in a Networked Age

I n 1962, a reporter asked President John F. Kennedy this question: "Somewhere in our land today there is a high school or college student who will one day be sitting in your chair. If you could speak to this future president, what advice and guidance would you give him or her?" Kennedy wisely replied, "It will help you to know the country you seek to lead," adding, "If you find the opportunity to know and work with Americans of diverse backgrounds, occupations, and beliefs, then I would urge you to take eagerly that opportunity to enrich yourself." Kennedy also advised his successor to see the world because "the future of your own country is bound to your capacity to exercise leadership and judgment on a global scale."[1]

Nearly five decades later most Americans agree with Kennedy's assessment of the qualities they would like their potential presidents to have, but have added even more qualifications to his short list. These include some prior executive experience (such as serving as a governor or mayor), being of sound character, and serving as an effective advocate of policies deemed to be in the "public interest." But how to devise a selection process that elevates such distinctive individuals to high office remains a mystery. In the nearly 50 years since John

F. Kennedy issued his job description for the presidency, would-be presidents have bemoaned the fact that to be a successful *candidate* one must foreswear any other occupation, abandon one's family, and single-mindedly devote every waking hour to seeking the office. In 1974, Democrat Walter Mondale appeared at a Johnstown, Pennsylvania, labor hall to test his potential 1976 presidential candidacy among a group of likely supporters. After delivering a stem-winder, Mondale sank into a floral couch at a local motel and wondered aloud, "Hell of a way to make a living, isn't it?"[2] All these years later, little has changed as would-be presidents typically devote two years (or more) to campaigning full time for the presidency—and that is *before* they become the nominees of their respective political parties.

WHAT KIND OF PRESIDENT?

During the twentieth and twenty-first centuries, the U.S. presidency survived two world wars, the Great Depression, the cold war, a presidential impeachment, wars in Iraq and Afghanistan, and an ongoing terrorist threat from Osama Bin Laden's al-Qaeda organization. Not surprisingly, Americans take considerable pride in the durability of the presidency. As one political scientist famously expressed it, "Only the Constitution overshadows the Presidency as an object of popular reverence, and the Constitution does not walk about smiling and waving."[3] But despite the presidency's unique place in our constitutional system, most Americans have an extremely low regard for how prospective presidents are chosen. In 2008, 65 percent said they wanted to completely overhaul the complex system of state primaries and caucuses used to pick presidents and replace it with one national primary that would select the party nominees.[4]

One reason for the profound public unhappiness with the current system is that it takes vast amounts of time, money, and energy to become president. Ever since Jimmy Carter won the Democratic Party's nomination in 1976, those who have entered the White House have checked "presidential aspirant" as their primary occupation. Bill Clinton and George W. Bush are two good examples. In the case of Bill Clinton, his presidential ambitions long predated his 1992 campaign. Back in 1963, the young Arkansan shook hands with John F. Kennedy—an encounter that Clinton's mother believed lit the fires of ambition within her son. A decade after that 1963 handshake, Clinton told Texas Democratic Party activist Billie Carr, "As soon as I get out of school, I'm movin' back to Arkansas. I love Arkansas. I'm going back there to live. I'm gonna run for office there. And someday I'm gonna be governor. And then one day I'll be callin' ya, Billie, and tellin' ya I'm running for president and I need your help."[5] Clinton biographer David Maraniss writes that the expectation and will to be president was always there "and it had built up year by year, decade by decade," climaxing in Clinton's 1992 victory.[6] Being governor did not deter Clinton from the campaign trail, since the Arkansas legislature met once every two years—and the legislature was out of session in 1992—thereby freeing Clinton to campaign for the presidency full time.

Like Bill Clinton, George W. Bush had lots of time on his hands to run for president, even though he served as governor of Texas from 1995 to 2000. Although Bush sought to convey the impression that the presidency was seeking him, just the opposite was true. During his second term as governor, Bush had a Republican lieutenant governor he could rely upon whenever he was out of the state. Moreover, the Texas constitution gives the governor few powers, placing much of the executive authority in the hands of the lieutenant governor and the legislature. Largely unburdened, George W. Bush devoted nearly every waking moment between 1998 and 2000 to seeking the presidency. Of course, his family ties helped—especially in providing organizational support and money needed to ensure his nomination. And Bush had been long exposed to the political process, having helped his father, George H. W. Bush, in his three previous presidential campaigns (1980, 1988, and 1992).

Besides those who list "full-time presidential candidate" on a job application, vice presidents have been successful players in the nomination game. Seven of the last 12 veeps have won their party's presidential nominations: Richard M. Nixon (1960), Lyndon B. Johnson (1964), Hubert H. Humphrey (1968), Gerald R. Ford (1976), Walter F. Mondale (1984), George H. W Bush (1988), and Al Gore (2000).[7] One reason these men captured their party's nod is that they are generally underutilized. A vice president's sole constitutional responsibility is to preside over the Senate and cast a vote in case of a tie. Even so, the Framers of the Constitution were reluctant to grant these minimal duties, but relented when delegate Roger Sherman noted that without them, the vice president would be "without employment."[8] Al Gore, who had been one of the country's more active vice presidents, all but withdrew from the day-to-day activities of the Clinton White House starting in 1999 to begin his quest for the presidency. Only the last two vice presidents, Dick Cheney and Joe Biden, have been viewed by the presidents they served as elder statesmen who likely would not seek the presidency on their own.

To limit prospective presidents to the unemployed, underemployed, and standby vice presidents excludes those who might be good chief executives but lack either the time, money, or determination to compete in today's presidential selection process—including a willingness to cede all privacy to inquiring reporters and subject themselves to round-the-clock protection from the Secret Service. In a meeting with his campaign team in 2006, David Plouffe, who would eventually manage Barack Obama's presidential campaign, told the putative candidate, "You have two choices. You can stay in the Senate, enjoy your weekends at home, take regular vacations, and have a lovely time with your family. Or you can run for president, have your whole life poked at and pried into, almost never see your family, travel incessantly, bang your tin cup for donations like some street-corner beggar, lead a lonely, miserable life."[9]

Despite Plouffe's admonition as to what life on the campaign trail would be like, Barack Obama concluded that 2008 was his time. He was hardly alone in making that choice: The other 2008 Democratic contenders included senators Hillary Clinton, Joe Biden, and Christopher Dodd; former senators John Edwards and Mike Gravel; Governor Bill Richardson (New Mexico); and Congressman Dennis Kucinich. The Republican list included senators John McCain and Sam Brownback; former governors Mitt Romney (Massachusetts), Mike Huckabee (Arkansas), and Jim Gilmore (Virginia); Congressmen Ron Paul, Duncan Hunter, and Tom Tancredo; former Health and Human Services secretary and Wisconsin governor Tommy Thompson; former New York City mayor Rudolph Giuliani; and former Tennessee senator and actor Fred Thompson. In nearly every instance (with the possible exception of Richardson), all of the contenders were either unemployed or underemployed, with the word *former* akin to being a first name. And all of the candidates could (and did) devote full time to seeking the presidency.

The 2012 election promises more of the same, with Republican contenders including former governors Mitt Romney, Jon Huntsman, and Tim Pawlenty; former House Speaker Newt Gingrich; congressional representatives Michelle Bachmann and Ron Paul; Godfather's Pizza executive Herman Cain; former senator Rick Santorum; and Texas governor Rick Perry—none of whom, with the exceptions of Bachmann, Paul, and Perry, held elective office in 2012. Moreover, the Texas governorship has been a historically weak office, thereby allowing both Perry and George W. Bush before him to pursue the presidency on a full-time basis. On the Democratic side, President Obama sought renomination without any serious opposition.

Time is a precious resource for would-be presidents. In fact, most successful candidates make more than one attempt before successfully winning their party's nomination. Thus, Ronald Reagan unsuccessfully sought the presidency in 1968 and 1976, before capturing the Republican nomination in 1980. George H. W. Bush unsuccessfully sought the Republican nomination in 1980, before winning it in 1988. And John McCain ran a losing campaign for the GOP nomination in 2000, before getting it in 2008. On the Democratic side, Al Gore unsuccessfully sought his party's presidential nomination in 1988, before securing it in 2000. One reason second-time candidates have a better chance of winning their party's nomination is that they have a greater degree of public recognition and, therefore, can raise more money than most unknown, first-time candidates.

To have even a chance of success, first-time presidential candidates must invest vast quantities of time and money in order to introduce themselves to the party faithful. Hillary Clinton found this out first-hand in Iowa in 2007. Although Mrs. Clinton had spent 35 years in the public eye—including campaigning for husband Bill in his 1992 and 1996 bids for the presidency—the New York senator found it surprising that Iowa voters were so intent on scrutinizing her every move. According to one account, Senator Clinton vented to aides after one Iowa visit, "I can't believe this! How many times am I going to have to meet these same people?"[10] Clinton staffers reported that their candidate complained about a system that gave the first-in-the-nation Iowa caucus such power in selecting the party nominees, remembering her as saying, "This is so stupid. So unfair."[11]

Barack Obama's 2008 candidacy provides an outstanding example of how a first-time candidate can successfully run for and win the presidency. After announcing his candidacy in 2007, the junior senator from Illinois practically relocated himself to the state next door, Iowa. Since 1976, the Iowa caucuses have been a first-run test of the potential strength the major candidates might have among the party faithful. Obama realized that winning Iowa was vital to his long-term success, and he practically lived in the state for more than a year. From February 10, 2007 (the date Obama declared his candidacy) until January 3, 2008 (the date of the Iowa caucuses), Obama held 174 campaign events in the Hawkeye State. One witness described the effects such a backbreaking schedule had on Obama personally:

The schedule was killing him. The fatigue was all-consuming. The events piled up on top of one another, making his temples ache. He tried not to bitch and moan too much, except when it got out of hand—meaning almost every day. Once, at five in the afternoon on the bus in Iowa, he turned to his body guy, Reggie Love, and asked, "How many more things do I have today?" Reggie: "Three." Barack: *"Are you kidding me?"*[12]

Yet thanks to his constant presence on the hustings, Obama won the Iowa caucuses, capturing 37.6 percent of the vote as compared to John Edwards (who campaigned full-time in the 2004 Iowa caucus and never left the state thereafter) who received 29.7 percent, and Hillary Clinton, the former first lady, who finished third with 29.5 percent.

FROM JOHN ADAMS TO BARACK OBAMA: THE PROBLEMS OF PRESIDENTIAL SELECTION

The grueling primary and caucus method for selecting presidents is relatively new, but changes to our nominating system are not. In fact, ever since the Constitution was ratified in 1789, the United States has had no consistent method for choosing its presidents. This failure to devise a selection system that recognizes the national character of the presidency, yet also provides some role for states and localities, has had enormous implications. For how a president wins an election will directly influence the direction of the federal government in Washington, D.C., and the ability of any given president to govern. Yet most Americans seem quite content to leave the definition of the electoral process to the whims of 50 state legislatures and the ambitions of countless would-be presidents. As a result, two questions that perplexed the Founding Fathers still remain largely unanswered: (1) What kind of president do we want? and (2) How do we devise a nominating system that produces "good" presidents?

The Framers understood that the challenge of consistently finding a good president was the single most conspicuous failure of the Constitutional Convention. Convening in Philadelphia in 1787, the delegates considered myriad schemes before finally settling upon the Electoral College. As devised by the Framers, each state would have a prescribed number of electors equaling its congressional delegation, based on the number of senators (two) plus the number of representatives (which varies from state to state based on its population). Under the Electoral College system, each elector would cast two votes for president. The Framers believed that state loyalties would determine the first vote (i.e., votes would go to "favorite sons"), but that the second vote would be for someone of national stature. Alexander Hamilton wrote in *The Federalist Papers* that the electors' "transient existence" and "detached situation" made the Electoral College a wise instrument for choosing the right kind of president.[13] In effect, the Electoral College would act as a presidential search committee.

However, the Electoral College only worked as planned in the first two elections of George Washington in 1788 and 1792. In those elections, Washington won unanimous victories—the only president ever to receive such a distinction. But by 1796, the Federalist and Republican parties were more organized and vigorously competing for votes—thereby negating the Electoral College's role of finding the best person with the greatest national standing to serve as president. In 1800, the system broke down completely when Thomas Jefferson recruited Aaron Burr to run with him as vice president. Burr broke his promise to defer to Jefferson and have him become president in the event of a tie vote. Instead, Burr sought the presidency outright with the result being a deadlock in the House of Representatives that was broken by the leader of the opposition party, Federalist Alexander Hamilton. By 1804, the Electoral College that had once been the object of Hamilton's effusive praise was completely overhauled when Congress and the states approved the Twelfth Amendment—that part of the U.S. Constitution creating "tickets" of presidential and vice presidential candidates.

Today the Electoral College remains one of the most flawed parts of the original Constitution (the other being how the Framers treated the issue of slavery), and 2 of that document's 27 amendments mention it directly. Each time it appears that a presidential candidate could win the Electoral College and fail to capture a majority of the popular vote—something that happened in 1828, 1876, 1888, and 2000, and nearly happened in 1960, 1968, 1976, and 2004—calls for abolishing the Electoral College mount. For example, after the Supreme Court made its infamous 2000 ruling in *Bush v. Gore* (thereby handing George W. Bush the presidency), 62 percent favored replacing the Electoral College with a direct popular vote for president (which would have made Al Gore the winner).[14] Other proposals to change the Electoral College include (1) prohibiting electors from voting for anyone other than the candidate who won their state; (2) having states cast their electoral votes on a more proportionate basis—for example, the winner of a particular congressional district (as is the case in Maine and Nebraska[15]); (3) creating bonus electors that would be awarded to the candidate who won the national popular vote; (4) allocating electoral votes on the basis of proportional representation; and (5) resorting to a popular vote count altogether with the proviso that if a candidate fails to win a majority, a runoff would take place between the top two finishers.[16] Yet for all of its flaws, none of these proposed reforms to the Electoral College has captured much public or congressional attention.

So the riddle that confronted the Framers still remains: How do we select the next president? Clearly, the president must be a national leader and able to articulate issues and solutions that are in the public interest. As Barack Obama reminded his weekly listeners on You-Tube, "One of the reasons I ran for president was because I believed so strongly that the voices of everyday Americans, hardworking folks doing everything they can to stay afloat, just weren't being heard over the powerful voices of the special interests in Washington. And the result was a national agenda too often skewed in favor of those with the power to tilt the tables .... And as long as I'm your president, I'll never stop fighting to make sure that the most powerful voice in Washington belongs to you."[17]

Yet even as presidents assert that only they can represent the national interest, it is also true that the United States consists of myriad interests, both special and regional. And as more money is needed to wage a successful presidential campaign, Americans increasingly resent the influence exercised by these so-called special interests. During the 2001 debate over the McCain-Feingold campaign finance reform bill, three-quarters of those polled supported tighter controls on campaign finances, and two-thirds thought there should be limits on the amount of money that political parties can spend during a federal election campaign.[18] Despite these sentiments, the Supreme Court voided much of McCain-Feingold in 2010—maintaining that corporations were persons and therefore entitled to their full rights to free speech under the First Amendment. In the case entitled *Citizens United v. Federal Election Commission,* the Court affirmed that speech and money went hand in hand; therefore allowing corporations to spend unlimited sums of money on behalf of their candidates, including those running for president.[19]

One possible outcome of the Supreme Court ruling is that even more money will flood presidential campaign coffers, surpassing recent records. In 2008, Barack Obama and Hillary Clinton raised more money in their nomination campaigns than all of their Democratic competitors *combined.* Obama garnered an astonishing $456.1 million, while Clinton amassed a war chest totaling $216.6 million. (For the entire presidential campaign, Obama raised $745 million, including $656 million from individual donors.[20]) On the Republican side, the two leading contenders, John McCain and Mitt Romney, were also numbers one and two in fundraising: McCain received $216.4 million in donations; Romney, $108.8 million. Despite all this money, Hillary Clinton, Mitt Romney, and John McCain each found it necessary to loan their campaigns even more money: Clinton, $13.2 million; Romney, $42.5 million; McCain, $4 million (see Figure 4.1).

One relatively new source of money is the proliferation of devoted followers on the Internet for several presidential candidates, many of whom are willing to donate $200 or less—often repeatedly. Figure 4.2 notes that in 2008, Barack Obama led the way, raising more than $200 million from his website. Republican Ron Paul also had a devoted cadre of Internet followers, raising $6 million on a single day, December 16, 2007, the date commemorating the historic Boston Tea Party.[21] Unlike contributions from wealthy or corporate donors, Internet contributions tend to be from ordinary people, who may feel they have a stake in the candidate's future in exchange for their contribution. One untested promise of Internet fundraising is that it may strengthen the bonds between candidates and voters. As Figure 4.1 demonstrates, the major party presidential candidates in 2008 together raised more than $1.2 *billion* to compete in the 2008 primaries.

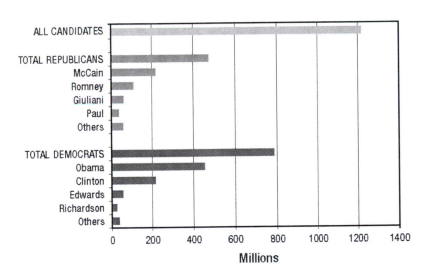

FIGURE 4.1 Campaign Funds Raised for Primaries in 2008 by Major Party Presidential Candidates
Source: Lydia Saad, "Among Recent Bills, Financial Reform a Lone Plus for Congress," Gallup Press Release, September 13, 2010.

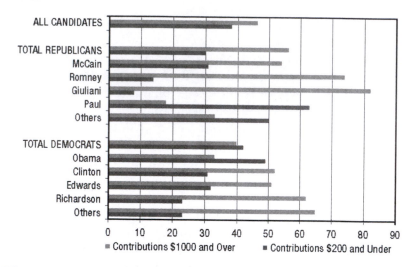

FIGURE 4.2 Campaign Funds Raised by All Presidential Primary Contestants in 2008

Source: Stephen J. Wayne, "When Democracy Works: The 2008 Presidential Nominations," in William J. Crotty, ed., *Winning the Presidency, 2008* (Boulder, CO: Paradigm Publishers, 2009), p. 58.

Internet fundraising aside, the vast amounts of time and money required to become president have created a strong public impression that the presidential selection system is broken. Accordingly, ideas for fixing it have flourished. But the various instruction manuals differ. When it comes to selecting a chief executive, Americans want the process to be fair, yet provide for majority rule; deliberative as well as quick; representative, but with some having a greater voice than others. Those in the national party establishments have tried unsuccessfully to resolve these contradictory impulses. Their discussions have centered around abstract details that have little to do with how best to pick a president, including (1) which state or states should go first in selecting presidential candidates; (2) how many party officeholders should attend the national convention; and (3) what proportions of men, women, blacks, Latinos, Native Americans, and other minority groups should constitute the various state delegations.

Political scientists have tracked how the major parties have addressed these issues. Scholars have found significant differences between the composition of the electorate and the makeup of the convention delegates. For example, Democratic Convention–goers in 2008 were less white than the general electorate, while Republicans were almost exclusively white. Blacks were twice as likely to

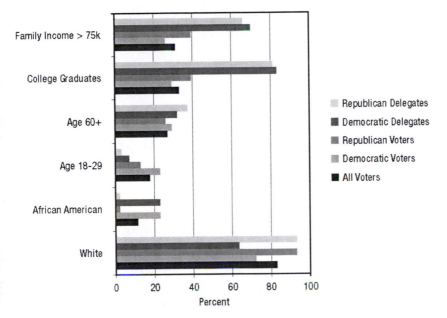

FIGURE 4.3 Demographic Representation at the 2008 National Nominating Conventions

Source: William J. Crotty, "Electing Obama: The 2008 Campaign," in William J. Crotty, ed., *Winning the Presidency, 2008* (Boulder, CO: Paradigm Publishers, 2009), p. 28.

be represented at the Democratic Convention than they were in the voting booths, while at the Republican Convention blacks were a minuscule presence. Young voters were under-represented at both party conventions in 2008, while older Americans were over-represented at both. Likewise, college graduates predominated at both national party enclaves, even though they constituted only one-third of the electorate. Wealthy Americans also found seats in numbers that vastly over-represented their electoral total (see Figure 4.3).

The over-representation of some groups at each of the national party conventions is hardly a new development. Since 1968, studies have shown both parties have disproportionate numbers of whites, college-educated people, males, and wealthy Americans who occupy important delegate seats in numbers that exaggerate their overall electoral influence. Nonwhites, those without college educations, older voters, and women have often been under-represented on the convention floors. Questions about adequate representation of key electoral groups have prompted both political scientists and party leaders to engage in an almost never-ending quest for a more perfect system of nominating presidents. This chapter focuses on the alternate roads taken in search of the best method for choosing a presidential candidate. Once again, the debates between Alexander Hamilton and Thomas Jefferson play a prominent role in the disagreements about which is the best path to take.

HAMILTON'S FAMILY VERSUS JEFFERSON'S COMMUNITY

Legendary party boss William Marcy Tweed once remarked, "I don't care who does the electin' as long as I do the nominatin'."[22] The issue of who should "do the nominatin'" has vexed the American polity for nearly 200 years. This argument, like so many others in American politics, is rooted in the dispute between Alexander Hamilton and Thomas Jefferson as to how best to implement the American ideology of classical liberalism. As we discussed in Chapter 1, Hamilton preferred to wed liberty to national authority—preferring a strong central government that could act on behalf of a national family. Jefferson, meanwhile, wanted to marry liberty with local civic authority, believing that America was a series of diverse communities and deference should be paid to local customs.

The King-Making Caucuses

The struggle between these two perspectives informs the controversy surrounding how presidents should be chosen. Throughout history, American political parties have at one time or another adopted either a Hamiltonian or a Jeffersonian approach to the exercise of power. Initially, they thought they had a solution in the Congressional Caucus. The caucus consisted of House and Senate members who belonged to the same party. They would meet, discuss the pros and cons of various candidates, and emerge with a nominee. As a national institution that represented state and local interests, it was thought that a gathering of congressional party leaders to choose a president made sense given the failure of the Electoral College. Moreover, it was generally assumed that presidents would come from the national legislature, so it seemed only natural that Congress would choose from among the prospective candidates.

The Congressional Caucus never functioned well, and the system completely broke down in 1824 after the last of the Founding

Fathers, James Monroe, had ended his presidency. That year, the caucus nominated William Crawford, who commanded little support outside the caucus and was badly beaten in the election. A five-way scramble for the presidency ensued, and John Quincy Adams, the son of John Adams, became president. By the late 1820s, the caucus system became a target of supporters of defeated candidate Andrew Jackson who vehemently argued that the entire nominating process epitomized aristocratic rule and thwarted the popular will.

Enter the Party Conventions

When the Congressional Caucus collapsed, the search for another mode of making presidential nominations began. Initially, the youthful parties gravitated toward a convention system that took local sensibilities into account. Thomas Ritchie, editor of the *Richmond Enquirer,* urged a national convention, in a letter addressed to Martin Van Buren dated January 2, 1824:

> Vain is any expectation found upon the spontaneous movement of the great mass of the people in favor of any particular individual, the elements of this great community are multifarious and conflicting, and require to be skillfully combined to be made harmonious and powerful. Their action, to be salutary, must be the result of enlightened deliberation, and he who would distract the councils of the people, must design to breed confusion and disorder, and to profit by their dissensions.[23]

In Ritchie's view, party conventions allowed for a successful fusion of Hamiltonian nationalism and Jeffersonian localism. The convention spoke with an authoritative voice in selecting the nominee, but individual states maintained their sovereignty in choosing the delegates. In 1831, the Anti-Masonic Party held the first political convention in Baltimore. A year later, the Democratic Party followed suit. The Democrats were driven toward the convention system not only because it seemed more "democratic," but because President Andrew Jackson wanted to replace Vice President John C. Calhoun, who had become an outspoken administration critic. One key Jackson operative pointed out "the expediency, indeed absolute necessity, of advising our friends everywhere to get up a national convention to convene at some convenient point, for the purpose of selecting some suitable and proper person to be placed upon the electoral ticket with General Jackson, as a candidate for the vice presidency."[24] Eventually, the convention was held and the delegates chose a Jackson loyalist, Martin Van Buren, for the vice presidential slot.

Over the years, nominating conventions became a vital party instrument—providing a forum for making key decisions about who would head the presidential ticket, what issues might be stressed, and how to support those persons once elected. Today, conventions are held in late August or early September before the general election, usually in one of the nation's largest cities in an important electoral state,[25] like Charlotte, North Carolina, the site of the 2012 Democratic convention, and Tampa, Florida, the Republicans' 2012 choice.

Until the 1970s, convention delegates were chosen by state and local party leaders. Party leaders ran the show, instructing delegates what platform planks to support and which candidates to back. Still, conventions were exciting affairs. Prior to the Progressive Era during the early twentieth century when party bosses wielded their greatest power, Democrats usually took 10 ballots to select their nominees; Republicans, 5. As boisterous and contentious as these gatherings could get, conventions were a way of aggregating the interests of local party leaders with the concerns of the national party to nominate a winner.

But the fusion of national party authority and states' rights was not completely harmonious and differed for each party. Initially, it was the Republican Party of the late nineteenth century that was most hospitable to Hamilton's notion of a national family. When it came to governing, Republican presidents paid attention to state concerns. But when it came to nominating, they viewed their party as a national organization that was all important in choosing their presidential ticket. During a credentials fight at the 1876 Republican Convention, one delegate asked "whether the state of Pennsylvania shall make laws for this convention; or whether this convention is supreme and shall make its own laws?" The delegate answered his own question, saying, "We are supreme. We are original. We stand here representing the great Republican Party of the United States."[26]

Democrats adopted a wholly different approach, believing they should adhere to the traditions of their progenitor, Thomas Jefferson. At their first convention in 1832, the party adopted the two-thirds rule under which no candidate could be nominated for president unless two-thirds of the delegates agreed. Whigs and Republicans eschewed calls for a supermajority, nominating their presidential candidates instead by a simple majority. Democrats also invented the unit rule, a device that allowed a state to cast all of its votes for one candidate if a majority so desired. These changes presented considerable difficulties in getting the southern and northern wings of the party to agree on a nominee. Thus, it took 49 ballots to nominate Franklin Pierce in 1852 and 17 to select James Buchanan 4 years later. Yet, the two-thirds rule and the unit rule accentuated the federal character of the Democratic Party's nominating process—something the party desperately sought to protect. Rising to defend the unit rule, a delegate to the 1880 Democratic Convention excoriated the Republicans as "a party which believes ... that the states have hardly any rights left which the Federal Government is bound to respect ... [and] that the state does not control its own delegation in a national convention. Not so in the convention of the great Democratic Party. We stand, Mr. President, for the rights of the states."[27]

At the beginning of the twentieth century, the debate over which approach to take in nominating presidents—one rooted in Hamilton's idea of nationalism, or Jefferson's preference for localism—intensified. The struggle took place not only between the two parties but within them. During the first years of the twentieth century, the Republican Party developed a growing Progressive faction that wanted to nationalize party affairs since local politics was often rife with corruption. Progressive leader Theodore Roosevelt advocated the creation of a national presidential primary in 1912. Failing that, Progressives wanted state parties to establish a direct primary, believing that Teddy Roosevelt would dominate them. Fourteen states followed this route, and Roosevelt beat incumbent William Howard Taft in all of the primaries. But Republican stalwarts, led by Taft, preferred having state GOP leaders retain their decisive voice in selecting presidential candidates. Taft's dismal third-place finish in 1912 resulted in a further nationalization of the nominating process. Progressive advocacy of the direct primary was extended to most elective offices, including the presidency. By 1916, 23 states with 65 percent of the delegates had adopted presidential primaries, though the party bosses still retained their power to decide the party nominee. Even so, the process had begun where slowly, but surely, party regulars were being shown to the convention exits.

Democrats, meanwhile, continued to support a Jeffersonian-like approach in choosing their presidents. Although Woodrow Wilson backed Theodore Roosevelt's call for a national primary, the 1912 Democratic platform upheld the rights of the states and condemned as a "usurpation" Republican-inspired efforts "to enlarge and magnify by indirection the powers of the Federal Government."[28] Thus, any attempt to nationalize the party's rules would be turned aside. In fact, Southern leaders blocked the nomination of Speaker of the House

Champ Clark, who was unable to obtain the two-thirds support from the delegates needed to win the nomination. Seeking a compromise, the delegates turned to New Jersey Democratic governor Woodrow Wilson, whose birthplace was Staunton, Virginia.

But not all was harmonious within the Democratic ranks. The coming of the immigrant—beginning with the Irish in the 1840s and eastern, central, and southern Europeans in the 1890s—wrought havoc in Democratic Party councils. These foreign-tongued Americans, mostly Roman Catholics, gravitated to the Democrats early and sought a voice in their state and national conventions. Most supported New York governor Alfred E. Smith in his quest for the Democratic presidential nomination in 1924. But the two-thirds rule prevented Smith from capturing the nomination. After 103 ballots, an exhausted convention finally turned to John W. Davis, a well-known lawyer whose views on race were acceptable to the South.

These internal party squabbles—and the many attempts to quell them—did not solve the nominating dilemma. This is because the argument between the Hamiltonian and Jeffersonian perspectives became linked to the ongoing debate about what kind of president we should have. Those advocating a national-centered system suggested leaders make the best presidents, not party bosses. As Theodore Roosevelt espoused, the true test of leadership rests in an ability to reason with followers in an open, public fashion. Therefore, a national system of presidential selection is preferable because it provides an environment in which candidates can test their mettle in such a way that successful contenders will maximize their ability to govern. Those who subscribe to a Jeffersonian approach hold that the selection of a presidential nominee must be consensual, and to accomplish this the deliberations must necessarily be private. Candidates should be judged by their peers, even if that verdict is rendered in a smoke-filled room. From these deliberations, a candidate will emerge with sufficient institutional backing to make the party instrumental in mounting a winning campaign and crucial in forming a successful administration.

THE RISE OF HAMILTONIAN NATIONALISM

During the nineteenth century, the youthful parties zigzagged between the Hamiltonian and Jeffersonian approaches to presidential nominating—never quite sure how to balance the two. But during the twentieth century, Hamiltonian nationalism gained the upper hand. Two individuals, both Democrats, were largely responsible: Franklin D. Roosevelt and George S. McGovern.

The movement toward a national-centered model was given its first push during the Progressive Era. A principal goal of this movement was to create a more open and democratic electoral process. One means to accomplish this was to allow average voters a say in nominations. By 1912 a dozen states adopted presidential primaries, and a few years later about one-half followed suit. Back then, however, the outcome of these primaries was only advisory, making them little more than political "beauty contests." The results provided information to the party leaders as to which candidates were popular, but the delegates were not bound to support these "beauty contest" winners. This gave local party leaders bargaining leverage at the conventions. So although the growth of presidential primaries at the turn of the twentieth century appeared to shift the nomination process in a national direction, the change was mostly symbolic.

Beginning with Franklin D. Roosevelt, the Democratic Party adopted a Hamiltonian approach to picking its presidential candidates. In 1936, Roosevelt succeeded in having the Democratic Convention strike down the two-thirds rule, despite the vigorous resistance from Southerners. Former navy secretary and ambassador to Mexico Josephus Daniels spoke for the administration: "The Democratic Party today is a national party, and Northern, Southern, and Western states would have greater representation in the party conventions under a majority rule."[29] Southerners argued that revoking the two-thirds rule would drastically reduce the role of individual states in the nomination process. On the surface, it was a call to a Jeffersonian-like system. Below the surface, Southerners realized that as long as a two-thirds majority was needed for the nomination, they could veto any nominee by acting in unison. Even in the 1930s, racial issues divided the Democratic Party and the country, so the end of the two-thirds rule was a blow to Southern party leaders.

Following Roosevelt's four terms in the White House, Democrats continued in the Hamiltonian tradition as their nominating process became increasingly nationalized. In 1952, a Democratic National Committee member lost his seat because he supported Republican Dwight D. Eisenhower for president. Four years later, the Democratic Convention passed a resolution that required a state to list the party's presidential nominee on its ballot in order for its delegates to be seated in the convention hall. (Some Southern states, in a protest to the Democratic Party's pro–civil rights stance, refused to list Democratic nominee Adlai Stevenson on the ballot in 1952.) A major step toward nationalizing the parties occurred in 1964, when the so-called Mississippi Freedom Democratic Party claimed to be more representative of that state's Democratic voters than the "regulars" who ran the state Democratic Party. Asked to settle the dispute between the two factions, the 1964 Democratic Convention passed a resolution forbidding discrimination in choosing delegates. Henceforth, delegates would be chosen without regard to their race, creed, or national origins. If a state delegation did not comply with the new rule, it could be ejected from the convention hall. A committee chaired by New Jersey governor Richard Hughes would be responsible for implementing the rule. On July 26, 1967, Hughes wrote to the DNC and all state Democratic Party chairs outlining six requirements each state must meet in order to comply with the charge of the 1964 convention. Failure would mean that the seats would be vacated and filled by the convention—an unprecedented act at that time.

THE MCGOVERN-FRASER COMMISSION

Not all states met Governor Hughes's criteria. In 1968, the Democratic Convention tossed out all of the Mississippi and half of the Georgia delegations for violating the Hughes resolution. In addition, the delegates abolished the 146-year-old unit rule that permitted a state to cast all of its votes for a presidential candidate even if other candidates had support within the delegation. The unit rule was a favorite among Southerners, who used it to maximize their power at Democratic conventions. But the pendulum toward a Hamiltonian-like nationalization of party affairs swung even further with the creation of the McGovern-Fraser Commission following the disastrous 1968 convention.

Nineteen sixty-eight was perhaps the worst year in the history of the Democratic Party. At first, it appeared that the convention would be a dull affair because Lyndon B. Johnson, the sitting Democratic president, gave every indication of seeking renomination. Not since Chester Arthur in 1884 had a party denied an incumbent president renomination. One lone Democrat had the temerity to challenge Johnson: a little-known U.S. senator from Minnesota, Eugene McCarthy. Propelled to oppose Johnson because of the Vietnam War, McCarthy had few resources and even less backing from party leaders. But with a battalion of antiwar activists drawn from several college campuses, McCarthy campaigned in New Hampshire, site of the first primary. Johnson defeated McCarthy, but the margin of victory was much smaller than expected—50 percent to 42 percent—an extremely poor showing for an incumbent president. In a dramatic turn of events, Johnson told a nationwide television audience, "I shall not seek, and I will not accept, the nomination of my party for another term as your president."[30]

Johnson's departure did not mean that most Democratic Party leaders were ready to back McCarthy—quite the contrary. If Johnson was out, their choice was Vice President Hubert H. Humphrey. Given the relative unanimity of party leaders supporting his candidacy, Humphrey did not need to campaign in any of the 17 states holding primaries in 1968. This infuriated anti–Vietnam War demonstrators within the Democratic Party, who charged that Humphrey was a member of the Johnson administration that had escalated U.S. involvement in Vietnam. Robert F. Kennedy, the brother of the late president and a U.S. senator from New York, entered the primaries and, along with McCarthy, fueled an anti–Humphrey movement. For a while, it looked as though Kennedy had a chance to win the nomination. He drew large crowds at every stop, received substantial media attention, and won most of the primaries he entered. Whether he would have been nominated is left to historical debate—on the night Kennedy won the California primary, an assassin ended his life. Needless to say, the nation was in a state of shock and the Democratic Party was essentially leaderless.

By the summer of 1968, the Democratic Party was in tatters. So deep were the divisions that two conventions were held: one in the hall, another in the streets of Chicago. Mayor Richard J. Daley, the Democratic boss of Chicago, refused to grant the crowds of young college students who descended upon the city a permit to demonstrate against the Vietnam War. Daley's police attacked the demonstrators with clubs and tear gas, creating what authorities subsequently described as a "police riot." Inside the hall, party leaders nominated Vice President Hubert H. Humphrey amid the usual hoopla and floor demonstrations. The jarring contrasts between these scenes led presidential chronicler Theodore H. White to describe Humphrey as "being nominated in a sea of blood."[31]

The protests in the streets, a widespread perception that Humphrey won his party's nod unfairly (because he did not compete in a single primary), and raucous dissent within the Democratic ranks led to the creation of the McGovern–Fraser Commission. As George McGovern, then a U.S. senator from South Dakota, recalled, "Many of the most active supporters of Gene McCarthy and Robert Kennedy and later of me, believed that the Democratic presidential nominating process was dominated by party wheel horses, entrenched officeholders, and local bosses. They believed that despite the strong popular showing of McCarthy and Kennedy in the primaries, a majority of the convention delegates were selected in a manner that favored the so-called establishment candidates."[32] The McGovern-Fraser Commission arrived at a similar conclusion. In evocative language, it urged Democrats to change their ways: "If we are not an open party; if we do not represent the demands of change, then the danger is not that the people will go to the Republican Party; it is that there will no longer be a way for people committed to orderly change to fulfill their needs and desires within our traditional political system. It is that they will turn to third and fourth party politics or the anti-politics of the street."[33]

First chaired by McGovern and later by Minneapolis mayor Donald Fraser, the commission was officially called the Committee on Party Structure and Delegate Selection. The McGovern-Fraser Commission adopted several recommendations that further nationalized presidential politics, including the following:

♦ A reaffirmation of the abolition of the unit rule, an action already approved by the 1968 Democratic Convention;
♦ Refusing to seat delegates chosen in back rooms;
♦ Prohibiting certain public or party officeholders from serving as delegates to county, state, and national conventions by virtue of their official position;
♦ Banning proxy voting, a practice used by party bosses to cast votes on behalf of absent delegates often without their knowledge;
♦ Ordering states to choose delegates during the calendar year in which the convention is held;
♦ Requiring states to post public notices announcing the selection of a delegate slate that would be committed to a particular candidate, and inviting the rank and file to participate in the selection process;
♦ Creating a Compliance Review Division within the DNC to ensure that states obeyed the McGovern-Fraser recommendations.

In effect, the McGovern-Fraser Commission told the party establishment to "reform or else." As McGovern recalled, "In public statements, speeches and interviews, I drove home the contention that the Democratic Party had but two choices: reform or death. In the past, I noted, political parties, when confronted with the need for change, chose death rather than change. I did not want the Democratic Party to die. I wanted our party to choose the path of change and vitality. That was the function of the reforms."[34]

But behind the reforms lay another agenda: removing the so-called Old Democrats—mostly white, middle-aged, establishment types who supported the Vietnam War—and replacing them with New Politics Democrats—younger, college-educated professionals, females, and minorities who were antiwar, antiestablishment, and antiparty. The commission exceeded all expectations in achieving this objective. At the 1968 Democratic Convention, just 14 percent of the delegates were women, 2 percent were under age 30, and only 5 percent were black. Four years later, women accounted for 36 percent of the delegates; those under age 30, 23 percent; blacks, 14 percent. But these increased numbers for women, blacks, and young voters came with a high price tag. In an unprecedented act, the 1972 Democratic Convention voted to exclude the delegates from Cook County, Illinois (including Chicago), led by Chicago Mayor Richard J. Daley, and replace them with pro-McGovern delegates led by a young, black civil rights activist named Jesse Jackson. In a subsequent legal action, the U.S. Supreme Court affirmed the convention's decision using decidedly Hamiltonian language: "The convention serves the pervasive national interest in the selection of candidates for national offices and this national interest is greater than any interest of any individual state."[35]

Establishment Democrats were astounded at the convention's actions and their ratification by the Supreme Court. Daley delegates had won the Illinois primary, whereas Jackson's slate had not even competed. Moreover, Daley was still viewed as key to winning this electoral vote–rich state in the fall. As it turned out, McGovern lost Illinois (and 48 other states) to Republican Richard M. Nixon. But by removing the Daley delegation on the grounds that it had less than the desired number of women, young voters, and blacks, the convention opened a Pandora's box of what became a virtual quota system for choosing delegates. As McGovern later acknowledged, "Whatever the commission originally intended, in administering the guidelines on minorities, women, and young people, it eventually moved very close to adopting a de facto quota system."[36]

Along with mandating specifics of the composition of each state's delegation, the commission also sought changes in how they were to be selected. The 1968 fiasco suggested that party regulars were excluded from the process in favor of party bosses who picked the president in smoked-filled rooms. The commission's proclamation that delegate selection must be "open, timely, and representative" was considered somewhat vague, but few states wished to jeopardize their role at the next convention. Most state Democratic Party leaders shrugged their shoulders and abandoned their state conventions in favor of primaries and caucuses where the rank and file would make their presidential preferences known. As compensation, however, Democratic leaders would retain a decisive voice in selecting their own candidates for state and local offices. The shift from party leaders deciding who would be the next president to primary voters has been significant. In most of the states that hold primaries, voters choose how many delegates will go to the nomination convention for each of the various aspirants. A candidate who nets 50 percent of the primary votes, for instance, will receive 50 percent of the state's delegation. The actual delegates themselves are usually selected by state party meetings and conventions, but, unlike the "advisory" primary system of the Progressive Era, they are bound to support the candidate they were sent to support, at least on the first ballot. Other states have a "pure" primary system whereby voters directly elect delegates to the national convention. Each would-be delegate's candidate preference is listed on the ballot. A delegate who has no preference is listed as "uncommitted." Delegates chosen under this system are duty-bound to support the candidate listed on the ballot.

REPUBLICANS FOLLOW THE MCGOVERN-FRASER LEAD

Although not subject to the recommendations of the McGovern-Fraser Commission, Republicans felt its effects when state legislatures passed laws mandating state presidential primaries. The gusts of change blowing through Democratic convention halls rattled Republican windows, too. Several state legislatures, largely controlled by Democrats, passed laws mandating presidential primaries for both parties. Republicans also engaged in a modest effort to alter their rules in the name of fairness. The 1972 convention authorized the creation of a Delegate-Organization (DO) Committee. The purpose of the DO Committee (called the "Do-Nothing Committee" by critics) was to recommend measures for enhancing the numbers of women, youth, and minorities at future Republican conventions. The committee proposed that traditional party leaders be prohibited from serving as ex-officio delegates; that party officials should better inform citizens how they could participate in the nomination process; and that participation should be increased by opening the primaries and state conventions to all qualified citizens. But the 1976 Republican Convention rejected several of the committee's more important recommendations, including (1) allowing persons under 25 years of age to vote in "numerical equity to their voting strength in a state"; (2) encouraging equal numbers of male and female delegates; and (3) having one minority group on each of the convention's principal committees. Later, the RNC rejected a recommendation that it review state affirmative action plans, and the GOP has refused to abolish winner-take-all primaries such as the one in California. Winner-take-all primaries helped John McCain wrap up the Republican nomination on March 4, 2008, even as Barack Obama and Hillary Clinton were still slugging it out in the Democratic primaries and caucus contests.[37]

THE UNINTENDED CONSEQUENCES OF THE MCGOVERN-FRASER REFORMS

Despite its intentions, the McGovern-Fraser reforms unleashed several unintended consequences, including the proliferation of primaries and caucuses, the emergence of outsider candidates, and a power shift from party elites to media elites.

A Proliferation of Primaries

One unintended consequence of the McGovern-Fraser reforms has been a substantial increase in the number of presidential primaries. In 1960, John F. Kennedy ran in only three state primaries: West Virginia, Wisconsin, and New Hampshire. In 2008, 34 states held caucuses or primaries on or before February 5, with 24 states conducting primaries or caucuses on February 5 itself, a date that now is known as "Super Tuesday"(see Table 4.1). Altogether, Democrats held 41 primaries; Republicans, 38 (the remaining states held caucuses). Skipping primaries and caucuses and relying on the party bosses to deliver delegates no longer works, as voters have seized control of the old party machines and use them at their will. In 2008, for example, former New York City mayor Rudolph Giuliani skipped both the Iowa caucus and the New Hampshire primary, deciding instead to make his stand in the Florida primary. But events would not wait: Former Arkansas governor Mike Huckabee won Iowa; Senator John McCain won New Hampshire; former Massachusetts governor Mitt Romney contested these primaries (winning second place in both) and was still in the hunt. Giuliani ran poorly in Florida and dropped out of the race after the votes were counted. As the Giuliani saga proved, waiting for more fertile ground to advance a candidacy no longer remains much of an option for would-be presidents. Under the current system, successful candidates have to run virtually everywhere, meaning that they often must be in two (or three) places at once.

As Table 4.1 demonstrates, the primary calendar is complicated and front-loaded. Candidates must know the dates of the scheduled state contests and plan their calendars accordingly. But candidates must do more than be in multiple places at once. They and their staffs have to know the state laws that govern the primaries and caucuses. In 2008, 17 states held closed primaries in which voters were required to declare their party affiliation before voting. Often, this declaration is done when one registers to vote. The idea behind a closed primary is to ensure that only loyal party members participate in selecting the nominee. Twenty-one states took a different route in 2008 and conducted open primaries. But how open the primary is varies from state to state. In some, registered party members can vote in a major party contest along with independents. In others, anyone who is a registered voter can decide on the day of the primary the contest in which he or she would like to vote.

Party Caucuses Also Become Popular

Caucuses are another popular means for selecting delegates. Instead of voting at one's leisure during the primary day, caucuses require the party's rank and file to appear at an organized meeting and publicly declare one's support for a candidate. The process is similar to a town hall meeting or a miniconvention, as people gather alongside neighbors and strangers to publicly declare their support for a candidate. In 2008, Democrats held caucuses in 13 states and the territory of Guam as well as Democrats Abroad; Republicans held caucuses in 13 states. For both parties, the most prominent of these is the Iowa caucuses, which provide the first test of a candidate's strength. On January 3, 2008, Democrats and Republicans gathered at libraries, town halls, and church basements across Iowa to declare their support for their preferred candidate and—if that candidate failed to garner a threshold level of support—to regroup and caucus with supporters of their

Table 4.1 2008 Schedule of Primaries and Caucuses

Date	Democratic Primary/Caucus	Republican Primary/Caucus
January 3	Iowa Caucuses	Iowa Caucuses
January 8	New Hampshire Primary	New Hampshire Primary
January 15	Michigan Primary*	Michigan Primary
January 19	Nevada Precinct Caucuses	Nevada Precinct Caucus
		South Carolina Primary
January 22		Louisiana District Caucuses
January 25–February 7		Hawaii Precinct Caucuses
January 26	South Carolina Party-run Primary	
January 29	Florida Primary*	
February 1–3		Maine Municipal Caucuses
February 5 (Super Tuesday)	Alabama Primary	Alabama Primary
	Arkansas Primary	Arkansas Primary
	California Primary	Arizona Primary
	Colorado Precinct Caucus	California Primary
	Connecticut Primary	Colorado Precinct Caucuses
	Delaware Primary	Connecticut Primary
	Georgia Primary	Delaware Primary
	Idaho County Caucus	Georgia Primary
	Illinois Primary	Illinois Primary
	Massachusetts Primary	Massachusetts Primary
	Minnesota Precinct Caucuses	Minnesota Precinct Caucuses/Nonbinding Straw Poll
	Missouri Primary	
	North Dakota Precinct Caucuses	Missouri Primary
	New Jersey Primary	Montana Caucus
	New Mexico Party-run Primary	North Dakota Caucus
	New York Primary	New Jersey Primary
	Oklahoma Primary	New York Primary
	Tennessee Primary	Oklahoma Primary
	Utah Primary	Tennessee Primary
February 5–12	Democrats Abroad Local Caucuses/Primary	
February 9	Louisiana Primary	Kansas Caucuses
	Washington Precinct Caucuses	Louisiana Primary
		Washington Precinct Caucuses
February 10	Maine Municipal Caucuses	
February 12	District of Columbia Primary	District of Columbia Primary
	Maryland Primary	Maryland Primary
	Virginia Primary	Virginia Primary
February 19	Washington Non-binding Primary	Washington Primary
	Wisconsin Primary	Wisconsin Primary
February 24		Puerto Rico Territorial Caucus
March 1	Automatic Selection of Unpledged (Super) Delegates	*(continued)*

Table 4.1 *(continued)*

Date	Democratic Primary/Caucus	Republican Primary/Caucus
March 4	Ohio Primary	Ohio Primary
	Rhode Island Primary	Rhode Island Primary
	Texas Primary	Texas Primary
March 11	Mississippi Primary	Mississippi Primary
March 15–April 11	Democrats Abroad Regional Caucuses	
April 22	Pennsylvania Primary	Pennsylvania Primary
May 3	Guam Territorial Caucus (Party-run primary)	
May 6	Indiana Primary	Indiana Primary
	North Carolina Primary	North Carolina Primary
May 13	Nebraska Advisory Primary	Nebraska Primary
	West Virginia Primary	West Virginia Primary
May 20	Kentucky Primary	Kentucky Primary
	Oregon Primary	Oregon Primary
May 27	Idaho Non-binding Primary	Idaho Primary
June 1	Puerto Rico Primary	
June 3	Montana Primary	Montana Advisory Primary
	South Dakota Primary	New Mexico Primary
		South Dakota Primary
June 3	Florida Do-Over Primary (canceled)	
August 25–28	Democratic National Convention (Denver, Colorado)	
September 1–4		Republican National Convention (Minneapolis-St. Paul, Minnesota)

Source: http://www.thegreenpapers.com/P08/events.phtml?s=c. Accessed January 23, 2010.

second or third choice. In addition, Iowa caucus-goers took positions on important issues of the day and forwarded them to the state party committees and the national convention. Not surprisingly, only the very committed from both parties resolved to come out on a cold, snowy night and remain at their caucus locations for several hours.

The caucuses worked in Barack Obama's favor in 2008. His strategy of organizing early on the ground paid rich dividends in his battle against Hillary Clinton. In most cases, Obama was able to win caucus-goers who were motivated to come to the polls and support his candidacy. Beginning in Iowa and continuing throughout the litany of states who chose their delegates based on the caucus system, Obama's organization was able to identify potential supporters in a low-turnout environment (compared to primary contests) and get them to the polls. The delegates from these caucus states proved crucial to Obama's win in the closely fought Democratic contest against Clinton.

A Surge in Outsider Candidacies

The McGovern-Fraser Commission facilitated a surge in outsider candidacies, beginning with McGovern's anti–Vietnam War candidacy in 1972. George McGovern admitted that the new rules spawned by the commission he led would fuel ideologically inspired candidacies: "My successful bid for the nomination in 1972 was based in part on the opportunity which the new rules offered to a candidate willing to take his case directly to rank-and-file voters rather than depending on big-name endorsements."[38] In fact, many who worked for the commission played key roles in McGovern's successful drive to win the Democratic nomination. But the exclusion of "big-name endorsements" has contributed mightily to a weakening of parties as institutions. By removing the most important function party leaders have—making the party's choice for president—what remained of the old establishment found itself with almost nothing to do. In the years since 1972, other outsider insurgent candidacies have included Pat Robertson and Ron Paul on the Republican side, and Jimmy Carter, Gary Hart, Jesse Jackson, and Al Sharpton on the Democratic side.

The Media Play an Important Role

The ongoing arguments about whether the rank and file or party leaders should exercise a dominant role in selecting presidential candidates are virtually meaningless today, given the new presidential nomination system engendered by the McGovern-Fraser Commission—one that is dominated by primaries and where most voters learn about politics through television and on the Internet. A key unanticipated result of the party reform process is that instead of shifting control over the nominating system from party elites to the rank and file, reform efforts made individual candidates free agents of sorts, who campaign for primary votes through the media. This, in turn, thrust journalists into the selection process, replacing party elites with media elites who have become unwitting king makers, running elections on their terms. Collectively, reporters exercise a form of "peer review," acting as political analysts and talent scouts.

Political reporters are often fascinated with two things: who has raised the most money and from what sources, and how the various candidates stand in public opinion polls. In fact, it can be said that

(((())))

PARTIES IN A NETWORKED AGE

The March of the Internet in Political Campaigns

By the dawn of the twenty-first century, the Internet had gone from being dismissed as a curiosity to being embraced as a political necessity. By 2000, every serious presidential candidate had a website. By 2003, the Howard Dean campaign had demonstrated the power of the medium for voter mobilization and campaign fundraising. By 2004, a few candidates and journalists had already begun to blog, and by 2006, bloggers were instrumental rather than incidental to political campaigns. Then, in 2008, Barack Obama ran a watershed campaign that engaged a variety of Internet-based outreaches from fan-base sites like MyBO, to personalized cell phone robo calling, to strategic text messaging. Upon his election, Obama issued a call for mass job applications to his administration via the Internet and continued many other Internet-based initiatives, turning them to the task of governing rather than campaigning. In 2012, tweeting and blogging will be accompanied by the proliferating use of computer apps on a variety of devices for everything from donating to candidates to finding one's polling place.

Source: Kerbel, Matthew R. 2009. *Netroots: Online Progressives and the Transformation of American Politics.* Boulder, CO: Paradigm Publishers.

even before the primaries begin, there is a pre-presidential primary whose criteria include how the candidates stand in the national polls, how much money they have raised, and the strength of their organizations. Making these judgments and declaring a winner is often the sole province of the national media.

Once the primaries begin, the press often plays a determinative role as to what constitutes a "win" or a "loss." For example, in 2008, Mike Huckabee's first-place finish in Iowa gave him a bump in media coverage and campaign donations. Mitt Romney's second-place finish there also gave him more media scrutiny. On the Democratic side, Barack Obama's Iowa win gave him enhanced media coverage going into New Hampshire, while John Edwards's disappointing second-place finish meant a corresponding loss in press coverage. Hillary Clinton continued to be a major story by virtue of being the first female candidate with a realistic shot at a major party nomination, but the press virtually wrote off the other Democratic candidates and departed from their campaign buses. Limited media resources means that journalists and their editors must make crucial decisions about which candidates they will cover and which ones they will not. In making these choices, journalists and their bosses are exercising a role once reserved for the party bosses.

THE MIKULSKI, WINOGRAD, HUNT, AND CHANGE COMMISSIONS

The unintended consequences of the McGovern-Fraser reforms have not stopped Democrats from continuously tinkering with their presidential nominating system. The 1972 Democratic Convention authorized the creation of a Commission on Delegate Selection and Party Structure to be chaired by then-Baltimore city councilwoman Barbara Mikulski. The Mikulski Commission reaffirmed the idea of choosing convention delegates through direct primaries and state party caucuses and of having a delegate's presidential preference clearly expressed on a state ballot. But even more radically, the commission recommended that anyone receiving 10 percent of the primary or caucus votes receive a proportionate share of the delegates. The DNC agreed with the basic thrust of the recommendation, but raised the threshold to 15 percent. Together, the McGovern-Fraser and Mikulski Commissions represented a revolution in the nominating process. Old bosses became extinct and individuals motivated more by ideology than pragmatism in both parties seized the reins of power.

As Democrats continued to lose presidential elections in the 1970s and 1980s, reform commissions continued. In 1975, Democratic National Chairman Robert Strauss created the Commission on the Role and Future of Presidential Primaries, chaired by Morley Winograd, the Michigan state Democratic chairman. The Winograd Commission recommended that each state Democratic Party "adopt specific goals and timetables" to carry out affirmative action programs, citing women, blacks, Hispanics, and Native Americans as groups for which remedial action was needed to overcome the effects of past discrimination. Upon receiving the commission report, the DNC immediately ordered that state delegations comprise equal numbers of men and women.

Taken together, these changes banished much of the Democratic Party establishment from the convention proceedings. Before the McGovern-Fraser Commission, 83 percent of Democratic governors, 68 percent of senators, and 39 percent of representatives attended the

1968 Democratic Convention as delegates or alternates; by 1976, only 76 percent of Democratic governors, 14 percent of senators, and 15 percent of representatives were delegates.[39] Proportional representation was introduced and soon engendered disputes among prospective nominees. The *New York Times* columnist Tom Wicker wrote that the Democratic Party's obsession with the purity of the process had overcome its desire to win presidential contests: "[Democrats have become] *a party of access* in which the voiceless find a voice while Republican control of the presidency has permitted them to maintain enough coherence and unity to become a *party of government*."[40]

Jimmy Carter's landslide 1980 loss to Ronald Reagan prompted the creation of the Hunt Commission, chaired by North Carolina governor James Hunt, which undertook to restore some modicum of federalism to the nominating process. It called for the creation of superdelegates—that is, Democratic officials and party officeholders who would be automatic convention delegates. In 2008, these so-called superdelegates cast nearly 20 percent of the total votes at the Democratic National Convention. Not officially bound to any candidate per se, these 795 delegates could, if they wished, reverse the verdict issued by the rank-and-file primary voters. At first, many of these superdelegates assumed that Hillary Clinton had a lock on the nomination. But as Barack Obama began to win many of the primary and caucus contests, it became evident that the superdelegates confronted two political dilemmas: (1) vote for Clinton, even if she lost the total primary and caucus vote, and be saddled with a nominee whose legitimacy would be questioned from the start; or (2) change their publicly stated support for Clinton and throw their weight behind Obama. If the superdelegates ignored the primary and caucus voters and backed the popular vote loser, a sizable 37 percent of registered voters said they would consider such a nominee to be illegitimate; only 31 percent said the nomination would have been won fair and square.[41] Other polls also showed strong support among Democrats for the notion that the superdelegates should take their direction from the voters: 62 percent believed the superdelegates should vote for the person with the most votes overall[42]; 36 percent said the superdelegates should vote for the person who won their state[43]; 25 percent thought the superdelegates should vote for whomever they wanted[44]; only 20 percent said the superdelegates should exercise independent judgment and vote for the candidate with the best chance to win in November[45]; and 50 percent thought the superdelegates were a bad idea, period.[46] In the end, the superdelegates moved toward Obama, and the roll call at the Democratic Convention was shortened when

Hillary Clinton asked the delegates to make Obama's nomination unanimous.

Despite their victory in 2008, Democrats plan to make more changes for their 2012 convention. The Democratic National Committee created a Change Commission, headed by Missouri senator Claire McCaskill and South Carolina representative James Clyburn, that recommended significantly reducing the number of superdelegates.[47] In addition, both parties adopted changes to their primary calendars that have the first contests begin in February 2012—with Iowa, New Hampshire, Nevada, and South Carolina going first and the remaining states to follow beginning the first Tuesday in March.[48] Republicans have also added an additional sanction: Any state holding its primary or caucus before April 1, 2012, will have its delegates chosen by proportional representation rather than the winner-take-all that has been customary in previous GOP contests.[49] Winner-take-all contests will resume after April 1, 2012. These changes make it possible that the contested 2012 Republican presidential contest will not be over until sometime in June. These changes adopted by Democrats and Republicans in the 2012 presidential selection process make this the twelfth time since 1968 in which there were significant alterations to the existing rules.

LOOKING TO 2012

Americans are ambivalent about political parties. That ambivalence stems, in part, from the accent on individualism that permeates the American polity. When it comes to choosing a president, a focus on the individual, not the party, has prevailed. This post-1968 emphasis on personalities has complicated the selection process. The Framers' attempt to devise a presidential selection system that would create a presidency free of partisan constraints resulted in the creation of the Electoral College, which many judge to have failed. By the mid-1800s, political parties became more firmly rooted in American tradition, and the party convention, which emphasizes group activity rather than individual choice, supplanted the Congressional Caucus. The party convention has enjoyed a long life, in part because it fused federalism with nationalism, and also because it became a source of social activity in an era when parties were an important socializing force. But the convention as a collective decision-making entity is no more—a victim of party decay, reform, and the ambitions of would-be presidents.

Today, conventions exist to ratify the choices made by voters in the party primaries and caucuses—choices that are made by a candidate's own desire to place his or her name into contention. Observers could see the first inkling of this phenomenon as early as 1960, when the reporter Richard Reeves wrote that the most important feature of John F. Kennedy's political career was his own ambition:

> He did not wait his turn. He directly challenged the institution he wanted to control, the political system. After him, no one else wanted to wait either, and few institutions were rigid enough or flexible enough to survive impatient ambition-driven challenges. He believed (and proved) that the only qualification for the most powerful job in the world was wanting it. His power did not come from the top down nor from the bottom up. It was an ax driven by his own ambition into the middle of the system, biting to the center he wanted for himself. When he was asked early in 1960 why he thought he should be president, he answered: "I look around me at the others in the race, and I say to myself, well, if they think they can do it why not me? 'Why not me?' That's the answer. And I think it's enough."[50]

Ever since John Kennedy uttered those words, every other presidential candidate in the decades since has said, in effect, "Why not me?" In presenting themselves to the public, these ambitious contenders have relied on their own personas, rather than their party affiliations, to help them get elected. Celebrity politics is entertaining, but it is not party politics. In 2008, for example, Barack Obama barely mentioned the word *Democrat.* Instead, his theme was "Change You Can Believe In"—a vague slogan that voters could interpret however they wished.

In an era of empty sloganeering, it is no wonder that party conventions hardly resemble the days of yore. In the 1965 edition of *The World Book Encyclopedia,* major party conventions were described as allowing "all citizens an opportunity to observe one of the processes of representative government. And when two strong candidates seek nomination, a national convention is more exciting than a World Series."[51] But it has been years since a convention has been more exciting than any World Series. The last gathering to take more than one ballot was in 1952, when the Democrats nominated Adlai E. Stevenson on the third ballot.

Still, party conventions continue on as spectacles. In 2008, numerous surveys found that Americans were paying attention to the

Table 4.2 Attitudes toward the 2008 Party Conventions

Plan to watch the Democratic Convention. Percentage answering "just a little" or "none of it."*	51
Plan to watch all or most of the Republican Convention. Percentage answering "just a little" or "none of it."†	56
Percentage "very interested" or "fairly interested" in watching Barack Obama's acceptance speech.‡	58
Percentage "very interested" or "fairly interested" in watching John McCain's acceptance speech.§	52
Percentage answering "the party conventions" most helped you decide your vote.°	8

Source: Pew Research Center for the People and the Press, poll, August 15–18, 2008; Marist College Institute for Public Opinion, poll, November 2, 2008.

* Pew Research Center text of question: "As you may know, both the Democratic and Republican parties will be holding their (2008) conventions over the next few weeks. How much television coverage of the Democratic Convention do you plan to watch? Do you think you'll watch all or most of the coverage, some of it, just a little, or none of it?" All or most of the coverage, 20 percent; some of it, 29 percent; just a little, 26 percent; none of it, 25 percent.

† Pew Research Center text of question: "As you may know, both the Democratic and Republican parties will be holding their (2008) conventions over the next few weeks. How much television coverage of the Republican Convention do you plan to watch? Do you think you'll watch all or most of the coverage, some of it, just a little, or none of it?" All or most of the coverage, 14 percent; some of it, 30 percent; just a little, 29 percent; none of it, 27 percent.

‡ Pew Research Center text of question: "As you may know, both the Democratic and Republican parties will be holding their (2008) conventions over the next few weeks. As I read some things that will happen at the (2008) Democratic Convention, tell me how interested you are in each event. Are you very interested, fairly interested, not too interested, or not at all interested in watching Barack Obama's acceptance speech?" Very interested, 33 percent; fairly interested, 25 percent; not too interested, 14 percent; not at all interested, 27 percent; don't know, 1 percent.

§ Pew Research Center text of question: "As you may know, both the Democratic and Republican parties will be holding their (2008) conventions over the next few weeks. As I read some things that will happen at the (2008) Republican Convention, tell me how interested you are in each event. Are you very interested, fairly interested, not too interested, or not at all interested in watching John McCain's acceptance speech?" Very interested, 24 percent; fairly interested, 28 percent; not too interested, 15 percent; not at all interested, 33 percent.

°Marist College Institute for Public Opinion text of question: "Which one of the following defining moments in the (2008) presidential (election) campaign most helped you decide your vote? The economic crash, the debates, the vice presidential selections, the party conventions, decided before party conventions?" The economic crash, 10 percent; the debates, 18 percent; the vice presidential selections, 10 percent; the party conventions, 8 percent; decided before party conventions, 47 percent; unsure, 7 percent.

acceptance speeches given by Barack Obama and John McCain, but less than a majority said they planned to watch either of the conventions, and only a small percentage said the party conclaves were a major factor in making their choices at the ballot box (see Table 4.2).

Given these numbers, it is not surprising that the major networks no longer deem the nominating conventions worthy of much coverage. In a celebrated incident, ABC anchor Ted Koppel walked out of the 1996 Republican Convention saying that there was no news there for him to cover. Four years later, the big three networks (ABC, CBS, and NBC) relegated their convention coverage to a mere hour each night (or folded it into their news magazine shows), a practice they have continued in the years since. Today, network executives defer to the cable news shows for comprehensive convention coverage and limit their precious air time to the candidates' acceptance speeches.

In a sense, we have never left square one, seeking to "fix" what many Americans see as a broken nominating system. Besides wondering about what kind of president we want, future tinkerers must also ask, "How do we get a president who can govern effectively?" The answers to both of these questions are harder to find as political parties become less able to control the selection process.

5

Party Brand Loyalty and the American Voter

E very four years Americans gather to follow a quadrennial series titled "Election Night" that answers an all-important question: Who will be the next president? Some Election Nights have become legendary for their suspense and high drama. For example, running for an unprecedented third term in 1940, Franklin D. Roosevelt saw trouble in the early returns. Breaking into a cold heavy sweat, the president abruptly ordered everyone to leave the family dining room at his Hyde Park, New York, estate. Seated in his wheelchair, Roosevelt calculated whether he had enough votes to win as news tickers clattered away with the latest results. After a few suspense-filled hours, the numbers turned in Roosevelt's favor, whereupon family and friends rejoined him as he became his familiar, cheery self.[1]

Twenty years later another Election Night was immortalized by journalist Theodore H. White. Spending the evening with John F. Kennedy at his Hyannisport, Massachusetts, compound, White described how the early figures were going Kennedy's way. At one point in the evening, Kennedy's wife, Jacqueline, exclaimed, "Oh, Bunny [her pet name for her husband], you're going to be president now!"[2] But as midnight approached, Kennedy's Republican opponent,

Richard M. Nixon, had cut dramatically into Kennedy's lead, leaving Kennedy a few electoral votes shy of a majority. As night turned to day, no one knew who had won. Only when Chicago mayor Richard J. Daley found enough votes to put Illinois into the Democratic column was Kennedy declared the winner. Final figures showed Kennedy beat Nixon by just 112,881 popular votes out of nearly 70 million cast—a margin of just one-tenth of 1 percent.

Eight years later Richard M. Nixon returned as a central character in another Election Night melodrama—this time defeating Hubert H. Humphrey by half a percentage point out of nearly 73 million popular votes cast. As in 1960, the lead seesawed between the two candidates throughout the night and into the next day. At midnight Humphrey was ahead. By 6 a.m. Nixon had taken a slim lead, but most television commentators were speculating that Mayor Daley was holding back Democratic votes in key Chicago precincts. When Mrs. Nixon heard that news, she became sick to her stomach.[3] Two hours later, Daley recognized that he could not stop Nixon and released his votes. Illinois and the presidency went to Nixon.

Perhaps the most exciting Election Night in modern times occurred in 2000. Early in the evening the television networks projected the state of Florida for Al Gore, only to recant a few hours later. At 2:17 a.m. Fox News, in a rush to judgment, awarded Florida and the presidency to George W. Bush. Not wanting to be left behind, the other networks concurred. But Bush's victory was premature because the votes for one Florida county showed Gore at *minus* 16,000 votes.[4] At 2:40 a.m., Gore telephoned Bush to concede, only to call back a short while later to say that his earlier concession had been based on Florida's faulty election returns. The conversation went like this:

Gore: Circumstances have changed dramatically since I first called you. The state of Florida is too close to call.

Bush: Are you saying what I think you're saying? Let me make sure that I understand. You're calling back to retract that concession?

Gore: You don't have to be snippy about it.

Bush: Well, Mr. Vice President, you do what you have to do. *Thanks for calling.*

Gore: You're welcome.[5]

Another 36 days would pass before the U.S. Supreme Court settled the matter, and Gore called Bush once more—this time to concede defeat.

Most Election Nights are not so melodramatic. Given the ease with which information travels over the Internet, the results of exit polls and the computer-based projections that accompany them are circulated on some political websites for curiosity seekers. It is also the case that partisan loyalties have hardened during the past decade, with fewer Democrats and Republicans defecting from their party moorings to support the opposition. In 2008, for example, only 9 percent of Republicans supported Democrat Barack Obama, while just 10 percent of Democrats backed Republican John McCain.[6] In 2008, the winner was known by 11 p.m. eastern time when the television networks unanimously projected Barack Obama to be the forty-fourth U.S. President. Two years later, a similar event occurred: By 11:00 p.m. eastern time the networks declared that partisan control of the U.S. House of Representatives had switched from the Democrats to the Republicans.

In many ways, today's fierce partisan rivalries are nothing new. In 1884, the *Philadelphia Inquirer* observed that "party lines were as strictly drawn as were the lines of religious sects."[7] Southerners coined the nickname "yellow dog Democrat," meaning they would vote for a yellow dog instead of a dreaded Republican. Northerners, meanwhile, were mostly rock-ribbed Yankees and firmly committed Republicans. For much of the nineteenth century, voting was not a soul-searching exercise because most Americans were creatures of political habit. The excitement on Election Night came not because there was much doubt about what individual voters might do—they were loyal partisans—rather, it was because the parties were so evenly matched.

This chapter examines how political consumers—the voters—relate to the parties. First, we review how party brand loyalty develops and examine ways scholars have sought to measure it. Second, we examine what political scientists call partisan realignment and how it affects the way electoral politics is studied. Third, we describe the electoral coalitions that have emerged to shape today's politics.

THE IMPORTANCE OF PARTY IDENTIFICATION

Few topics have received more scholarly attention over the last seven decades than political behavior, an area of research that focuses on the attitudes, beliefs, and actions of individuals. Among the first to study how individual voters behave in the voting booths were Bernard R. Berelson and Paul F. Lazarsfeld, who contributed to *The People's Choice* (1940)[8] and *Voting* (1948).[9] Berelson and Lazarsfeld developed a sociological model in which socioeconomic standing (education, income, and class); religion (Catholic, Protestant, or Jewish); and place of residence (rural or urban) formed an "index of political predisposition" that often determined party identification, which, in turn, strongly influenced choices made at the ballot box. Thus, a well-educated, white, upper-class Protestant from upstate New York would most likely be a Republican, whereas a black, blue-collar worker from Detroit would most likely be a Democrat. Using this index of political predisposition, demography mattered most and political campaigns counted for little. Joining a political party was, in essence, a declaration about who you were and where you were born. During the campaign season, Republicans shouted at other like-minded Republicans to vote for their candidates, and Democrats did much the same—with few minds being changed in the process.

The sociological model was best suited to explain the strong party era that existed from the post–Civil War period until the New Deal. But a weakening of party loyalties, which began during the 1950s and accelerated in the 1960s and 1970s, helped make the sociological model obsolete. In 1952, millions of Democrats voted for Republican and World War II hero, Dwight D. Eisenhower, giving him a comfortable 10-point victory over Democrat Adlai Stevenson. What influenced many people (including Democrats and independents) to back Eisenhower were *issues*—especially the Korean War. Gallup polls found 65 percent chose Eisenhower as the best person able to break the stalemate in Korea.[10] In 1956, Eisenhower defied the existing Democratic majority to beat Stevenson again—this time with 57 percent of the vote to Stevenson's 43 percent. As in 1952, Eisenhower's advantage on cold war–related foreign policy issues proved decisive.

Eisenhower's landslide victories illustrated the deficiencies associated with the sociological model. While race, ethnicity, and location mattered in helping to form partisan identifications, it was also true that voter attitudes about particular candidates and issues were also important factors in determining who won or lost on Election Night. Two questions remained: What individual political attitudes were important, and how could they be measured?

Some answers were contained in *The American Voter,* published in 1960.[11] Authors Angus Campbell, Philip Converse, Warren Miller, and Donald Stokes created a sociological-psychological model of voting behavior. They agreed with Lazarsfeld that demographics still mattered, but the authors also believed that partisanship had a strong psychological dimension. Thus, most Americans identified with their parents' party, whereas the children of parents without a clear partisan preference were ambivalent about politics. Once established, party identification frequently persisted throughout a person's adult life. Using data gathered in the 1950s, Campbell and his colleagues found that nearly 85 percent of respondents stuck with the same party throughout their adult lives, and a majority had never voted for a candidate of the other party.[12] It is in this vein that many political analysts consider the 2008 election to be historically important, since Barack Obama won 66 percent of the votes from those aged 18 to 29.[13] The thinking goes that if Obama can get their support for a second time in 2012, the Democratic Party could have an enduring majority for decades to come from the all-important age cohort that pollster John Zogby has dubbed the "First Globals."[14]

The American Voter is considered a seminal work because it introduced a new way of understanding how people vote. Ethnicity, race, region, religion, different economic structures (including education, occupation, and class), and historical patterns (including parental partisanship and social class) converge into a single act of voting. Together they create a person's party identification, which is usually long lasting. Once partisanship is formed, voters selectively screen information using the lenses of their preferred party. For example, following passage of a sweeping health care reform bill proposed by President Obama and congressional Democrats, support for the new measure depended on which political party a survey respondent identified with. According to one poll, 71 percent of Democrats backed the new law; 82 percent of Republicans were opposed.[15] This enormous partisan divide was replicated on many important issues that confronted the Obama administration.

From its inception, The American Voter provided a baseline to measure how a person's party identification influenced individual voting choices. This is not to say that refinements were impossible and challenges were not forthcoming. In 1971, Gerald Pomper found a significant increase in the correlation between policy and party from the results reported in The American Voter. Using seven issues— (1) federal aid to education, (2) government provision of medical care, (3) government guarantees of full employment, (4) federal enforcement of fair employment, (5) housing, (6) school integration, and (7) foreign aid—Pomper found that in 1956 a linear relation between issue and party identification existed only for medical care. By 1968, there were correlations on all of the aforementioned issues except foreign aid. In addition, the proportion who viewed the Democrats as the more liberal party had risen on every question. Pomper concluded that between 1956 and 1968 "considerable political learning" had taken place.[16]

Building on Pomper's work, Norman Nie, Sidney Verba, and John Petrocik argued in *The Changing American Voter* (1976) that issues were important influences on voting behavior.[17] This approach, called the cognitive voter model, assumed that citizens supported a particular candidate based on issue positions. For example, as the Vietnam War and civil rights debates of the 1960s and 1970s were given increased public prominence and the two political parties nominated conservative Republican Barry Goldwater and liberal Democrat George McGovern who had strong positions on these issues, voters began to use candidate and party stances on the key issues of the day as their voting guides. Candidate-centered politics, with its focus on issues, replaced party-centered politics. This did not mean that party identification no longer mattered; rather, voters paid attention to issues when candidates took clear, unequivocal stands on them. But if candidates adopted similar positions, then party identification reemerged as the primary determinant of vote choice. It was a two-step process: issues first, party second.

Since the 1950s, several scholars have approached the study of parties and party identification using the rational choice model, which postulates that voters establish goals and achieve them using cost-benefit calculations. For example, someone might aspire to become rich, but finds that working 18-hour days to acquire wealth is not worth it. Applying the same rationale to party identification, Anthony Downs in his 1957 book titled *An Economic Theory of Democracy* argued that the benefits of arriving at a "correct" voting decision may not be worth the costs of compiling extensive information on the candidates.[18] Most voters want to cast an informed vote, but often lack the time and energy to sift through the complex details of each candidate's policy stands and personal character. Party identification gives the busy voter a quick and easy solution. Voters can take an information shortcut by understanding the basic contours of what each party stands for, matching that information with their own values (thereby developing a party identification), and then associate particular candidates with their party labels. Thus, an election day decision can be made in a few quick seconds, because the voter need only know each candidate's party in order to cast an "informed" vote.

Measuring Party Identification

If the scholarly quarrel over how party identification is acquired and how it influences vote choice has dominated the study of political behavior, a close second has been the controversy over how to measure party identification. The most commonly used technique employs a seven-point ordinal scale developed by public opinion pollsters. Voters are classified by their answers to two questions. First, respondents are asked if they consider themselves Republicans, Democrats, or independents. Those who answer that they are either Republican or Democrat are asked a follow-up question about how strongly they identify with their chosen party. Those who classify themselves as "independent" are subsequently asked whether they are closer to the Republican Party or the Democratic Party. Respondents are then grouped into one of seven categories: (1) strong Democrat, (2) weak Democrat, (3) independent-leaning-Democrat, (4) true independent, (5) independent-leaning-Republican, (6) weak Republican, and (7) strong Republican. The advantage of this approach is that it suggests degrees of partisanship. It is reasonable to assume that some Democrats and Republicans are more closely connected to their parties than others, and that many so-called independents lean more toward one of the parties. According to one poll taken during the 2010 midterm campaign, 16 percent of all adult respondents said they were strong Republicans; 20 percent identified themselves as moderately Republican; 19 percent said they were strong Democrats; and 26 percent said they were moderately Democratic. Only 14 percent said they were truly independent. Overall, 36 percent of voters preferred the Republicans; 45 percent were inclined toward the Democrats.[19]

But party identification is more complex and depends on a variety of other factors beyond whether a respondent is a Democrat, Republican, or independent. Herbert Weisberg offers three variables: (1) attitudes toward the Republican Party, (2) attitudes toward the Democratic Party, and (3) attitudes toward political independence.[20] Another approach to measure the strength of party identifiers is to have survey respondents rank each party on a "thermometer," with zero degrees representing very negative feelings and 100 degrees signifying very positive feelings. Scores for each party are compared, and a partisan preference is determined.[21] Others believe yet another way to gauge citizens' dispositions toward the parties is to ask how they vote on election day.

PARTIES IN A NETWORKED AGE

The Internet as a Force of Decentralization

From local newspapers to wire services to radio and television networks to international media conglomerates (including book publishing), the effect of technology has been to centralize media and political power, dilute partisanship, and shift the source of political funding from party patronage to political action committees (PACs) and now Super PACs. The Internet is the first mass medium in history with the potential to reverse these centralizing trends. The Internet is, by nature and structure, a highly decentralized electronic bazaar with unlimited opportunities for users to find content to match their interests. It is the anti-television, a place where all politics is intensively local, intrinsically grassroots in character, and stridently partisan in tone.

Source: Kerbel, Matthew R. 2009. *Netroots: Online Progressives and the Transformation of American Politics.* Boulder, CO: Paradigm Publishers.

The debate surrounding the validity of and ways to measure party identification is likely to continue, given the new technologies and modes of communication associated with today's networked age. Whereas voters once got most of their political information through interpersonal communications or daily newspapers, today's plugged-in electorate has vastly more options for obtaining election information through the media and on the Internet. CNN, for example, has a politics tab on its website that the online browser can summon at a moment's notice. The other major networks—CBS, ABC, MSNBC, and Fox News—also have sophisticated websites that contain vast amounts of political information. Each evening, MSNBC viewers can watch *Hardball* with host Chris Matthews querying an array of political guests. For a more conservative view, Fox News Channel viewers can tune in to Bill O'Reilly and Sean Hannity for their takes on politics in their daily shows, *The O'Reilly Factor* and *Hannity.* During the same time period, liberals can tune in MSNBC's Lawrence O'Donnell and Rachel Maddow or Current TV's Keith Olbermann for very different points of view. The *Washington Post, New York Times, Congressional Quarterly, Political Wire, Politico,* and *National Journal* also provide websites for interested voters. In addition, there are dozens of Web sites for individual newsletters and candidate organizations that today's networked voters can access (see Table 5.1).

Table 5.1   Political Websites, 2010

Website/Address	Description
Political Wire: www.politicalwire.com	Provides a running account of the latest political headlines.
Politico: www.politico.com	Offers analysis of contemporary politics by Washington insiders.
CNN Politics: www.cnn.com/politics	Supplies web users with a supplement to CNN television reports, with analyses provided by CNN correspondents and a look at public opinion polls.
Congressional Quarterly: www.cq.com	Analyzes voting trends in Congress and the American electorate.
Huffington Post: www.huffingtonpost.com	Analyzes politics from a liberal perspective.
Daily Kos: dailykos.com	The largest online political community site that serves as a virtual home for progressive activists.
Townhall: www.townhall.com	Analyzes politics from a conservative perspective.
Drudge Report: www.drudgereport.com	A portal for political news and information with a conservative bent.
Daily Beast: www.dailybeast.com	A website run by Tina Brown in conjunction with *Newsweek* magazine.

THE MAKING OF AN IDEA: PARTY REALIGNMENT

So far, we have discussed how individuals form partisan attachments, but what of the electorate as a whole? Taken together, the party affiliations of the entire body politic form an underlying structure of voting behavior. Thus, for political scientists, Election Nights in today's networked age still retain an aura of their former excitement. Besides knowing whom the next president is going to be, the next most important question to be answered is what the election means. Surely, there must be something more behind the collective Xs placed next to a candidate's name. Thus, after Franklin D. Roosevelt's 1936 landslide victory, one analyst declared that he could "see no interpretation of the returns which does not suggest that the people of America want the president to proceed along progressive or liberal lines."[22] Similarly, after Ronald Reagan's stunning 1980 victory, many agreed with Reagan pollster Richard Wirthlin when he interpreted the result as "a mandate for change ... [that meant] ... a rejection of the New Deal agenda that had dominated American politics since the 1930s."[23] In both cases, political scientists argued that the structure of the U.S. party system had undergone a significant transformation. In 1936 and 1980, Americans came to very different conclusions about the role of government in our society. These contests gave way to historic changes in overall partisan identification and the coalitions that comprised the Democratic and Republican parties. Realigning elections (like those of 1936 and 1980) provide important clues to a simple question: What does party change look like?

V. O. Key and Party Realignment

Behind the speculation about what votes in any given election mean and which political party is favored, it is clear that some elections have far-reaching consequences. Political scientist V. O. Key Jr. was the first to argue that some elections were more important than others. Who remembers, for example, whether Franklin Pierce won the presidency in 1852, or James Buchanan in 1856, or James Garfield in 1880? Although the results of these contests might provide interesting material for a game of Trivial Pursuit, from Key's perspective realigning elections are those in which catastrophe plays a significant role. For example, in 1860 the impending Civil War consumed everything in its wake. Lincoln's successful prosecution of that war, along with his proclamation of a "new birth of freedom" in the Gettysburg Address, convinced most voters that the Republican Party could be trusted to steer the ship of state.

Likewise, in the next century the Great Depression and Franklin Roosevelt's collection of New Deal programs to combat it convinced most voters that the Democratic Party could best handle the nation's economy and look after the interests of the average American. When asked in 1951 what they would tell young people about whom the parties stood for, most said that the Democrats represented the "working man" whereas the Republicans promoted the "privileged few."[24]

Building on this idea, in 1955 Key developed a category of elections he described as "critical elections"—that is, contests characterized by sharp reorganizations of party loyalties over short periods of time. In these contests, voter turnout is quite high, and new, long-lasting

PARTIES IN A NETWORKED AGE

Howard Dean on Parties and the Internet

"Our tendency in the Democratic Party—amplified by the new generation, which is more and more Democratic—is decentralizing democratization. The Internet is fundamentally a democratizing tool, which is why Net neutrality is so important. If you start fettering it either commercially or politically, it destroys itself as a democratizing tool. The Republicans are inherently not interested in (small *d*) democratic organization; they tend toward top-down centralization and organization. The Democrats tend toward true democracy. The truth is, we probably need to be a bit more organized (you know the joke, "I'm not a member of an organized party, I'm a Democrat!"), but we do not need to become more centralized. Decentralization should not be mistaken for disorganization. The Republicans do a good job of being organized, but they do a terrible job being decentralized, and so they have a hard time with the Internet. The Net is a tool that works best for people who believe in decentralization."

Source: Teachout, Zephyr, and Thomas Streeter, et al. 2008. *Mousepads, Shoe Leather, and Hope: Lessons from the Howard Dean Campaign for the Future of Internet Politics.* Boulder, CO: Paradigm Publishers.

party coalitions are formed. Studying the election outcomes of several New England towns from 1916 to 1952, Key found that when the Democrats nominated Catholic New York governor Alfred E. Smith in 1928, party support in urban areas increased significantly and remained high, whereas Democratic backing in rural, Protestant-dominated enclaves fell to record lows, where it remained in the years that followed.[25]

Shortly after Key introduced the concept of critical elections, he published a major modification of his original idea. In 1959, he wrote that changes in partisanship are sometimes not as dramatic as those that occurred in 1928. Instead, he noted, party loyalties can erode among some groups and regions over many years. Key termed these changes *secular realignments*, defining them as "a movement of the members of a population category from party to party that extends over several presidential elections and appears to be independent of the peculiar factors influencing the vote at individual elections."[26] Key placed no time limit on the pace of this change, noting that it could take as long as 50 years. But the premise was clear: Gradual alterations in voting behavior, not a sharp reorganization of party loyalties, characterized secular realignments. Again, using election returns from some New England towns, Key found instances where the shift from Republican dominance to sustained Democratic victories during the New Deal era was slow, but steady. Key attributed the snail-like pace of change to the increased industrialization and urbanization of the region, as well as to the last wave of European immigrants who became acclimated to their new country and over time came to the polls in support of the Democrats.

Key's ideas about critical elections and secular realignments gained widespread popularity in the political science community. Enhancing its appeal was the proparty argument that underpinned realignment theory. Instead of resorting to arms or tearing up the Constitution when catastrophe struck, political scientists believed that voters used political parties to engineer significant policy changes. Parties were often credited with being important agents in maintaining the stability of the constitutional order. The U.S. Constitution works because political parties work, or so went the argument. Given this line of reasoning, political scientists had much at stake in making the case for party realignment.

As analysis of electoral change expanded to include polling data that could pinpoint changes within narrowly defined population groups (e.g., white male Catholics between the ages of 18 and 24), party realignment took on added significance. Walter Dean Burnham, a major proponent of the realignment concept, published *Critical Elections and the Mainsprings of American Politics* (1970), in which he transformed Key's simple idea of critical elections into a generalized theory of party realignment. Burnham outlined five conditions that characterized the "ideal-typical" partisan realignment:

1. There are short, sharp reorganizations of the major party voter coalitions which occur at periodic intervals nationwide.
2. Third-party revolts which often precede party realignments and reveal the incapacity of "politics-as-usual."
3. There is abnormal stress in the socioeconomic system which is closely associated with fundamental partisan change.
4. Ideological polarizations and issue distances between the major parties which become exceptionally large by normal standards.
5. Realignments have durable consequences and determine the general outlines of important public policies in the decades that follow.[27]

Using this classification scheme, Burnham cited the elections of Andrew Jackson in 1828, Abraham Lincoln in 1860, William McKinley in 1896, and Franklin D. Roosevelt in 1932 as having met the conditions of party realignment. In each case, voter interest and turnout was high, there were significant third-party revolts either in the actual election or in the contests leading up to it, and the differences between the parties were exceptionally large by U.S. standards. In making his calculations, Burnham discovered a rhythm to U.S. politics—namely, that realigning elections occur once every 28 to 36 years. Thus, if a realigning election happened in 1932 (as Burnham suggests) or in 1928 (as Key found in New England), one could expect another realignment to occur circa 1968.

Indeed, many believe that Republican Richard M. Nixon's close victory over Democrat Hubert H. Humphrey in 1968 met the conditions of a classic party realignment. The issue differences between the two parties on civil rights, the Vietnam War, and what became known as the "social issues" (crime, abortion, pornography, etc.) were significant. Moreover, there was a major third-party revolt in the person of Alabama governor George C. Wallace, whose presidential candidacy garnered 14 percent of the popular vote—a feat not surpassed until 1992 when Ross Perot captured 19 percent of the ballots cast. Kevin Phillips, an astute Republican political analyst, wrote in his 1969 book *The Emerging Republican Majority*, "Far from being the tenuous and unmeaningful victory suggested by critical observers, the election of Richard M. Nixon as president of the United States in November 1968 bespoke the end of the New Deal Democratic hegemony and the beginning of a new era in American politics."[28] The Election Nights that followed Nixon's 1968 win gave credence to Phillips's vision of a Republican realignment. From 1968 to 1988, Republicans won five of the six presidential contests (Nixon in 1968 and 1972, Reagan in 1980 and 1984, and George H. W. Bush in 1988). Only Nixon's misadventures in the Watergate scandal permitted a Democratic victory—Jimmy Carter in 1976—and that was for only one term. The Republican hold on the presidency was so great that some analysts thought the GOP had an impenetrable lock on the Electoral College that would prevent future Democratic victories.

But this Republican realignment had a very different feel from those that preceded it. Far from being vanquished, Democrats retained comfortable majorities in both houses of Congress for most of this period. Democrats controlled the Senate from 1968 to 1980—narrowly losing control in the 1980 Reagan landslide, but reclaiming majority status in 1986. The House showed an even greater Democratic advantage.

After Ronald Reagan won reelection in 1984, Democrats held a 71-seat margin in the House—the largest edge given to a party that did not control the White House since 1895. Thus, while the party system created by Franklin D. Roosevelt had died, the "ideal-type" of partisan realignment forecast by Burnham failed to take its place. Many wondered what happened. Some attributed the Republican failure to produce a classic realignment to the aftereffects of Watergate. In 1974, Democrats added 49 seats in the House—enough to ensure control until Newt Gingrich and his Republican allies took over 20 years later. Others attributed the failure of either party to achieve a classic realignment to presidents who were all too willing to eschew their party affiliations in order to win more votes.

Some believe that a realignment is already in the making. As Burnham noted in his review of history, realignments occur once every 28 to 36 years. If Nixon's 1968 election marked the beginning of a realignment, then we might have expected another realigning election to have occurred by 2004 (the outside limit of the 36-year period). Karl Rove, a key advisor to George W. Bush, maintained that Bush's 2000 and 2004 victories resembled those of Republican William McKinley, whose election in 1896 strengthened what had been a tenuous Republican majority, although that perspective is contradicted by strong gains by congressional Democrats in 2006 and 2008, and by Barack Obama's comfortable victory.[29]

An opposing view was articulated in 2002, when John B. Judis and Ruy Teixeira published an influential book titled *The Emerging Democratic Majority.* Judis and Teixeira asserted that the rise of Hispanic and Asian immigrants, the continued support of Democrats by African Americans, the emergence of a well-educated professional class, and the support given to Democrats by women created a new demography that would ensure future Democratic victories.[30] One of the authors of this book, John Kenneth White, argues that Barack Obama's 2008 victory highlights the new demographic terrain outlined by Judis and Teixeira. Obama won overwhelming support from nonwhites, who will comprise the majority of the U.S. population by 2050. More-over, Obama won support from so-called nontraditional families (i.e., families comprised of single parents, cohabiting adults, and blended families), religious seculars, and college graduates—especially those with more than four years of college. These demographic entities are on the rise, and their strong support for Obama suggests that the makings of a new Democratic era could be underway.[31]

While many still believe that demography is destiny in politics, the argument that Obama's 2008 victory signaled a partisan realignment was tempered by the 2010 midterm elections, when Republicans added more than 60 House seats (wiping out the Democratic gains made in 2006 and 2008) and retook control of the U.S. House by a wide margin. Republicans also added six Senate seats (not enough to win control of that body) and six governorships (including control of the key electoral vote–rich states of Ohio, Pennsylvania, and Florida). These gains by the minority party were the largest since 1948, when the Democrats roared back to power on a ticket led by President Harry S Truman.[32] It is possible that 2008 was like 1968, in that the election signified a lasting shift in partisan strength that nonetheless did not guarantee one-party control of the federal government.

Party Realignment: The Death of a Concept?

Despite the attempts of V. O. Key Jr. and Walter Dean Burnham to develop a theory of party realignment (and predict when it would occur), one problem persisted: Voters refused to cooperate. During the 1970s and early 1980s, new terms to describe how the electorate was behaving came into vogue. The most common of these was *dealignment*—a term meaning that voters were moving away from both political parties. The widespread belief that parties did not count for much was reflected in public opinion surveys. One 1983 poll found most respondents said there was "no difference" between Democrats and Republicans when it came to reducing crime, stopping the spread of communism, dealing effectively with the Soviet Union, providing quality education, reducing the risk of nuclear war, providing health care, reducing waste and inefficiency in government, or protecting the environment.[33] Instead of rooting for their "home team" Democrats or Republicans, voters adopted neutral attitudes toward them. No wonder that more than one-quarter of the electorate at the time classified itself as being "independent."

The failure of party realignment to live up to expectations during the Nixon and Reagan eras caused many political scientists to question the concept. In a major critique of party realignment theory entitled "Like Waiting for Godot," Everett C. Ladd maintained that Key and Burnham's emphasis on a party realignment modeled after the New Deal had been "mostly unfortunate."[34] In Ladd's view, the New Deal was a unique period when parties mattered and Franklin D. Roosevelt loomed over the political horizon. Key, Burnham, and other adherents to the party realignment idea grew up during the New Deal era and were shaped by it. Thus, said Ladd, by focusing on whether or not a party realignment happened in such interesting contests as 1968, 1980, 1992, or 1994, political scientists had been asking the wrong question. Rather than wonder whether each of these elections constituted a party realignment, Ladd suggested that it would be better to ask the following:

1. What are the major issues and policy differences between the two major parties, and how do these separate political elites and the voting public?
2. What is the social and ideological makeup of each major party at both the mass and elite levels?
3. What are the principal features of party organization, nomination procedures, and campaign structure?
4. In each of the previous three areas, are major shifts currently taking place? What kind? What are their sources?
5. Overall, how well is the party system performing?[35]

Political scientist David R. Mayhew recently echoed Ladd's criticism of party realignment theory. In a powerful book titled *Electoral Realignments: A Critique of an American Genre* (2002), Mayhew argues that the application of realignment theory misses the important context found in many other elections—including the midterm elections of 1874, which resulted in a Democratic takeover of the House of Representatives, the surprising victory of Harry S. Truman in 1948 (thanks to a shift within the Democratic Party in favor of civil rights), and many others. Mayhew tests the assumptions made by realignment advocates and concludes that they hardly measure up to close scrutiny. Only the New Deal realignment of the 1930s comes close, and that, Mayhew argues, was a unique moment in U.S. political history.[36]

Ladd and Mayhew's critiques notwithstanding, political scientists persist in seeking elections that conform to their understandings of a traditional partisan realignment. They have done so despite Key's 1955 admonition that "the actual election rarely presents in pure form a case fitting completely any particular concept."[37] Instead of abandoning realignment, political scientists are busily refurbishing the idea. During the Reagan era, John Kenneth White and Richard B. Wirthlin coined the phrase "rolling realignment" to describe the electoral changes that were taking place.[38] Building on Key's concept of secular realignment, they described party realignment as a process involving four distinct stages:

1. A change in the political agenda. During the 1930s, Americans had a simple political agenda: Big government works. By 1981,

most Americans agreed with Ronald Reagan when he declared in his inaugural address, "In this present crisis, government is not the solution to our problem. Government is the problem."[39] The Reagan Revolution consisted of limiting the expansion of federal responsibilities and returning power to state and local governments and to the individual.

2. A change in partisan self-identification as expressed in public opinion polls. How one answers the question, "In politics do you think of yourself as a Democrat, Republican, independent, or something else?" is a subjective query. When the political agenda changes, one's partisan identification will inevitably change as one party or another becomes identified with the new political thinking.

3. Changes in party registration. All states regulate party membership. In some places, people must visit a local town hall and formally declare to which political party they belong. In other states, voting in a primary is a form of party registration. Either way, the commitment to a party involves an overt act. Frequently, alterations in party registration are lagging indicators of partisan change. For example, although Ronald Reagan had been campaigning for Republicans since 1952, it took him 10 years to formally switch his California party registration from Democrat to Republican. As the Reagan illustration indicates, formal party registration is an imperfect barometer of how the electorate thinks about politics at any given moment.

4. Changes at the bottom of the ballot. Every state ballot lists offices that are usually invisible. New Yorkers, for example, elect their local county coroners; Texans vote for railroad commissioners and judges; in Illinois, state university trustees are elected posts. In such races, party identification means everything, whereas the campaigns of individuals who seek these posts count for little. Thus, when voters place an X next to the names of these obscure candidates, they are expressing a partisan preference. Alterations in the outcomes of these races are suggestive that a party realignment has at last taken place.

The stages White and Wirthlin described were not linear—voters could move back and forth from step to step. But the final result was an inevitable realignment—however slowly and imperfectly that process rolled along. Yet the rolling realignment they envisioned that would help the Republicans failed to materialize. By the time Reagan left office in 1989, Republicans held fewer seats in the House and Senate than they did after Reagan won the presidency in 1980. Moreover, George H. W. Bush suffered a massive rejection at the polls in 1992, winning just 38 percent of the ballots cast. Even after Republicans seized Congress in 1994, GOP identifiers in the public opinion polls failed to increase measurably. In 2000, George W. Bush *lost* the popular vote to Al Gore. And in 2004, Bush was able to muster a bare majority of the popular vote (51 percent) and only 286 electoral votes—this despite the overwhelming public support Bush received following the September 11, 2001, terrorist attacks. Although White and Wirthlin were right to suggest that successive realignments to the New Deal were not going to be the short, sharp reorganizations of party loyalties akin to those of the 1930s, something went awry in the inevitable steps toward a Republican realignment that, however slowly, they believed would follow in Reagan's wake.

The 1994 midterm election gave party realignment theorists new ammunition with its apparent reorganization of voter loyalties—and right on schedule, 26 years after Richard Nixon's 1968 victory. For the first time in 40 years Republicans won majorities in both houses of Congress, gaining 52 seats in the House and 8 seats in the Senate. Newt Gingrich and his fellow Republicans campaigned on a simple theme—the Contract with America, a document signed by all but four Republican House contenders in a flashy Capitol Hill ceremony. The contract promised that if Republicans won, party leaders would schedule votes during the first 100 days of the new Congress on such issues as term limits, a line-item veto for the president, and a balanced budget amendment (see Chapter 8). Walter Dean Burnham claimed that the 1994 results closely resembled an old-fashioned party realignment and challenged his critics to disagree: "Those who have stressed partisan dealignment will now have to consider how this abrupt emergence of something remarkably like an old-fashioned partisan election fits their models. And those who have placed their bets on the argument that critical-realignment analysis is irrelevant to this modern candidate-driven electoral universe will have to reconsider their position."[40]

Still, the debates about party realignment persist. Is realignment, as conceived by Burnham and Key, still possible? Does Barack Obama's election herald a long-term change in electoral preferences? Can a Republican rebound be meaningful and lasting? And does any of this mean that a new realignment is imminent—or happening before our eyes?

WHERE ARE THE VOTERS GOING?

Today, the decision as to which political party a voter belongs to is as much about which lifestyle and values they prefer, as it is about the particular candidates and issues that surround a given campaign. This has given rise to a "values divide," that became evident in the dramatic 2000 Bush-Gore race and has persisted in every presidential contest held since.[41] In 2000, Democrat Al Gore won strong backing from Democrats, women, African Americans, Latinos, unmarried voters, those who did not attend church services, working women, union members, liberals, gays, those who did not own guns, voters who preferred that abortion be legal in all situations, and those who resided in big cities. George W. Bush got majority support from Republicans, men, whites, voters who were married and had children, those who attended religious services more than once a week, stay-at-home moms, nonunion members, conservatives, heterosexuals, gun owners, those who say abortion should be illegal in all cases, and rural voters. The same patterns have persisted in subsequent presidential elections, despite the fact that the Democrats had different nominees in the persons of John F. Kerry and Barack Obama in 2004 and 2008, respectively, and the Republicans had a different candidate in John McCain in 2008 (see Figure 5.1).

THE RISE OF HAMILTONIAN NATIONALISM IN TODAY'S NETWORKED AGE

Barack Obama entered the presidency in 2009 determined to rise above the partisanship of the George W. Bush years. But, thus far, his call for an end to excessive partisanship has fallen on deaf ears. Democrats still strongly support Obama (including the rank and file and members of Congress), while Republicans have unified in their opposition to Obama (both inside Washington and in the country at large).

The result is not only a more polarized electorate but stronger national parties. The twenty-first century has given rise to an enhanced Hamiltonian-like party system wherein partisan activities are directed from the top down. Organizational competence—such as the ability to raise money and aid candidates with high-technology

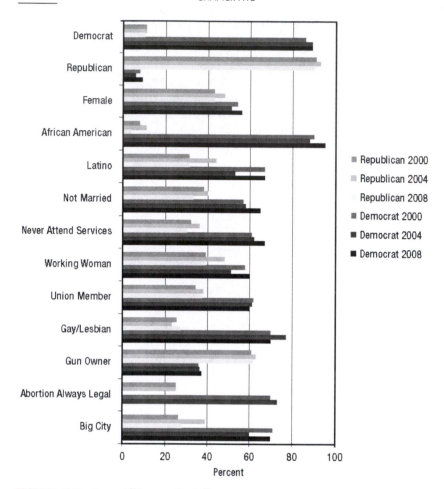

FIGURE 5.1   Party Affiliations for Different Voter Groups in 2000, 2004, and 2008

Sources: Voter News Service exit poll, November 7, 2000; Edison Media Research and Mitofsky International exit poll, November 2, 2004, and November 4, 2008.

services—has become an indicator of party accomplishment. The partisanship exhibited by these organizations is synonymous with the partisanship held by voters. In short, the national parties excel at mobilizing their respective bases and motivating them to vote.

At the same time, this resurgence of a Hamiltonian-like party system has an interesting Jeffersonian twist to it. The Internet has become a partisan device, but unlike the parties whose strong organizations dwarf their state and local counterparts, voters can visit a variety of partisan websites where they can offer their own thoughts and analyses. Moreover, they can even "tweet" their own critiques and analyses on Twitter.com to anyone and everyone who shares their interests. Thus, the nationalization of party politics from the top down has been accompanied by a strong bottom-up component.

If politics is about "who gets what, when, where, and how," to use political scientist Harold Lasswell's famous phrase, we know what candidates want: votes at election time.[42] With the assistance of new technologies, candidates have found new ways to target and reach out to voters. But these same technologies have also served to strengthen partisan attachments, as evidenced by the natural division of cyberspace into left and right blogospheres. While the debates about party realignment theory (and its various iterations) continue, the fact is that the U.S. electorate is overcaffeinated. Partisanship matters, and the parties' abilities to use the new tools of the Internet and mobilize supporters inside and outside of Washington, D.C., are the subjects of the next three chapters.

6

Parties and Social Media

One of the recurring themes in the history of American parties is that they have been willing to change their modes of operation as conditions dictate. It is no wonder, then, that both parties have moved full steam ahead into today's networked age. However, as with any new technology, the emergence of the Internet has left political practitioners struggling to figure out how to maximize the political potential of social media and keep up with its rapidly changing scope and shape. Just as Republicans proved adept at harnessing the power of television advertising in the 1950s and direct mail and cable technology in the 1980s, they took an early lead over Democrats in the use of the Internet in the 1990s. By the end of the first decade of the twenty-first century, however, Democrats and their allies on the left had emerged as more skillful practitioners of Internet politics.

During the 1996 election season, the RNC homepage received 75,000 hits a day—a meager number by contemporary standards but a huge figure back then. Republicans used the Internet to broadcast immediate responses to Bill Clinton's State of the Union address in 1997, and the RNC chair held regular online chats. By 2000, the GOP site boasted numerous links to facilitate making financial contributions, fact finding on policy topics, buying GOP-related products, and—significantly—enabling rudimentary grassroots email efforts by ordinary users. The site was regarded as so substantive that it was dubbed "Best Party Site" by *Campaign and Elections* magazine. That publication noted:

> The RNC gave its all into an "e-campaign" this year, not only creating a meaty, updated home page for interested Republicans but by an effective use of banner advertisements on outside sites. The RNC also led a successful grassroots email campaign, collecting around 935,000 addresses. Larry Purpuro, the RNC's deputy chief of staff who led the "e-GOP" efforts, likes to point out that the RNC had 32,000 "email activists" in Florida, where Texas Gov. George W. Bush won the election with little to spare.[1]

By 2002, the RNC had spent some $60,000 to create gopteam leader.com, designed to give nearly 100,000 activists information on how to contact radio stations and newspapers to disseminate Republican views on a range of issues. The site also offered incentives such as mouse pads and fleece pullovers for users who completed "action items" listed on the site. Points were awarded, for example, for recruiting GOP activists or for emailing members of Congress to support Republican initiatives.[2]

Once again, Democrats found themselves playing catch-up. In 1996, the DNC's website received only 50,000 hits per day. One year later, the DNC updated its homepage to include a user survey, volunteer sign-up sheet, and a help page that downloaded voter registration forms from the Federal Election Commission. By 2002, visitors could access daily news briefings and links to other state and local Democratic Party organizations, and even take a chance at winning $1,000 for the most creative flash animation. Taking a cue from Republicans, they turned to the Internet to organize rudimentary grassroots efforts on their website, democrats.org.[3] But the Internet didn't emerge as a contemporary political force or reveal its potential for grassroots mobilization until an obscure former Vermont governor named Howard Dean came out of nowhere on the strength of an Internet campaign to become the frontrunner for the 2004 Democratic presidential nomination.

DEAN UNLOCKS THE GENIE

Howard Dean did not set out to run the first national Internet campaign. In fact, he wasn't particularly proficient with computers when

he and a small group of supporters set up a small office in Burlington, Vermont, for what would have to be considered the longest of
long-shot presidential campaigns. It would be more accurate to say
that Dean's Internet supporters found the candidate rather than the
other way around.

Dean was an opinionated politician who was not afraid to challenge his party's orthodoxy, and his outspokenness contributed
significantly to his online appeal. At the Democratic National Committee's Winter Meeting in February 2003, Dean appeared with
other Democrats vying to challenge President George W. Bush the
following year. Where the others made safe political speeches, Dean
used the opportunity to appear before party activists to give voice to
what many in the room were likely thinking or saying privately to
one another about how Democrats had been approaching the Bush
administration and its economic and military policies. "What I want
to know," a full-throated Dean told his audience, "is why in the world
the Democratic Party is supporting the president's unilateral attack
on Iraq." He continued:

What I want to know is why are Democratic Party leaders
supporting tax cuts ....What I want to know is why we're
fighting in Congress about the Patient's Bill of Rights when the
Democratic Party ought to be standing up for health care for
every single American man, woman, and child in this country.
What I want to know is why our folks are voting for the
president's No Child Left Behind bill that leaves every child
behind, every teacher behind, every school board behind, and
every property tax payer behind. I'm Howard Dean, and I'm here
to represent the Democratic wing of the Democratic Party.[4]

Dean's remarks struck a nerve with the audience and reverberated beyond the party gathering. For disenchanted liberals, Dean
offered something new: a Democrat not afraid to take on his party
in full view of key party figures. All they needed was a way to find
each other and express their support, and the Internet provided them
with a vehicle. The venue was as unlikely as the candidate himself:
Meetup.com, a non-political site designed to unite people with common interests. The concept was simple: Type in the activity you're
interested in and your zip code, and the website returned a date and
time for like-minded others to meet in the real world and discuss their
common interest. By making it possible for disparate people with the
same concerns to find each other and facilitate in-person meetings,

Meetup.com coincidently addressed the initial organizational problem faced by supporters of an obscure candidate, and soon after Dean's DNC address, "Howard Dean" rapidly became a prominent meet-up category (Dean would eventually become the most requested meet-up topic, surpassing the previous record holder, witches).[5]

The Dean meet-up effort expanded exponentially in the spring and summer of 2003, and the candidate's small staff struggled to remain one step ahead of what their supporters were building. Working around the clock, they launched the weblog "Blog for America" in March to serve as a nerve center for the blossoming online campaign.[6] The blog provided a way for the Burlington staff to keep supporters apprised about what they were doing, but more importantly it gave supporters a way to connect with each other and self-organize. Blog for America hosted diary and comment features, permitting supporters to initiate their own topics and respond to what others were writing. And respond they did—to everything ranging from policy ideas to the candidate's polling numbers to how the mainstream media was covering their candidate to ideas for political action they could take on behalf of the campaign.[7] At its peak, hundreds of thousands of ordinary supporters had taken it upon themselves to engage in Internet-based campaigning on behalf of Dean, creating a citizen army that multiplied the efforts of the candidate's staff and propelled the Vermont governor to frontrunner status weeks before the 2004 Iowa caucus.[8]

They also raised money in unprecedented amounts and in an entirely new way—through small-dollar contributions made by ordinary citizens who responded to the candidate's online pitch for cash. As a sign of their level of investment in the candidate and in what would have to be considered a campaign manager's dream, Dean's online activist core asked and at times *begged* the campaign to ask *them* to contribute money. The campaign had developed a convention whereby they would post a baseball bat icon on the blog whenever they wanted to raise funds, and fill the bat in with red ink proportional to the percentage of the goal they had achieved. After a while, some blog readers began asking the campaign to "put up a bat" to raise money off an achievement like strong polling numbers or a particularly impressive public performance by their candidate. When blog readers believed they were being invaded by a "troll"— someone supporting an opposing campaign who masquerades as an online community member in order to stir up trouble in comment threads—supporters would respond by trying to raise money for the campaign in the troll's name (they called it a "troll goal"), thereby undermining the troll's subversive purpose.[9]

Despite these virtues, Internet activism came with risks to the campaign's leadership. Giving supporters the means to mobilize on behalf of Howard Dean also meant relinquishing control over their actions while having to take responsibility for anything done or said in the candidate's name. If a supporter said something off-message or did something embarrassing that was caught on video, the campaign organization would have to address it. Furthermore, the rapid acceleration of Dean's online movement outpaced the campaign's ability to hire and train full-time staff, leaving Dean's staff exhausted and always trying to keep pace with its Internet growth.[10] These factors combined to make Dean's Internet supporters both a necessary blessing and a source of constant strain as they powered his drive toward the nomination even as they unintentionally threatened to swallow it.

For much of 2003, the Dean campaign was a phenomenon and the talk of the political world. Few could remember the last time a candidate had bolted from obscurity to the doorstep of a major party presidential nomination. High-profile competitors like John Kerry and Joe Lieberman and their seasoned Washington advisors watched the Dean juggernaut with a mixture of envy, anger, and dread, trying to understand what Dean was doing and figure out how to stop it. Because no one had ever succeeded at this level on the strength of new media, many conventional political advisors were baffled. "Other than raising money, the [other] campaigns generally continued to treat the Internet like a TV with keys," wrote Dean campaign manager Joe Trippi, "and ignored the ways that this technology actually invites people to be involved, rather than just throwing pictures and slogans at them in the hope they donate money."[11]

Ultimately, Dean's opponents resorted to traditional political methods—a withering television advertising attack on the frontrunner—to undermine his campaign. Dean experienced the limitations of Internet politics as well. As the primary season approached, the once-exponential growth in his supporters flattened considerably, in part a reflection of the limited reach of high-speed Internet access in 2003. For all its novelty, the Dean campaign still had to reach voters through traditional means, and the candidate who was a folk hero online had difficulty communicating on television. As a result, the candidate was unable to withstand the assault waged by his opponents, and finished a distant third in Iowa when just weeks before he was favored to win. His fate was sealed when he addressed his supporters with a loud yelp of support designed to lift their spirits that made the candidate appear unhinged on camera. Video of the moment went viral on the Internet overnight; in an ironic twist, the medium that made the Dean campaign possible had helped bury it.

Although Dean had failed, something new had happened that turned traditional campaigning on its head. Ever since party reforms turned presidential campaigns into candidate-centered affairs with the rise of primaries and concomitant decline in the influence of party elites, ingenious long-shot candidates like Jimmy Carter had occasionally succeeded in upending more seasoned opponents. But, no one had ever done it like Howard Dean, on the strength of bottom-up political fundraising and citizen-initiated organizing channeled through the Internet. It set the stage four years later for a more advanced Internet effort by another long-shot candidate, Barack Obama. And, it heralded the rise of the political influence of online blogs and organizations, which would self-organize in a manner similar to the Dean campaign and challenge the autonomy of the two parties from without.

OBAMA SETS THE STANDARD

During the 2008 presidential campaign, Republican vice presidential nominee Sarah Palin mocked Barack Obama for having been a community organizer. It turned out that Obama's knowledge of bottom-up organizing meshed perfectly with the advantages of Internet politics, enabling him to leverage the medium to identify and mobilize millions of new voters en route to the first successful Internet-fueled presidential victory.

Like Dean, Obama was a relative newcomer to national politics, having emerged from obscurity in 2004 when he gave the keynote address at the Democratic National Convention while still an Illinois state senator. That speech showcased Obama's oratorical abilities and thrust him into the national spotlight, where he continued to shine after he was elected to the U.S. Senate in November 2004. Although this gave Obama a larger platform than serving as the governor of a small, obscure state, he was hardly in a commanding position to challenge his party's presidential frontrunner for the 2008 nomination—especially when that frontrunner was senator and former first lady Hillary Rodham Clinton.

Obama entered the campaign with a host of disadvantages that in an earlier time would have been fatal to his hopes. He had neither the money nor the likelihood of raising the sums of money that Clinton could command by virtue of a network built over decades in politics.

PARTIES IN A NETWORKED AGE

Entertainment Television and the Parties

During the 2008 election, entertainment television played a bigger role than ever before. According to the Center for Media and Public Affairs at George Mason University, 2008 presidential candidates appeared 110 times on late night talk shows including *The Daily Show* and *The Colbert Report*. The three major candidates of the election season—Barack Obama, Hillary Clinton, and John McCain— also appeared on *Saturday Night Live*. But whether the candidates and the parties were using the shows or the shows were using the candidates and abusing the parties is an active question. SNL's repeated parody of Republican vice presidential nominee Sarah Palin, by Tina Fey, is the premier case in point. Even though Palin appeared live with Fey after several send-ups at Palin's expense, it did not counteract the conflation of news and nonsense as journalists came to regularly invoke the inane claim, "I can see Russia from my house," despite the fact that it was Fey—not Palin—who had said it. Moreover, even Fox News had trouble differentiating between the two. The network accidentally used a photo of Fey emulating Palin *twice*. The first occasion was in 2009 when Palin was promoting her book, and Fox subsequently erred in a segment discussing Palin's potential presidential run for 2012.

Sources: Baym, Geoffrey. 2010. *From Cronkite to Colbert: The Evolution of Broadcast News*. Boulder, CO: Paradigm Publishers.

Roberts, Christine. "Fox News Mistakenly Airs Image of Tina Fey in Sarah Palin Segment—New York Daily News." *Featured Articles from the New York Daily News*. New York Daily News, June 6, 2011. http://articles.nydailynews.com/2011-06-06/news/29648606_1_sarah-palin-palin-rally-fox-news.

Similarly, he lacked the extensive number of political IOUs amassed by his opponent, who built an impressive list of early endorsements from Democratic officials who were either loyal or obligated to her or her husband from their days in the Clinton White House. Where Hillary Clinton enjoyed universal name recognition and a double-digit lead in early national polls, Obama struggled to establish sufficient public support to be taken seriously by reporters as a credible challenger. And, while Clinton battled monumental barriers in her quest to be elected the first female president, Obama confronted long-standing racial prejudices compounded by a thin national resume. He had to convince voters that an African American candidate could be elected president while fending off charges from his critics that he was too inexperienced to serve in the office.

Obama's shrewd understanding and skillful manipulation of the Internet served as a critical counterweight to these disadvantages, generating unprecedented amounts of money while identifying and mobilizing millions of voters. Like Dean before him, Obama excelled at building an online presence that encouraged his partisans to form an army of supporters to campaign in his name. But, unlike Dean, the Obama online effort struck an effective balance between centralized control and decentralized activism, making it more manageable and ultimately more successful. Benefitting from a more advanced Internet that reached more people and a campaign team that had learned from Dean's successes and failures, Obama blended traditional candidate-centered, television-based campaigning with a powerful Internet operation that proved effective enough to topple the Democratic Party's biggest name and go on to capture the presidency.

Obama sought to avoid the pitfalls that dogged the Dean campaign without extinguishing his supporters' enthusiasm and initiative. The effort required finding the right combination of empowerment and control, balancing a campaign's need for top-down coordination with the decentralization necessary to take advantage of the Internet's social networking capabilities. The engine running this effort was Obama for America (OFA), a state-of-the-art website offering a host of online tools through which supporters could customize their contribution to the campaign without the risk that their actions would run the campaign off the rails.

Where the Dean campaign outsourced its networking through Meetup.com, Obama's website integrated social networking tools. An icon labeled "Make a Difference" directed users to a campaign event finder and a tool for making calls to voters in competitive states. A "Take Action Now" icon served the interests of supporters who wanted to email friends or strangers to share positive impressions of the candidate. Through MyBO (pronounced "my boh" and standing for "my Barack Obama"), supporters could customize their web presence and participate in the campaign's version of Facebook—or link directly to Obama's actual Facebook page. On MyBO, users could establish a profile, write their own campaign blog, comment on the blog posts of others, find other Obama supporters in their zip code, and identify and join local Obama groups with people who had similar interests, ranging from Veterans for Obama to Environmentalists for Obama.[12] As the *Washington Post* noted, the Obama campaign made sure it had a presence anywhere you could find possible supporters:

Obama was the first candidate to have profiles on AsianAve
.com, MiGente.com and BlackPlanet.com, social networking
sites (a.k.a. socnets) targeting the Asian, Latino and black
communities. His presence on BlackPlanet, which ranks behind
MySpace and Facebook in terms of traffic, is so deep that he
maintains 50 profiles, one for each state. On ALforObama, his
Alabama page on BlackPlanet, for example, supporters can read
an updated blog, watch YouTube videos and learn more about his
text program. It's difficult to measure the value of these socnets
in persuading voters to choose Obama. What's clear, however, is
that online networking—how supporters communicate with one
another within their online communities—has its advantages. A
Facebook group called Students for Barack Obama, started in
July 2006 by Bowdoin College student Meredith Segal, was so
successful that it became an official part of the campaign.[13]

This organizational structure liberated Obama from relying on
local party operatives to perform the fieldwork for primary and caucus
challenges, enabling him to build his own organizational structure
from the ground up with the help of volunteers who came to the
campaign through the Internet. The same held true for the campaign's
sophisticated turnout operation, which funneled responsibility for
identifying and mobilizing voters to low-level volunteers operating
within a highly differentiated organizational structure, balancing
the freedom of supporters to self-motivate with traditional elements
of campaign command-and-control. The Obama campaign made
the unprecedented decision to share its turnout goals—considered
confidential by campaigns worried about underperforming—with
volunteers who in turn felt empowered by the campaign's decision
to entrust them with getting voters to the polls. "If we tell a team
leader that the vote goal for this neighborhood is 100 votes," said one
of the campaign's state directors, "and we give them a list with 300
names of supporters and persuadable voters on it, they respond with,
'Wow, I can make this happen.'"[14]
    After he was elected president and became de facto head of the
national Democratic Party, Obama retooled his website and folded
it into the everyday operation of the DNC, as we mentioned in
Chapter 3. This signaled his intention to keep a social networking
presence alive during his presidency while remaking the party in
the image of his successful Internet model. Rechristened Organizing for America, OFA worked alongside the administration from its
new home inside Democratic National Committee headquarters in

Washington to build support for key Obama initiatives, notably the healthcare reform effort that dominated politics in 2009. As the 2010 congressional midterm elections drew near, OFA went to work on behalf of congressional Democrats, applying social networking tools to mobilize first-time voters who were inspired by Obama in 2008, gambling that Obama's bottom-up mobilization approach would work without the president's presence on the ballot. The results were not good. Facing a strong headwind in the form of a poor economy and widespread anger from swing voters who felt the administration had over-reached and overspent, OFA was unable to mobilize the 2008 electorate that put Obama in office, and Democrats suffered historic losses in congressional and state contests.

THE NETROOTS CHALLENGE DEMOCRATS

Advances in the availability of high-speed Internet access during the first decade of the twenty-first century facilitated the growth of a virtual space where ordinary people could engage in political discourse, venting about things they did not like and planning to take action to change them. As like-minded individuals on the left and right began publishing political blogs, and as a few of these blogs developed into sizable virtual communities, a political blogosphere took shape. Reflecting deeply held partisan feelings on both sides, bloggers on the left would link to each other with abandon while generally refusing to link to bloggers on the right in order to avoid giving them additional traffic that would inflate the size of their community. Bloggers on the right reciprocated, generally refusing to link to liberal blogs. As a result, two distinct hemispheres evolved in political cyberspace: a conservative or "right blogosphere" and a progressive or "left blogosphere."

Although they emerged simultaneously, they differed in size and structure. Like the Republican Party, conservatives were first to establish a notable presence in cyberspace; in the years immediately following the turn of the century, the largest and most active blog communities were on the right[15]; as with previous technological innovations, the left found itself playing catch-up. However, animated by opposition to the Iraq War in particular and the Bush Administration in general, a vital left blogosphere took shape by 2005, and between 2003 and 2005, a period when overall political blog traffic increased six-fold, progressive online sites increased their traffic at a much sharper rate than comparable conservative sites.[16]

Moreover, the left blogosphere was developing in a horizontal fashion suitable to taking advantage of the social networking capabilities of the Internet. Toward the end of the first decade of the century, the top blogs of the left were all community blogs, meaning they permitted ordinary users to post original ideas in diaries rather than restricting that function to "front page" bloggers formally affiliated with the sites, and allowed people to post comments about blog posts, diaries, and even the comments of other users.[17] This facilitated virtual discussions in "comment threads" where people could respond to the ideas of others. On the left blog with the largest readership, Daily Kos, it is commonplace to find threads with hundreds of comments, reflecting the size and level of engagement of that online community.

Over time, this structure birthed a movement, which self-consciously modeled itself on the twentieth-century reform-minded Progressives we discussed in Chapter 3. Emerging online from the grassroots, the progressive "netroots" (or "Internet grassroots") movement came to life via the left (or progressive) blogosphere. Structurally, the netroots encompass a web of national, state, local, and issue-oriented blogs, along with like-minded progressive organizations with a strong web presence, like Moveon.org (which formed to oppose Republican efforts to impeach Bill Clinton during the modern Internet's infancy in the late 1990s), Act Blue (a website for directing small-dollar campaign contributions to progressive candidates), and Democracy for America (an online organization devoted to identifying, recruiting, and funding progressive candidates that grew out of the Dean campaign). By linking to each other, these sites can enhance each other's visibility and effectiveness. But, in keeping with the horizontal structure of the netroots, the effort lacks central coordination. It is the organic product of many people using the Internet to work toward a shared set of goals.[18]

The right blogosphere emerged differently, owing in part to the existence of a long-standing conservative movement operating within and outside the Republican Party. From elected Republicans to conservative think tanks, talk radio, and other media outlets, conservatives had fashioned over time an idea and messaging apparatus that operated with great efficiency and effectiveness. The right blogosphere developed within this vertically organized structure, offering conservatives a new outlet for messaging and maintaining interest among the faithful. However, the hierarchical structure of the existing conservative movement had the effect of limiting the development of community blogs on the right, restricting the emergence of new voices, and limiting the number of venues where many voices would gather to argue and debate as in a virtual town hall.[19] Consequently, the preeminent ideas expressed in the right blogosphere typically mirrored those expressed by Republican politicians.

Not so for the netroots. As a movement that developed online without mainstream party support, netroots progressives often find themselves at odds with elected Democrats. Animated by challenges to corporate influences they feel tip the political balance of power away from ordinary citizens, netroots activists have shown themselves willing to take on the Democratic Party whenever they feel it tilts too heavily toward the interests of the privileged, to the point of re-cruiting and raising funds for primary challenges to Democrats who otherwise would not feel the heat of accountability to progressive interests. During the 2006 election cycle, the netroots channeled their organizing and fundraising toward winning a Democratic majority in the House and Senate, but once that objective was realized, their attention shifted to pushing Congress in a progressive direction by supporting "better Democrats" over incumbents who in their view worry more about what others in Washington think about them than the concerns of progressive voters. Daily Kos founder Markos Moulitsas put it this way in a blog post in 2007:

> Too many bad Democrats in DC don't feel they need to fulfill campaign promises on Iraq and other national priorities. They don't care about you or their constituents. They are more concerned about what [*Time* magazine columnist] Joe Klein and George Bush think. They are afraid of Republicans, but figure they can take you for granted. What are you going to do, vote for Republicans? They know we don't have that option. Are we going to withhold our money? The lobbyists will be more than happy to pick up the slack. We're going to call them, or email them, or write them? Their staff can deal with those inconveniences.
>
> What we CAN do is to threaten their jobs. And you do that with primary challenges. We've seen how good [Democratic representative] Jane Harman became after hers, and how merely a threat of a primary challenge to [Representative] Ellen Tauscher whipped her into proper shape. That's the *only* tool we have to keep our caucus accountable. So it's important we win these races, to send a message that we don't just threaten, but can actually deliver real pain. And the more successful we are, the more challengers we'll have to bad Democrats in 2010, and we can continue on this long and arduous path toward a more responsive and accountable Democratic Party.[20]

In recent years, the netroots have proved to be a factor in Democratic primary contests, occasionally inflicting the "pain" Moulitsas addressed. In 2009, they emerged on the victorious side of a challenge to Senator Arlen Specter of Pennsylvania by a netroots favorite, Representative Joseph Sestak (whose election to the House in 2006 was supported by netroots efforts, and who went on to lose a close general election contest to Republican Pat Toomey). Specter, a former moderate Republican who had switched parties the previous year to avoid a difficult primary challenge from his right by Toomey, enjoyed widespread institutional support including the DNC and the Obama administration.

That same year, the netroots failed to unseat their number one target, Arkansas senator Blanche Lincoln, although their candidate, Arkansas Lieutenant Governor Bill Halter, kept the incumbent below 50 percent of the primary vote, forcing a run-off that he narrowly lost. Lincoln provoked the ire of progressives by opposing a public healthcare option and for opposing strong climate change and financial reform legislation because, in the view of the netroots, she was beholden to large corporate interests for her campaign funds. These positions had done nothing to improve her position with general election voters, and she faired poorly in polling match-ups with all Republican comers. Netroots activists felt she would make a good test case for their opposition to "corporate Democrats" in that they felt if she lost the primary, the Democratic Party would be in *better* shape to hold the Arkansas seat.

In their efforts to unseat Lincoln, they were opposed by an array of powerful forces, including the U.S. Chamber of Commerce, the White House, and Arkansas' favorite son, Bill Clinton. Even though these forces proved too strong to get Halter over the finish line, the netroots in defeat realized an important policy achievement. Joan McCarter, writing at Daily Kos, explained that

> The repercussions of Blanche Lincoln's hotly contested primary are playing out in the Wall Street reform effort in a complex and potentially massive way. Because of Bill Halter's challenge, Lincoln proposed—and passed in her Ag[riculture] committee—a very tough derivatives reform package. So tough, in fact, that it has strong opposition from the White House and from key Senate Dems. But, they can't strip it now, because it's too important for Lincoln to use in her primary.[21]

Throughout the progressive blogosphere, the stronger Wall Street reform package—one of the netroots' key legislative objectives—was a sign of vindication for their strategy of running Halter against Lincoln, coming as it did at the hands of one of their most disliked Democrats. "It's very possible," blogged McCarter, "that we'll have Bill Halter to thank for a tough Wall Street reform bill."[22]

One of the ironies of these efforts is how they came at the expense of a Democratic president who owed his election victory to a sophisticated understanding of Internet politics. In Pennsylvania and Arkansas, President Obama was on the other side of the fight, supporting the incumbent against a netroots-endorsed challenger. This rift owes more to the inside-outside dynamic separating the Washington political establishment from the netroots than to an appreciation of how to use the Internet as a political tool.

As party leader, it is Obama's responsibility to protect the Democratic congressional majorities he inherited when he was elected in 2008. Given the high rate of incumbent reelection over time, the path of least resistance to maintaining that majority would ordinarily be to discourage primaries that, if successful, create open seats that the party would have to defend without the advantages of incumbency. From the president's perspective, stumping for Democratic incumbents is in the best interest of the party. It is also a given in Washington that members of the same party will work for mutual political self-preservation. When Arlen Specter switched sides, he temporarily gave Democrats a 60-seat Senate supermajority, enough to block Republican filibusters should Democrats vote in concert. It was not surprising that Obama would want to reward that effort with his political support.

However, bloggers and activists on the political left do not see things this way. Instead, they believe that a candidate who is not hamstrung by corporate obligations and who is therefore free to campaign on behalf of middle- and working-class interests will always do better on Election Day, even if that candidate lacks the track record, name recognition, and fundraising capability of an incumbent. They regard blind support for incumbents as counterproductive to maintaining congressional majorities, believing that select open seat challenges can have a better chance of success despite the aggregate odds favoring incumbents. And, they believe that having more such candidates in Congress would work to strengthen the long-term political prospects of the Democratic Party. These strategic differences put them at odds with many party regulars, including the president.

Differences between mainstream Democrats and netroots activists extend beyond campaigning to legislating. Nowhere was this more evident than during the long campaign to enact healthcare reform in 2009 and 2010, when an online push for reform often clashed with administration efforts, and bloggers who had supported Barack Obama's election found themselves deeply at odds with his governing approach.

Netroots engagement in the healthcare policy debate was impressive and demonstrated that Internet-based organizing could be applied to policymaking. Their objective was to secure passage of healthcare reform with a strong public component—initially a single-payer plan, then, when the administration took this option off the table, a plan with a strong government component, like a public insurance option or wider accessibility to Medicare. As progressives, they believed that private, for-profit insurance operated to the benefit of insurance companies first, the public second, and they felt that government was the only institution that could effectively address these perceived inequities.

A sophisticated inside-outside strategy developed online through the network of progressive sites that had previously engaged in political action. Working on the inside, the netroots partnered with the congressional progressive caucus, a large but—in the view of netroots activists—generally ineffectual group that tended to give in to more conservative Democrats. Led by several bloggers who rose to the forefront, but supported by a large network of less visible individuals connected online, they coordinated strategy with congressional progressives while simultaneously pressuring them to hold the line on progressive objectives. This included cajoling progressive Democrats to publicly pledge to reject legislation that did not include a public healthcare plan, and keeping a "whip count" of who was on board and who was not, akin to how the House or Senate Democratic Whip would keep track of his caucus. Simultaneously operating from the outside, they used their online resources to raise money for Democrats who supported a public option while organizing against sending progressive dollars to those who did not, utilized online social networking tools to keep the pressure on wavering Democrats, and even threatened progressive primary opponents to wavering Democrats in safe districts who might be successfully opposed from the left.[23]

Their chief opposition came from the White House, where President Obama was fixed on getting Congress to pass healthcare legislation whether or not it met progressive goals. To this end, the White House launched its own Internet campaign, engaging Organizing for America through its perch at the Democratic National Committee to stimulate some of the people who had participated in Obama's online campaign to work for passage of healthcare legislation. Unlike the campaign, however, and in sharp contrast to the horizontally organized netroots, the White House effort was top-down, with the administration asking people to go to the OFA website and lobby Congress to pass healthcare legislation. By the numbers, the results of their efforts were impressive: mobilizing volunteers in every congressional district, with 2.2 million supporters working for passage; over 1.5 million testimonials of support for Obama's priorities; over 230,000 letters submitted to newspaper editors; over 238,000 personal healthcare stories shared online.[24] The dilemma, as netroots activists were quick to point out, is that the president was intentionally vague on exactly what his priorities were.

While never closing the door to a public option, Obama also never pushed for one. Working on a highly complex piece of legislation in a difficult political climate—the longer congressional debate dragged on, the less popular healthcare reform became—required maximum flexibility. The lack of responsible parties and the sometimes divergent political interests between the president and some members of his own congressional caucus made it difficult for the president to shepherd the legislation through the political process without making compromises and adjustments. Billions of dollars were at stake, and those who stood to lose money lobbied strongly to members of the president's party to have their interests represented. Against this backdrop, Obama's Internet effort amounted to an additional source of pressure to keep the reform process moving forward and counterbalance those forces which might pull it apart, but—unlike the netroots' efforts and in contrast to Obama's Internet election campaign—it was not a grassroots movement designed to accomplish an objective any more specific than passage of some form of healthcare legislation. That meant it was not specifically a progressive effort, differentiating and putting it at odds with netroots goals.[25]

Ironically, the netroots at times were one of the forces threatening to undermine the process, particularly when an eleventh-hour Senate deal to expand Medicare eligibility fell apart. For a brief moment, the netroots were divided between those who wanted to scrap healthcare policy and start from scratch and those who wanted to take what they could get, even though it fell short of what they wanted. Ultimately, most netroots voices expressed support for the bill that eventually passed, with the caveat that it was simply a first step as they continue to push the Democratic Party and a Democratic president in a progressive direction.

THE "TEA PARTY" CHALLENGES REPUBLICANS

Although sometimes equated in the press with netroots progressives for their mirror-image political objectives, "Tea Party" conservatives—who emerged as a visible force during the healthcare debate—are not exclusively an online movement. Several websites lay claim to a version of the Tea Party name and claim to be home to the movement, including Tea Party Patriots (teapartypatriots.com) and Tea Party Nation (teapartynation.com). These sites, like their counterparts on the left, include discussion forums, provide action alerts and information on movement activities, and house blogs with discussion threads. Unlike the netroots, however, some groups flying the Tea Party banner have Washington connections, like Freedom-Works, a group run by former Republican House majority leader Dick Armey, which funded and organized a Tea Party march on Washington in 2009.[26]

Where netroots activists work to reduce corporate influences in the Democratic Party as they pursue progressive legislation, Tea Party activists have emerged as an ideologically conservative influence on mainstream Republicans. In a brief time, they have made their mark on electoral politics, advancing a brand of libertarian conservatism that challenges the constitutionality of all but the most essential activities of the federal government, condemns deficit spending and high taxes, and rejects Obama administration efforts to expand the government's role in healthcare and energy policy.

Like the progressive netroots, Tea Party candidates have targeted wayward incumbents for defeat, and with visible success. Notable among these is Senator Bob Bennett of Utah, a reliably conservative Republican who was defeated in his bid for renomination to a fourth term at the 2010 Utah Republican Party Convention because of Tea Party opposition and a $200,000 advertising and mail campaign directed against him by the Club for Growth, a conservative Washington-based organization. Bennett's adversaries accused him of being insufficiently conservative; for his part, the senator expressed the sentiment that his problem was less about ideology and more about his willingness to strike a conciliatory tone with his colleagues across the aisle.[27]

In Florida, Republican Governor Charlie Crist was the de facto incumbent for an open Senate seat in that state in early 2010. Popular with Democrats and sporting high overall approval ratings, Crist looked ready to sail to victory in the Republican primary against

Marco Rubio, a former Florida House Speaker who had enthusiastic Tea Party backing. As Rubio hammered away at Crist for being too moderate, his standing among Republican voters shot up at the expense of his better-known opponent. Crist had welcomed President Obama to Florida with a hug in early 2009, and the gesture—caught on video that circulated on the Internet—served as a symbolic reminder to conservative voters of the governor's larger transgressions, such as his support for the $787 billion federal stimulus package that helped ignite Tea Party anger.[28] By the spring of 2010, Crist's once commanding lead in the Republican primary had collapsed, and he chose to withdraw from the primary, leave his party, and run (unsuccessfully) as an independent candidate in a three-way race against the eventual victor Rubio and Democrat Kendrick Meek.[29] Doing so meant foregoing all party support, a huge challenge for a statewide candidate. But, it also liberated Crist to move leftward to appeal to moderate voters and Democrats who gave him high job approval ratings as governor, raising the possibility that Crist would have caucused with Senate Democrats had he been elected.

In other high-profile primary contests, Tea Party–backed candidates upset candidates who had the normally decisive backing of national Republican Party officials. In Kentucky, Senator Mitch McConnell, the powerful Senate Republican leader, was backing Secretary of State Trey Grayson in the race for his party's nomination for an open U.S. Senate seat in McConnell's home state. Ordinarily, having the support of a powerful party figure like McConnell would be sufficient to make Grayson the prohibitive favorite in his party's primary. But, Grayson was opposed by Tea Party favorite Rand Paul, son of libertarian Republican representative Ron Paul, who generated a small but intense online following during his 2008 quest for the Republican presidential nomination. The primary results were stunning: Paul, an ophthalmologist with no previous political experience, handily defeated McConnell's hand-picked candidate by a wide margin.[30]

In Nevada, former state assemblywoman Sharron Angle, a long shot who had previously run unsuccessfully for Congress, was trailing badly to Sue Lowden, languishing in single digits two months before the primary. Lowden, a former chair of the Nevada Republican Party, was the preferred candidate of the Republican establishment to run against incumbent Democratic senator Harry Reid, the Senate majority leader. Then, Angle was endorsed by the Tea Party Express and rapidly won the backing of Tea Party enthusiasts for her deeply conservative views. When Lowden's campaign stumbled, Angle capitalized on her Tea Party support and shot into the lead, eventually winning the Republican nomination over her more established opponent.

Given Kentucky's right-leaning tendencies and with Reid deeply unpopular among his constituents, both Paul and Angle emerged from their nomination battles as viable general election candidates. Paul would go on to win his contest; Angle would lose hers. However, both general election races started out close, owing in part to the limited reach of Tea Party ideology among nonlibertarian independent voters and making the Tea Party movement simultaneously a boon to the Republican Party and a potential electoral problem. Energized and mobilized, Tea Party supporters were reliable general election voters, eager to turn out during a normally low turnout off-year election. However, as they picked off more mainstream Republican candidates in primaries, they made it harder for Republicans to win over voters in the political middle who are decisive in close contests, while forcing the Republican Party to expend resources contesting elections that might not be close with more conventional nominees. Primary victories by Tea Party–backed candidates over mainstream Republicans in Delaware and Colorado may have prevented Republicans from taking control of the Senate in an otherwise strong Republican year when they lost to Democrats in the general election.

Another cautionary tale of the relationship between the Republican Party and the Tea Party movement may be found in a remote congressional district in upstate New York, where in a special election held in late 2009 a Tea Party uprising cost the Republican Party a House seat it had held since Reconstruction. The local Republican Party nominated State Assemblywoman Dede Scozzafava to run against Democrat Bill Owens in what normally would have been the end of the story: No Democrat had been elected from New York's 23rd congressional district since Ulysses S. Grant was president. However, there was a third candidate in the race. Accountant Doug Hoffman, who had been passed over for the Republican nomination by local party officials, accepted the nomination of the Conservative Party, which has a dedicated ballot line in New York State, insuring Hoffman a place on the ballot without having to perform the cumbersome tasks of circulating and filing petitions for ballot access.

Hoffman attacked Scozzafava from the right, painting her as too moderate for the district. Accordingly, Tea Party support rapidly coalesced behind Hoffman, who was promoted by Dick Armey's FreedomWorks group. The results were similar to what would happen the following year in Florida, Nevada, and Kentucky: The establishment Republican's support cratered, making Hoffman the de facto Republican candidate in the race. The weekend before the election, Scozzafava dropped out of the race and endorsed her *Democratic* rival. However, her name remained on the ballot, and she ended up siphoning off 6 percent of the vote, enough to put Democrat Bill Owens in Congress with a plurality of the vote, despite the feverish efforts of Hoffman's Tea Party supporters, who had flooded the district in an effort to mobilize conservative voters.[31] Some Tea Party activists saw Scozzafava's loss as a victory for ideology over party loyalty,[32] not exactly music to the ears of Republican leaders. And, Owens was seated in time to vote in favor of a bill that was a premier target of Tea Party anger, the healthcare reform measure.

INTERNET POLITICS: JEFFERSONIAN POLITICS ON A HAMILTONIAN SCALE

For Tea Party activists and netroots progressives, the image of an ideal America could not be more different. The Tea Party would move America in the direction of a rugged individualism without much taxation or the social safety net it supports, where states would be free to make decisions without the interference of the national government, businesses would be less burdened by regulatory control, and individual and corporate tax burdens would be reduced. Netroots progressives envision an America based on community, where taxes and regulation are necessary to support a commons that would be destroyed if government were downsized and where government would serve popular rather than corporate interests. It is a vision rooted more directly in Hamiltonian nationalism, where the nation is a family presided over by a strong central government, than in Jeffersonian localism, which in turn is closer to the libertarian bent of the Tea Party. In this regard, the two groups line up with the long-standing alignment of Hamiltonian-minded Democrats and Jeffersonian Republicans. Beyond these generalizations, however, distinctions between the two groups are less clear. Tea Party activists are far more comfortable with the unfettered capitalism promoted by Hamilton, while netroots activists share with Jefferson an abiding faith in the goodness of ordinary citizens. And, each group poses a bigger threat to the party to which it is closest than to the other side.

As for their means, Internet politics—regardless of the ends to which they are applied—enable people to come together in virtual gatherings for the purpose of taking collective social action. It is in this respect a sort of twenty-first century town meeting—the Jeffersonian commons in cyberspace—where anyone of like mind with Internet access can read a blog, post a diary, engage in spirited exchanges on comment threads, plot strategy, give money, and mobilize and motivate friends, relatives, and strangers. By virtue of its scale, however, it is something more than a town hall; rather, it is a national forum independent of location, an organic meeting that people enter and exit at will, unbounded by the limitations of space or time. It is something neither Jefferson nor Hamilton could have imagined: a town meeting with national reach, Jeffersonian localism on a Hamiltonian scale.

As Internet-based activists on the left and to some degree on the right engage the new media to push the parties to move in new directions, the parties have no choice but to respond. Even an Internet-savvy president found that he could not ignore the efforts of an animated netroots as they attempted to move him in directions he felt his fellow partisans in Congress were not willing to go. If netroots activists continue to win electoral battles, party regulars will take note and make adjustments. Republicans are already making adjustments to avoid being victims of Tea Party anger, refusing to make themselves targets by reaching across the aisle. In the short term, the distinctions symbolized by the two separate blogospheres that do not link to each other have been manifested in greater party polarization in government.

In the long term, it is possible that both parties will turn more and more to the Internet to air and iron out differences. If, as we said in Chapter 1, many people do not like to choose between Jeffersonian localism and Hamiltonian nationalism, politics on the Internet offers a new set of possibilities through the creation of a virtual national commons. As a matter of means rather than ends, both parties are struggling to understand the new technology and make it work for them. Recall that we also said that parties have evolved before, sometimes dramatically, in the wake of social changes and technological advances. As they feel continued heat from Internet communities that have already realized a fair degree of political success, it is hard to imagine they will not evolve again.

7

Campaign Finance and Networked Political Parties

s parties are buffeted by a changing media environment, so
are they shaped by a gusher of money that has been flood-
ing the political system at an increasingly rapid pace. In late
January 2010, Barack Obama stepped forward to the rostrum to give
his official State of the Union address. Before him were assembled
members of Congress, the Cabinet, and the justices of the U.S. Supreme Court. As expected, Obama spoke of the economic and foreign
policy challenges facing the country. But, in an unusual move, the
president directly attacked the Supreme Court. Only days before, the
Court had rendered a five-to-four opinion in a case entitled *Citizens
United v. Federal Election Commission*. This decision eliminated much
of the campaign finance regulatory system assembled by previous
congresses and presidents following the Watergate scandal in the
1970s. Staring directly at the Court justices, Obama took aim at the
Republican-appointed jurists who wrote the opinion, saying, "With
all due deference to separation of powers, last week the Supreme Court
reversed a century of law that I believe will open the floodgates for
special interests—including foreign corporations—to spend without
limit in our elections."[1] Immediately, the television cameras zoomed

in on Justice Samuel Alito, who could be seen mouthing the words, "Not true."

The debate concerning the ability of the federal government to regulate the flow of money in politics is a long-standing one. For nearly two centuries, the tension between the rights of individuals, corporations, and labor unions to participate in the political process, and the interest of the federal government in making sure that candidates and campaigns participate on a level playing field, is one that has been the subject of much debate in the U.S. Congress and ongoing litigation in the courts (see Table 7.1). Today, 82 percent maintain that the impact of special-interest money is a "major problem," and 76 percent "agree strongly" that "there is too much money spent on political campaigns and elections today, and limits should be placed on campaign spending."[2]

Table 7.1   Issues Raised by Federal Campaign Finance Laws

Monetary Issues

1. How much money given to a political candidate is too much?
2. Are corporate donations inherently corrupt?
3. What limits, if any, should be placed on corporate and/or individual donations to political candidates?
4. Should federal campaigns rely mostly on local contributions?
5. Should the national parties have greater involvement and help candidates with out-of-state monies?

Constitutional Issues

1. Is money truly a form of speech that deserves protection under the First Amendment to the U.S. Constitution?[3]
2. Do corporations fall under the protection of the First Amendment as conceived by the Framers?

This chapter traces the history of money in political campaigns in the United States. Over the past two centuries, there has been a torrent of dollars funneled into partisan campaigns and numerous efforts by Congress to regulate and stem the flow of dollars. At the same time, these laws have raised profound constitutional questions that have been repeatedly addressed by the Supreme Court. During the twentieth century and extending into the present era, a pattern has emerged: As the major parties become stronger nationally, more dollars from outside a given state have flowed into political campaigns. It is, therefore, not surprising that the growing role of money in party politics is conceivably the most powerful force pushing the system toward the Hamiltonian pole. It is, we argue, the fulcrum of a new professionalized and centralized party system.

A BRIEF HISTORY OF MONEY
AND POLITICAL CAMPAIGNS

The dominant means of reaching voters during the early days of campaigning was the print media, namely, newspapers. As discussed in Chapter 1, the surest way to win favorable attention for candidates was either to own a newspaper or sponsor the editor. Thus, in 1791, Thomas Jefferson gave Philip Freneau a part-time clerkship in the State Department so that he would move to Philadelphia to become editor of the *National Gazette,* the paper that became the mouthpiece for Jefferson's Democratic–Republican Party. Alexander Hamilton, meanwhile, was a major financial backer of the competing *Gazette of the United States.* As late as the mid-nineteenth century, newspapers were a major source of campaign expenditures. For example, when a wealthy backer wanted to aid the presidential candidacy of James Buchanan in 1856, he contributed $10,000 to start a sympathetic newspaper. Likewise, Abraham Lincoln secretly purchased a small Illinois newspaper to advance his presidential ambitions in 1860.[4]

"Treating" was another common form of electioneering during the early days of the republic. Candidates would sponsor events at which voters would be treated to lavish feasts.[5] Thus, when George Washington ran for the Virginia House of Burgesses in 1751, he reportedly purchased a quart of rum, wine, beer, and hard cider for every voter in the district (there were only 391 voters).[6] In 1835, Ferdinand Bayard, a Frenchman traveling in the United States, commented that "candidates offer drunkenness openly to anyone who is willing to give them his vote."[7] Besides owning newspapers and treating potential supporters, candidates also sent mailings to voters, printed pamphlets for distribution, and organized rallies and parades. By the 1840s, pictures, buttons, banners, and novelty items were widely distributed.

Although controlling newspapers and treating and distributing campaign paraphernalia were costly endeavors, collecting massive sums of money was unnecessary. Prior to 1828, only white males could vote, there were property qualifications in some states, and voting was even restricted in some places to those belonging to a particular religious denomination.[8] Fewer voters meant fewer expenditures. Modes of communication were limited to word of mouth and the print media. After the formation of the spoils system in the 1830s (whereby party workers were rewarded with government jobs), volunteers were called upon to organize parades and get voters to the polls.

Finally, because party loyalty was extremely pronounced for much of the nineteenth century, there was very little movement from one election to the next, and straight-ticket voting was the norm. At the same time, party politics was truly local politics. Jeffersonian localism provided the means by which candidates sought federal offices: control of local newspapers, local party jobs, and local volunteers. It was amateur based, but also very effective.

Mark Hanna, the Campaign of 1896, and the Rise of Hamiltonian Nationalism Politics

Mark Hanna is often credited with being the first campaign consultant in U.S. history, having orchestrated William McKinley's 1896 presidential victory. He also helped transform the role of money in politics, once famously saying, "There are two things that are important in politics—the first is money, and I can't remember what the second one is."[9] This was an astonishing statement, given the secondary role of money in elections during the first century of our nation's history. Why did things change so quickly?

The reasons for the tremendous surge in campaign funds were linked to the vast transformation of the U.S. economy following the Civil War. By the 1870s, the Industrial Revolution was in full swing. The nation's industrial infrastructure was booming, and Americans were migrating to the nation's largest cities. Relationships were forged between party machines and captains of industry, in which the latter pumped money into party coffers in exchange for preventing elected officials from interfering with the so-called free market. The election of 1896 marked a turning point in the tale of money and politics. William McKinley pledged to continue the GOP's laissez-faire economic policies, whereas William Jennings Bryan, McKinley's Democratic opponent, wanted more government regulation of business.

Fearing a Democratic Party groundswell and the ruin of the free-market economic system should Bryan become president, Republicans mounted the best-bankrolled campaign ever. For the first time, corporations made political contributions directly from their company treasuries. The Republicans' massive war chest, estimated at $3 million, allowed Hanna and the Republicans to sponsor hundreds of speakers for small gatherings and debates; produce more than 200 million pamphlets (the GOP headquarters employed over 100 full-time mail clerks) as well as hundreds of thousands of posters, buttons, and billboards; invest heavily in newspaper advertising; and hire legions of workers to register new Republicans and get them to the polls.[10] McKinley simply stayed at home in Canton, Ohio, where trainloads of supporters, many carrying envelopes of cash, were brought to his front porch. The Democrats, meanwhile, raised a mere $650,000. Not surprisingly, McKinley won with 51.7 percent of the vote.[11]

Mark Hanna's efforts were significant in two ways. First, the 1896 election was the first time that systematic fundraising techniques were used in a presidential campaign. No longer would party operatives wait for the money to come in; instead, they would go out and get it. Second, Hanna demonstrated that political advertising could rule the day. Word-of-mouth campaigning, relying on volunteers, and placing newspaper ads were becoming passé. Press releases, direct mail, billboards, and soon radio (and later television and the Internet) would transform electioneering by creating national messages that were developed by strategists at the highest levels and could be disseminated to voters using new messaging tools.

In addition to a shift in campaign tactics, the U.S. was experiencing a rapid expansion of the electorate thanks to immigration and women's suffrage. With more voters to reach, political parties needed more resources, and so an age of aggressive fundraising began. It was once reported that when a union leader came to a U.S. senator to urge support for protections against child labor at the turn of the century, the senator supposedly replied, "But, Sam, you know damn well as I do that I can't stand for a bill like that. Why those fellows this bill is aimed at—those mill owners—are good for $200,000 a year to the party. You can't afford to monkey with a business that friendly."[12]

In short, Hanna and the Republican Party created a new type of Hamiltonian nationalism in politics. By centralizing power at the top of a federal campaign, and using new, top-down techniques to communicate with a mass electorate, Hanna and his colleagues began a movement away from locally based politics—a movement that grew with the passage of time and vastly transformed U.S. politics. In this new era, political parties became more professionally based and were a central point for gathering large sums of money. Elections were conducted by party professionals, and the party machines exerted considerable control over policymaking. Party bosses expected those in government to ante up, and anyone interested in shaping public policy was expected to woo them. Party coffers were filled through small numbers of huge contributions from the so-called fat cats. During the presidential race of 1928, for example, over half of both the Democratic and Republican treasuries came from contributions of

$5,000 or more—a sum that could buy 10 family cars at that time.[13] In sum, the cornerstone of Hamiltonian parties is money—lots of it.

Television Marketing and the Skyrocketing Costs of Campaigns

If the cost of elections rose during the Industrial Revolution, it sky-rocketed during the technological revolution that was well underway by the 1960s. By 2008, for the first time in history, the major party presidential candidates raised more than *$1 billion.*[14] Altogether, more than *$5 billion* was spent by all candidates seeking office in 2008.[15] And future years are likely to see even more expenditures. Indeed, the cost of running for any political office has grown at a staggering rate. In 2010, winning candidates in House races raised an average of more than $1.2 million; victorious senators averaged $8.3 million.[16]

The single greatest force behind this change has been the way candidates communicate with voters. Today, most voters hear from politicians through the electronic media—television, radio, and now the Internet. The first television advertisements for presidential candidates appeared in 1952. By the 1980s, nearly all candidates for public office relied on television advertisements to spread their messages. But television advertising is extraordinarily expensive: in 1860, Abraham Lincoln's campaign cost just over $100,000; a century later, that amount bought only 30 minutes of television airtime.[17]

Another reason for the growing cost of elections is the emergence of professional campaign consultants. Prior to the 1950s, most campaigns were headed by candidates, their spouses, or party activists—usually the most seasoned "hacks" in the party organizations. With the advent of television advertising, product marketing experts became useful. By the 1960s, a new profession blossomed—campaign consulting. Over time came a greater specialization within the consulting profession that included media gurus, pollsters, fundraising professionals, and direct mail experts. As the professionals took over the mechanics of campaigning, the cost of elections further escalated. In 2008, for example, political consultant David Axelrod's firm was paid $2.5 million to handle the Barack Obama presidential campaign.[18]

The Rise of Political Action Committees

Interest groups have played an important role in funding elections for over a century. During the Industrial Revolution, businesses, trade associations, and labor unions channeled large donations to parties and their candidates. Even though reform measures limited direct contributions from corporations, banks, and labor unions, many loopholes existed. In 1943, the Congress of Industrial Organizations (CIO) circumvented contribution restrictions by creating a separate fund to receive and spend voluntary contributions—a new organizational unit it called the political action committee (PAC). It was legal, the CIO argued, because none of the monies used to support the group or given to candidates came directly from the labor union itself.

By the late 1950s, scores of business and professional associations began to develop their own PACs.[19] But the real growth period began in the 1970s. In 1974, there were roughly 600 PACs; by 2008, there were more than 5,200. During the same period, PAC expenditures grew from $12.5 million to $600 million.[20] And most PACs gave to incumbents. During the past decade, PACs gave a minimum of 70 percent of their contributions to incumbents; less than 15 percent went to challengers.[21]

Overall, labor union PACs tend to support Democrats and business-related organizations generally help Republicans. During the 2006 elections, when Republicans still held their congressional majorities, corporate PACs gave 66.6 percent of their contributions to Republicans, while labor PACs gave 88.9 percent of their funds to Democrats.[22] In 2008, things were different as Democrats had majorities in both houses of Congress. Thus, only 51.9 percent of corporate PAC contributions went to the GOP; 48.1 percent went to the Democrats (many of them incumbents). Meanwhile, 92.5 percent of labor PAC money went to the Democrats in 2008; only 7.5 percent found its way into the coffers of Republican congressional candidates.[23] In 2010, signs pointed toward a reversal as corporate PACs swung their political giving to the GOP by the start of the fall campaign, when all signs pointed to large Republican gains in the congressional midterm contests.[24]

CONGRESS, THE SUPREME COURT, AND CAMPAIGN FINANCE

What difference does it make that some groups and individuals give money during elections while others do not? One could argue that contributing money is one way citizens participate in the democratic process. This argument is often heard from opponents of campaign finance reform who claim that the more money there is in electoral politics, the better off the system is. After all, they reason, is not the act of contributing money an exercise of freedom of speech guaranteed in the First Amendment? Viewed from this perspective, the massive influx of money into campaigns is nothing more than democracy churning along on all cylinders.

Most Americans do not share this upbeat view. In 2007, 64 percent believed the U.S. government should put restrictions on the amount of money that a private individual can contribute.[25] Today, 65 percent are opposed to giving corporations and unions the right to spend money either to support or oppose specific candidates.[26] These results are not surprising, as there is a long-standing belief that money plays a corrupting role in the development of public policy. Moreover, most Americans never send a check either to a candidate or to a political party. One 2008 study found only 17 percent of voters contributed to one of the presidential candidates; 83 percent did not.[27]

Prior to the Progressive Era, there were few efforts to curb the flow of money in elections. In 1867, Congress passed legislation prohibiting assessments on navy yard workers. Nine years later, the ban was extended to all federal employees.[28] The most prominent of these reforms occurred in 1883 when Congress, prompted by the 1881 assassination of President James A. Garfield by a disappointed office seeker, passed the Civil Service Reform Act. Besides creating the civil service, the law continued the ban on assessing federal government employees for political contributions.[29]

In 1907, Congress passed the Tillman Act, which made it a crime for any corporation or national bank to contribute to either congressional or presidential candidates. A Senate report concluded that "[t]he evils of the use of [corporate] money in connection with political elections are so generally recognized that the committee deems it unnecessary to make any argument in favor of the general purpose of this measure. It is in the interest of good government and calculated to promote purity in the selection of public officials."[30] Three years later, Congress required House candidates to disclose the source of their party committee contributions if they operated in two or more states—but only after the elections. The law, passed by a Republican-controlled Congress, was strengthened in 1911 when the Democrats came to power. The new law established spending limits and required preelection disclosure of finances in House and Senate races.[31]

The Teapot Dome scandal that gripped the Warren Harding Administration led to additional cries for reform. In 1925, Calvin Coolidge signed the Federal Corrupt Practices Act into law. This legislation required quarterly reports (even in nonelection years) of contributions to federal candidates and to multistate political committees. The law reaffirmed the spending limits, but it was easily circumvented as candidates established a multitude of supporting committees, thus making it hard to determine the total amount of receipts and expenditures in any given campaign.[32]

Another flurry of reform measures occurred during the late 1930s and early 1940s—most notably the Hatch Act of 1939, officially called the Clean Politics Act. This measure made it a crime for any federal employee to become an active political participant, and for anyone to solicit funds from people receiving federal relief. Within a year, several amendments were added—including the first federal limit on contributions from individuals (they could give no more than $5,000 to a candidate for federal office), and a prohibition against contributions to federal-level candidates from any business doing work for the U.S. government. By 1943, Congress extended the prohibition on contributions from banks and corporations to include labor unions as part of the Taft-Hartley Act. In enacting the measure, Congress overrode the veto of President Harry S. Truman who warned that the expenditure ban was a "dangerous intrusion on free speech."[33]

But these reform efforts proved to be meaningless. The flow of large sums of money into campaigns did not slow down; it was simply channeled along different paths.[34] Although these statutes sounded impressive, they failed to create public authorities responsible for collecting disclosure reports and prosecuting any illegal activity. In addition, the laws were fraught with loopholes. For example, reporting requirements were limited to "campaign periods." Thus, contributors evaded the law by donating to candidates prior to the start of any designated period. Moreover, expenditure limits applied only to a particular candidate, not to the separate committees that sprang up on a candidate's behalf (e.g., "Friends to Elect Mary Smith to Congress"). In addition, corporations evaded contribution prohibitions by reimbursing corporate executives who sent money to candidates. Under-the-table gifts were also commonplace. Finally, there was a lack of will among elected officials to enforce the existing regulations. It is no wonder that from the passage of the Corrupt Practices Act of 1925 until the 1970s, there is no record of a single prosecution for campaign contributions violations.

Watergate and Campaign Finance Reform

By the 1970s, reform was back on Congress's agenda. First, the cost of elections was rising owing to the growing use of television. Second, incumbents from both parties were worried that well-financed challengers could connect with voters through the mass media and toss them out. Finally, there were shocking disclosures of fat-cat contributions, including businessman Clement Stone's $3 million gift to Richard M. Nixon's 1968 presidential campaign.

Two significant measures became law in 1971. First, the Revenue Act created a fund for presidential campaigns and allowed voters to check off a one-dollar donation on their tax forms to help support the fund.[35] (To get around a veto threat posed by President Nixon, the act did not go into effect until the 1976 election.) Second, the Federal Election Campaign Act (FECA) was an ambitious attempt to tighten reporting requirements and limit media expenditures. Unlike prior disclosure laws, FECA mandated that all expenditures and contributions of over $100 be disclosed, regardless of when they were given. Moreover, reports would be filed with the General Accounting Office and made public within 48 hours. Media expenditures—including television, radio, billboards, and newsprint—would be limited to $50,000, or 10 cents per voting-age resident (whichever amount was larger).[36]

The FECA did increase disclosure levels, but the law had little impact on the 1972 elections. As before, candidates found different channels through which to spend their funds. But the story of finance reform was about to take a dramatic turn. During the course of investigating Richard M. Nixon's involvement in the cover-up of the break-in of the Democratic National Committee headquarters located at the Watergate Hotel, it was discovered that the Committee to Re-elect the President (CREEP) had established its own secret fundraising program. Many of the donations to Nixon's 1972 reelection campaign war chest were illegal—ranging from the $200,000 delivered in an attaché case, to nearly $1 million in illegal corporate donations. Of the $63 million collected by Nixon, $20 million came from 153 donors who gave $50,000 or more. Commenting on the breadth of the Watergate scandal, John Gardner, head of Common Cause, said in April 1973, "Watergate is not primarily a story of political espionage, nor even of White House intrigue. It is a particularly malodorous chapter in the annals of campaign financing. The money paid to the Watergate conspirators before the break-in—and the money passed to them later [to keep quiet]—was money from campaign gifts."[37]

A shocked public and a Democratic-controlled Congress led a reform effort and passed legislation that established contribution limits and created a regulatory system for enforcement (see Table 7.2).

Table 7.2   Highlights of the 1974 Campaign Finance Reforms

1. Created a Federal Election Commission consisting of six members and charged them with enforcing federal election statutes.
2. Set an individual contribution limit of $1,000 per primary, runoff, and general election not to exceed $25,000 to all federal candidates annually.
3. Set a contribution limit of $5,000 per political action committee (PAC) to federal candidates with no aggregate limit.
4. Set a $1,000 independent expenditure limit on behalf of a federal candidate.
5. Banned any contributions to federal candidates from foreign sources.
6. Set a $10 million spending limit per presidential candidate for all presidential primaries.
7. Set a $20 million limit per presidential candidate for the general election.
8. Set a $100,000 limit for U.S. Senate primary candidates.
9. Set a $150,000 limit for U.S. Senate general election races.
10. Set a $70,000 limit for U.S. House primary races.
11. Set a $70,000 limit for U.S. House general elections.
12. Limited party spending to $10,000 per candidate in U.S. House elections.
13. Limited party spending to $20,000 per candidate in U.S. Senate elections.
14. Limited party spending to 2 cents per voter in presidential general elections.
15. Expanded public funding of presidential elections (both primary and general). Primary elections would allow private funds to be matched with public funds to a certain level.
16. Created an extensive list of disclosure and reporting requirements. Each campaign must have one central committee through which all contributions and expenditures on behalf of a candidate must be reported to the Federal Election Commission.

Source: Cited in Mary W. Cohn, ed., *Congressional Campaign Finances: History, Facts, and Controversy* (Washington, DC: Congressional Quarterly, 1992), p. 44–46. These were amendments to the 1971 FECA law.

Despite his reservations, President Gerald R. Ford signed it into law, noting that "the times demand this legislation."[38]

A Challenge in the Supreme Court: *Buckley v. Valeo*

The jubilation over enacting the new reform laws did not last long. As soon as FECA took effect in 1976, it was challenged in the courts. The case comprised a diverse set of plaintiffs, including U.S. senator James Buckley, a conservative Republican from New York; U.S. senator Eugene McCarthy, a liberal Democrat from Minnesota; the New York Civil Liberties Union; and *Human Events,* a conservative publication. In *Buckley v. Valeo* (Francis R. Valeo was the secretary of the Senate),[39] the core arguments were rather simple. Buckley and his allies maintained that campaign spending was a form of speech protected by the First Amendment. The government argued that the democratic process compelled a level playing field, and this meant limits must be placed on both campaign contributions and expenditures.

On January 30, 1976, the Supreme Court rendered its decision. The Court found that some, but not all, of the FECA restrictions were constitutional. They let stand limits on how much money individuals and political committees could contribute; they allowed public financing of presidential elections, so long as it was voluntary (meaning that candidates could refuse public monies and spend their own money instead); and they required disclosure of campaign contributions and expenditures of more than $100. But the Supreme Court also struck down several features of the new law, including the overall spending caps; limits on what candidates and their spouses could contribute to their own campaigns; and limits on independent expenditures.[40] Concerning its rejection of overall spending limits, the Court noted, "A restriction on the amount of money a person or group can spend on political communication during a campaign necessarily reduces the quantity of expression by restricting the number of issues discussed, the depth of their exploration and the size of the audience reached."[41]

REFORMING THE REFORMS: THE BIPARTISAN CAMPAIGN REFORM ACT OF 2001

Public opposition to the increased amounts of money given to candidates and campaigns during the 1980s and 1990s gave rise to new reforms. Several novel types of campaign contributions found their way around existing laws. One of these was soft money, which is money not regulated by the Federal Elections Commission. Rather, it is money collected by the national parties—including the Democratic National Committee, the Republican National Committee, and their corresponding House and Senate committees—and is used for party-building activities ranging from public education to voter mobilization. Hard money refers to contributions made by individuals to federal candidates that are subject to the caps imposed by FECA and are monitored by the Federal Elections Commission.

From 1994 to 2000, the total amount of soft money raised by the Democratic and Republican parties rose more than fourfold from $102 million to $495 million.[42] Disgusted by the bipartisan evasions of FECA, consumer activist Ralph Nader ran for president in 2000, contending that the campaign finance system was broken and had corrupted the system of checks and balances created by the Framers of the U.S. Constitution. Said Nader: "If we don't have a more equitable distribution of power, there is no equitable distribution of wealth or income. And people who work hard will not get their just rewards. And the main way to shift power, if you had to have one reform, is public financing of public elections."[43]

Prior to the 2000 election, senators John McCain, a Republican from Arizona, and Russ Feingold, a Democrat from Wisconsin, led a bipartisan effort to change the campaign finance laws. The two senators were joined in the House by Representatives Christopher Shays, a Republican from Connecticut, and Martin Meehan, a Democrat from Massachusetts. But their collaborative efforts, despite overwhelming public support, were to no avail. In the Republican-controlled House, parliamentary procedures were used to forestall debate. High-ranking Republicans in both the House and Senate offered countless amendments that either weakened the proposed bills or broke up the bipartisan coalition that supported stronger measures. Spearheading the opposition to any changes was Senator Mitch McConnell, a Republican from Kentucky. Clinging to the idea that donating and spending money to campaigns is a form of free speech, McConnell, along with a handful of Republicans, filibustered any reforms. Unless McCain and Feingold could somehow muster 60 votes needed to end a McConnell-led filibuster, campaign finance would go nowhere.

The election of 2000 was pivotal to the reformers. Democrats made gains in both houses, with many newcomers pledging to "clean things up." Moreover, after John McCain failed to secure the 2000 GOP presidential nomination against George W. Bush, he set his sights on campaign finance reform. McCain became the darling of the media during his presidential bid, and a growing number of citizens seemed ready to follow his lead. McCain used his newfound popularity to help dozens of Republican House candidates win election. In exchange, he received their pledge of support for his campaign reform efforts.

The debate was set for March 2001. After nearly two weeks of compromise, McCain and Feingold were able to break the filibuster—thereby bringing the bill to a vote, and winning over some moderate Republicans by increasing the cap on individual contributions from $1,000 to $2,000. But the battle was far from over. House Republicans offered an alternative to the Shays–Meehan plan that allowed for contributions to the party committees above the proposed $90,000 limit. This less sweeping measure was meant to appeal to black and Hispanic Democratic legislators, since the national party committees were instrumental in mobilizing minorities to vote. But Shays and

Meehan knew that their bill would have to be identical to the one passed in the Senate in order to avoid a House–Senate conference committee that could potentially kill the measure. As 2001 turned into 2002, most congressional observers were pessimistic that the Shays–Meehan bill would ever come to a vote.

The break came with the Enron scandal in which monumental accounting fraud led to the energy company's bankruptcy. George W. Bush, whose campaign benefitted from Enron's generous contributions, stated he would support the bill if it passed Congress.[44] Armed with this presidential endorsement, Shays and Meehan were able to collect enough signatures to force a vote, and in February 2002, the House passed the bill by a 51-vote margin. One month later the Senate approved the most sweeping campaign finance bill in more than 25 years. On March 27, 2002, the Bipartisan Campaign Reform Act (BCRA), more popularly known as the McCain–Feingold law, was approved by George W. Bush.

The final version of the law included a ban on contributions to any national political party. The bill also banned issue-advocacy ads 30 days before primary elections and 60 days prior to a general election. However, the ban on soft money did not apply to PACs, which were free to raise unlimited amounts of money. Even so, the passage of the McCain–Feingold law created its own set of controversies. The very day that the BCRA was signed into law, Senator Mitch McConnell and a host of other federal legislators, along with various interest groups and minor parties, challenged it in the federal courts. The core of their complaints was that McCain–Feingold represented an assault on free association and expression. This was based on the restrictions on issue advocacy and expressed advocacy for a given candidate 60 days prior to an election.[45] Previously, the Supreme Court had ruled in 1996 that political parties could spend unlimited amounts on issue advocacy advertisements so long as they were not done in concert with any candidate's campaign.[46]

Constitutional arguments in support of the law stressed that limits on contributions may be imposed without being a burden on the First Amendment. Supporters noted that Congress's interest in limiting corruption had been previously endorsed by the courts, including *Buckley v. Valeo*. As Trevor Potter, a former Federal Election Commissioner, observed, "The Supreme Court has accepted that large contributions to political parties and candidates … is a serious national problem, contributing to both corruption and the appearance of corruption, and to diminished public faith in government. The Court has also consistently held that those concerns amply justify reasonable regulation."[47]

By the end of 2002, the complaints against McCain-Feingold were merged into one case, *McConnell v. Federal Election Commission*. On December 10, 2003, the Supreme Court ruled that McCain-Feingold's ban on soft money contributions was constitutional. Writing for a five-to-four majority, justices John Paul Stevens and Sandra Day O'Connor abhorred the use of soft money in political campaigns:

> Just as troubling to a functioning democracy as classic *quid pro quo* corruption is the danger that officeholders will decide issues not on the merits or the desires of their constituencies but according to the wishes of those who have made large financial contributions ....The best means of prevention is to identify and remove the temptation. The evidence set forth ... convincingly demonstrates that soft-money contributions to political parties carry with them just such a temptation.[48]

But the final paragraph of the majority opinion contained a prescient prediction: "Money, like water, will always find an outlet."[49] The flow of money into campaigns would continue, and *McConnell v. FEC* would not be the last word from the Supreme Court on the issue of campaign finance.

THE DEBATE BEGINS ANEW

Evidence that the Supreme Court decision in *McConnell v. FEC* was beginning to fray mounted during George W. Bush's second term. Justice Sandra Day O'Connor decided to retire to help her ailing husband, and President Bush initially asked John Roberts to succeed O'Connor. But in the interregnum, Chief Justice William Rehnquist died, and Bush elevated Roberts to that position while naming Samuel Alito to succeed O'Connor. This rapid turnover proved decisive. For 11 years, the composition of the Supreme Court had not changed. But with the additions of Roberts and Alito, the Court further shifted to the right.[50]

In 2007, the Roberts Court ruled that the McCain-Feingold ban on using a candidate's name in issue advocacy advertisements 30 days before a primary and 60 days prior to a general election was unconstitutional. In its five-to-four decision, the Roberts-led Court declared, "Discussion of issues cannot be suppressed simply because the issues may also be pertinent in an election. Where the First Amendment is implicated, the tie goes to the speaker, not the censor."[51] Meanwhile, the flow of money into campaign coffers became a torrent. In 2000, George W. Bush became the first Republican presidential candidate to refuse federal financing for his primary campaign, a stance he repeated four years later.[52] In 2004, Democrat Howard Dean raised an astounding $45 million dollars, becoming the first Democratic presidential primary candidate to forgo federal matching funds.[53] Four years later, no serious presidential contender accepted federal funding. In fact, Barack Obama and Hillary Clinton raised more money in 2008 than all of their Democratic competitors *combined*. Obama garnered an astonishing $456.1 million; Clinton amassed a war chest totaling $216.6 million. For the entire presidential campaign, Obama raised $745 million.[54] On the Republican side, the two leading contenders, John McCain and Mitt Romney, were also numbers one and two, respectively, in fundraising: McCain received $216.4 million in donations; Romney, $108.8 million. In the fall, Barack Obama became the first major party nominee since 1976 to forgo federal financing of his general election campaign—a move sure to be emulated by both the Democratic and Republican presidential nominees in 2012. Obama could easily afford to forgo the $84 million in federal dollars to which he was entitled, having raised $745 million, including $656 million from individual donors.[55] The sizable contributions Obama amassed from individuals were unforeseen by writers of federal campaign finance laws in the 1970s, an era when individual contributions (when they came) were through a slow-moving postal system rather than the instantaneous Internet contributions of the twenty-first century. Back then, legislators were focused on corporate donations and their potentially corrupting influence, as witnessed by the 1972 Nixon reelection campaign.

Meanwhile, money continued to flow in new ways designed to evade federal laws. So-called 527 groups, a name that refers to a provision in the federal tax code, began to sprout. These tax-exempt organizations have a goal of affecting election outcomes and are not subject to any limits in the amount of monies they receive or how they spend them. Citizens United, on the right, and MoveOn.org, on the left, are examples of such organizations. And the McCain-Feingold ban on soft money made these organizations even more attractive to political activists. Thus in 2004, philanthropist George Soros gave $15 million to two liberal organizations—MoveOn.org and America Coming Together—hoping to defeat George W. Bush for reelection.[56] While these organizations could not expressly advocate for the Democratic nominee, John Kerry, they could point out why they believed Bush did not deserve another term. On the Republican

PARTIES IN A NETWORKED AGE

The Parties and Internet Fundraising

There are many differences in the way the Democrats and Republicans have approached using the Internet. Campaign fundraising in 2004 is one example. Howard Dean's campaign is known for a variety of Internet innovations, but none was as vital or long-lasting in its effect as Dean for America's drive to dig into the untapped font of small donors who had perhaps never given to a political campaign in their lives. On a summer day in 2003, when Republican vice president Dick Cheney was holding a $2,000-a-plate luncheon on behalf of Bush-Cheney '04, the Dean campaign countered with an Internet challenge to its supporters to match the vice president's take with small contributions. While impishly streaming a video of Democrat Howard Dean munching on a turkey sandwich, the campaign managed to collect $500,000 from 9,700 people willing to brown bag it with the governor. It was twice what Cheney brought in from his wealthy supporters, and the world of campaign fundraising has not been the same since.

Source: Kerbel, Matthew R. 2009. *Netroots: Online Progressives and the Transformation of American Politics.* Boulder, CO: Paradigm Publishers.

side, a 527 group entitled "Swift Boat Veterans for Truth" ran advertisements raising questions about Kerry's service record during the Vietnam War. In 2008, 527 groups spent $258 million to influence the outcome of federal elections.[57]

In addition, campaign money found still another way to flow like water. So-called 501c groups (also named after a provision of the Internal Revenue Service code), labor unions, trade associations, or social welfare organizations can raise and spend virtually unlimited sums of money so long as it is not their "primary activity" or "major purpose."[58] In other words, electioneering is not the primary purpose of the organization. The principal difference between 527 groups and 501c groups is that 527s are required to disclose the identities of their donors; 501cs are not. Moreover, 501cs are not required to disclose their expenditures. This makes the 501c group preferable to a 527 group among contributors who wish to remain in the shadows.

A Final Denouement? *Citizens United*
v. *Federal Election Commission*

Perhaps the final denouement on the issue of campaign finance came in 2010 when the Roberts-led Court issued a landmark decision in *Citizens United v. Federal Election Commission.* The case arose in 2008 when Citizens United, a conservative group led by longtime Republican activist David Bossie, created a movie about then-presidential candidate Hillary Clinton. For much of 2007 leading into 2008, Clinton was a leading contender for the Democratic presidential nomination. Long a polarizing figure, Clinton evoked the ire of conservatives—even more so as she seemed on the verge of becoming George W. Bush's successor. The film created by Bossie and Citizens United was entitled *Hillary: The Movie* and, not surprisingly, it depicted Senator Clinton in the most negative light, claiming she was "steeped in sleaze."[59]

In January 2008, Citizens United sought to broadcast its movie on the video-on-demand channels provided by cable service providers. To implement its plan to air the movie, Citizens United was prepared to pay for the video-on-demand channel, and it wanted to promote the film on the cable networks in two 10-second advertisements and one 30-second advertisement. The advertisements and movie were scheduled to air within 30 days of the first presidential primaries, violating the provision in the McCain-Feingold Act prohibiting third-party groups from broadcasting advertisements that advocated against a candidate immediately before an election. Although the words "vote against" were not found in *Hillary: The Movie,* the message contained in the film was that Senator Clinton did not merit any votes in her quest to become president. The case quickly reached the Supreme Court.

At the Supreme Court, the outcome was not initially clear. In fact, *Citizens United v. Federal Election Commission* was argued twice before the Court, partly because President Obama appointed Justice Sonya Sotomayor to succeed Justice David Souter, who had heard the initial argument. Expectations were that the Court would issue a narrow ruling. Citizens United had a $12 million budget that included corporate donations, and it was this money that was illegally used to finance and promote *Hillary: The Movie.* But Citizens United also had its own political action committee, and if that entity had been employed to promote the film it would have not violated the provisions of McCain-Feingold.[60]

But the Supreme Court decided to issue a much broader ruling. In its five-to-four decision, the Court sought to demonstrate that the

First Amendment as conceived by the Founders included the right for corporations to engage in free, unregulated speech.[61] By making it a felony for corporations to expressly advocate either the election or defeat of candidates (either 30 days before a primary or 60 days prior to a general election), the Court determined that this portion of McCain-Feingold violated the First Amendment and was therefore unconstitutional.[62] Writing for the majority, Justice Anthony Kennedy declared, "No sufficient governmental interest justified limits on the political speech of non-profit or for-profit corporations. ... For these reasons, political speech must prevail against laws that would suppress it, whether by design or inadvertence .... There is simply no support for the view that the First Amendment, as originally understood, would permit the suppression of political speech by media corporations."[63] Chief Justice Roberts agreed, saying, "The First Amendment protects more than just the individual on a soapbox and the lonely pamphleteer."[64]

The Court also rejected the argument that corporate political speech was inherently corrupt. Reversing the decision in *Buckley v. Valeo* that found otherwise, Justice Kennedy wrote, "[W]e now conclude that independent expenditures, including those made by corporations, do not give rise to corruption or the appearance of corruption."[65] Kennedy added,

> Our Nation's speech dynamic is changing, and informative voices should not have to circumvent onerous restrictions to exercise their First Amendment rights. Speakers have become adept at presenting citizens with sound bites, talking points, and scripted messages that dominate the 24-hour news cycle. Corporations, like individuals, do not have monolithic views. On certain topics corporations may possess valuable expertise, leaving them the best equipped to point out errors or fallacies in speech of all sorts, including the speech of candidates and elected officials.[66]

Virtually the only portion of McCain-Feingold the Court majority left intact was its disclosure requirements. Justice Kennedy found that disclosure did not inhibit political speech, noting that "disclosure permits citizens and shareholders to react to the speech of corporate entities in a proper way. This transparency enables the electorate to make informed decisions and give proper weight to different speakers and messages."[67] This point was vigorously contested by Justice Clarence Thomas, who argued that disclosures of political contributions supporting California's Proposition 8, a 2008 law that overturned the state supreme court's decision legalizing gay marriage, had resulted in intimidation and harassment. Said Thomas: "I cannot endorse a view of the First Amendment that subjects citizens of this Nation to death threats, ruined careers, damaged or defaced property, or pre-emptive and threatening warning letters as the price for engaging in core political speech, the primary object of First Amendment protection."[68]

The majority view was countered by Justice John Paul Stevens. In his opinion, Stevens ridiculed the majority's view that corporations are akin to persons and are therefore subject to First Amendment protections, saying, "Corporations have no consciences, no beliefs, no feelings, no thoughts, no desires. Corporations help structure and facilitate the activities of human beings, to be sure, and their 'personhood' often serves as a useful legal fiction. But they are not themselves members of 'We the People' by whom and for whom our Constitution was established."[69] By treating them as such, Stevens maintained that "corporations and unions will be free to spend as much general treasury money as they wish on ads that support or attack specific candidates, whereas national parties will not be able to spend a dime of soft money on ads of any kind."[70] Stevens concluded that the ruling "enhances the role of corporations and unions—and the narrow interests they represent—vis-à-vis the role of political parties—and the broad coalitions they represent—in determining who will hold public office."[71] He maintained that Congress was entirely correct to view corporate money as a corrupting influence:

> [O]ver the course of the past century Congress has demonstrated a recurrent need to regulate corporate participation in candidate elections to "[p]reserv[e] the integrity of the electoral process, preven[t] corruption, … sustai[n] the active, alert responsibility of the individual citizen, protect the expressive interests of shareholders, and [p]reserv[e] … the individual citizen's confidence in government." …Time and again, we have recognized these realities in approving measures that Congress and the States have taken.[72]

Stevens further noted that corruption "can take many forms," adding, "Bribery may be the paradigm case. But the difference between selling a vote and selling access is a matter of degree, not kind. And selling access is not qualitatively different from giving special preference to those who spent money on one's behalf."[73] Thus, Stevens argued that unrestricted use of corporate money in political campaigns would result in a loss of public confidence in government:

When citizens turn on their televisions and radios before an election and hear only corporate electioneering, they may lose faith in their capacity, as citizens, to influence public policy. A Government captured by corporate interests, they may come to believe, will be neither responsive to their needs nor willing to give their views a fair hearing. The predictable result is cynicism and disenchantment: an increased perception that large spenders "call the tune" and a reduced "willingness of voters to take part in democratic governance."[74]

Stevens issued this final broadside: "While American democracy is imperfect, few outside the majority of this Court would have thought its flaws included a dearth of corporate money in politics."[75]

Reaction to *Citizens United* was swift. As mentioned at the outset of this chapter, President Barack Obama repudiated the Court for its decision, and he repeated his denunciations often during the 2010 midterm campaign. Obama was hardly the only critic. When asked about the case, former Justice Sandra Day O'Connor tartly responded, "If you want my legal opinion, you can go read *McConnell* [*v. Federal Election Commission*]."[76] Others, however, supported the Roberts Court. Republican Senate leader Mitch McConnell, for one, was ecstatic, claiming that the outcome in *Citizens United* was "an important step in restoring the First Amendment rights."[77]

A Failed Congressional Response

Republican lawyer Jan Baran observed in the wake of *Citizens United,* "Regulating campaign finance is now going to hit a brick wall."[78] But that did not stop the Democratic-controlled Congress in its final days from trying to scale it. A bill proposed by New York senator Chuck Schumer and Maryland representative Chris Van Hollen entitled DISCLOSE (shorthand for "Democracy Is Strengthened by Casting Light on Spending in Elections") sought to restrict the *Citizens United* decision (see Table 7.3).

But the Schumer–Van Hollen bill died in the 111th Congress when it failed to gain a single Republican vote in the U.S. Senate, thereby failing to win the 60 votes required to break a GOP filibuster. In the meantime, other nongovernmental organizations are seeking to eliminate all contribution limits and reporting requirements for political committees that make independent expenditures in federal elections. David Keating, the executive director of the Club for Growth, has formed SpeechNow.org, an online entity that seeks to strike down

Table 7.3 Provisions of the 2010 DISCLOSE Proposal

1. Disclosure of all independent spending related to federal elections, even if the advertisement or publication did not expressly call for the election or defeat of a named candidate.
2. Independent spending must be reported to the Federal Election Commission within 24 hours for any spending of $1,000 or more within 20 days before an election.
3. Corporations, unions, or non-profit groups that make at least $10,000 in campaign-related expenditures in a year are required to report all donors of $1,000 or more.
4. Radio and television advertisements must include a disclaimer recorded by the corporate chief executive officer or a union or non-profit group taking responsibility for the ad.
5. For advertising sponsored by a coalition, the top funder of the ad must personally appear in the advertisement.
6. A "pay-to-play" provision bans federal contractors with contracts of more than $1 million from making any federal campaign–related expenditures.
7. Bars federal campaign expenditures by a company if a foreign national owns 20 percent or more of its stock.
8. Bars federal campaign expenditures by a company if a majority of the board of directors are foreign nationals.
9. Bars federal campaign expenditures by a company if foreign nationals can control a U.S. subsidiary's decision-making or activities with respect to U.S. elections.

Source: See Kenneth Jost, "Campaign Finance Debates," CQ Researcher 20: pp. 457–480. Retrieved July 7, 2010, from CQ Researcher Online, http://library.cqpress.com.proxycu.wrlc.org/cqresearcher/cqresrre2010052800.

all laws that limit political contributions to either a candidate or to a political party. SpeechNow.org took its case to court, and in March 2010, the U.S. Court of Appeals for the District of Columbia Circuit struck down the contribution limits, but upheld disclosure requirements. Judge David Sentelle spoke for the court: "Given this analysis from [the Supreme Court in] Citizens United, we must conclude that the government has no anti-corruption interest in limiting contributions to an independent expenditure group such as SpeechNow."[79] More court action is likely, and many believe the Supreme Court will revisit this issue once more—although the outcome is likely to be no different from Citizens United.

The immediate result of Citizens United was an infusion of cash into the 2010 midterm elections. According to published reports, the U.S. Chamber of Commerce spent $75 million in the congressional contests, with the vast majority of its funds supporting Republican candidates opposed to the Obama agenda.[80] Other corporate and labor groups also entered the fray and spent a total of $293 million, the most ever.[81] The most prominent of these newly formed outside groups was American Crossroads, a group founded by former George W. Bush political advisor Karl Rove and former Republican National Committee chairman Ed Gillespie. American Crossroads raised more than $24 million (including $14.5 million from just *three* contributors), all of it in support of Republican congressional candidates and used in television advertisements.[82] This outside money, combined with $1.2 billion raised by the national party committees, made the 2010 elections the most expensive biennial contest in U.S. history, with a total cost of $4 billion.[83]

In sum, we are back to where we started prior to the Watergate scandals. Despite the herculean efforts of Congress to regulate campaign finance, the Supreme Court in *Citizens United* has undone much of the legislation. By taking the position that corporate money is not a corrupting influence, the Court has asserted that money is a legitimate form of speech that is subject to little or no federal regulation. It has been noted previously in this chapter that money in politics is akin to water. You can change the direction of its flow, but never eliminate its presence or, apparently, reduce its volume. All of this has made the national parties important players in local politics. Hamiltonian nationalism continues its ascent, ironically aided by the ability of individuals to log onto their computers and contribute to the national parties with a simple click of a mouse.

8

Elected Officials and the New Partisanship

On Thanksgiving eve 1994, a buoyant Newt Gingrich drove along the country roads of Georgia with his then-wife, Marianne. Only two weeks earlier, House Republicans added 52 representatives to their ranks—enough to form a congressional majority for the first time in 42 years. Not since 1946, the year John F. Kennedy and Richard M. Nixon entered Congress, had there been this many new Republicans. As the car raced along the road, an excited Gingrich exclaimed, "This is really a big change!" At this, Marianne turned to her husband and gently reproved him, "You don't have any clue how big this change really is."[1]

Six months later the change seemed very real as House Republicans strutted down the steps of the U.S. Capitol and a partisan crowd held small American flags and signs that read, "Contract with America—Promises Made—Promises Kept—Restoring the American Dream."[2] The occasion was to mark the one-hundredth day since Gingrich put the U.S. House under new management. The rally's highpoint came when Speaker Gingrich strode to the podium and proudly declared, "Editorial writers and pundits scoffed. But we did mean it. We made promises and we kept promises."[3]

There is an old adage that says, "Winning is not everything—it's the only thing." But what happens *after* the ballots are counted is often even more important than winning elections. In the United States, the victor wins an office, but elections alone do not confer power. Specifically, the Framers of the U.S. Constitution did not want political parties to become instruments of government, believing that parties corrupt and prevent leaders from doing the right thing. Instead, the Founders agreed with Alexander Hamilton that the best thing is to eschew parties and rely on the outstanding characters of distinguished citizens who would act in the public interest. Defending the Electoral College as a means for choosing a president, Hamilton wrote in *The Federalist Papers* that "there would be a constant probability of seeing the station filled by characters pre-eminent for ability and virtue," adding that "the true test of a government is its aptitude and tendency to produce a good administration."[4] Hamilton's equation of character with effective administration still appeals to many Americans. Over the years, would-be presidents have promised to put the interests of their country ahead of their party. In 2008, for example, Republican John McCain's campaign slogan was "Country First," a reference to the many times he had previously bucked the GOP, and an indication that he would do so again should he be elected president.

Yet the pages of American history are suffused with examples demonstrating that character alone is an insufficient basis for good administration. During his single term as president, Jimmy Carter was extolled for his honesty and trustworthiness. But Carter's outstanding character did not translate into effective leadership.[5] The separation of powers among the executive, legislative, and judicial branches; the "special interests" that populate Washington, D.C.; and getting 535 members of Congress to agree on anything are huge obstacles to making things happen—as Carter and many of his successors have learned to their regret.

THE PRESIDENT AS PARTY LEADER

Historically, political parties have been viewed as necessary mechanisms that make government work. During the New Deal, Democrats led by Franklin D. Roosevelt were unified and passed a sweeping list of government-aid programs during a breathtaking 100 days in 1933. In his inaugural address, Roosevelt called for "action, and action now," noting that the Great Depression created conditions whereby he would "wage a war against the emergency, as great as the power that would be given to me if we were in fact invaded by a foreign foe."[6] When Roosevelt's bank reform bill was introduced shortly afterwards, a Democratic House member reportedly said, "Here's the bill. Let's pass it!"[7] And that's what happened without a word of the new law being read by most legislators.

Another example of a political party uniting to change the course of government happened after Ronald Reagan assumed the presidency in 1981. This time, it was the Republicans who rallied to effect a conservative change. The "Reagan revolution" cut taxes, raised the federal deficit, and substantially increased defense spending. In 2001, George W. Bush took a page from Reagan and won quick congressional approval of tax cuts and education reforms during a brief five-month period when Republicans controlled both houses of Congress and were united in support of the new president.[8]

The Roosevelt–Reagan–Bush effect was so powerful that would-be presidents wanted to emulate it. In 2008, Democratic presidential candidate Barack Obama lauded Reagan, telling reporters, "I think Ronald Reagan changed the trajectory of America in a way that, you know, Richard Nixon did not, and in a way that Bill Clinton did not," adding that it was "fair to say the Republicans were the party of ideas for a pretty long chunk of time there over the last 10 to 15 years, in the sense that they were challenging the conventional wisdom."[9] And when Obama became president, he beseeched the Democratic–controlled Congress to enact a healthcare reform bill—something that had been part of every Democratic Party platform since 1948. In fact, when it came to passing a $787 billion stimulus package, healthcare reform, and financial reform, Obama received almost no Republican support and had to rely on a unified Democratic congressional party to make these changes happen. Former Democratic congressman turned White House chief of staff Rahm Emanuel summarized the administration's thinking when he declared that "no crisis should go to waste." According to Emanuel, "Things that we had postponed for too long, that were long-term, are now immediate and must be dealt with. This crisis provides the opportunity for us to do things that you could not do before."[10] In little more than two years, Obama and the Democrats enacted their $787 billion stimulus bill, passed healthcare reform, and overhauled the financial regulatory system.

Franklin Roosevelt, Ronald Reagan, George W. Bush, and Barack Obama form a quartet of presidents who paid attention to their party. They are hardly alone in the pages of history. Back in 1912, Woodrow Wilson and his fellow Democrats promised to create a Federal Reserve Board to control the flow of the nation's money supply and a Federal Trade Commission that would rein in corporate interests. He promised to pass workmen's compensation for those injured on the job and ease the way for the abolition of child labor. Voters agreed with Wilson and the Democrats, giving Wilson a plurality of 42 percent and, more significantly, adding 73 more Democrats in the House and 6 Democrats in the Senate. Wilson made much of the Democratic victory in his inaugural address: "No one can mistake the purpose for which the Nation now seeks to use the Democratic Party. It seeks to use it to interpret a change in its own plans and point of view."[11] More than a decade later, a conservative Republican president, Herbert Hoover, also saw his party as an indispensable partner in governing: "We maintain party government not to promote intolerant partisanship but because opportunity must be given for the expression of the popular will, and organization provided for the execution of its mandates. It follows that Government both in the executive and legislative branches must carry out in good faith the platform upon which the party was entrusted with power."[12]

But as the twentieth century progressed and television allowed presidents to become personalities, the effect was to liberate presidents from their party obligations. Voters saw Dwight D. Eisenhower, John F. Kennedy, Richard M. Nixon, Jimmy Carter, Ronald Reagan, and Bill Clinton as television personalities that became part of their living rooms. As a result, all of these presidents felt free to ignore their party-in-government when it suited them. Nixon, for example, advocated a guaranteed annual income for the poor and national health insurance that were designed to mollify his Democratic opponents over the opposition of most Republicans.[13] Years later, Bill Clinton adopted a strategy of "triangulation"—setting himself above the partisan wrangling when Republicans assumed control of Congress in 1994, and sometimes siding with the Democrats; other times, the Republicans; and, at other moments, neither party. Both Nixon and Clinton were reelected in part because they distanced themselves from their respective political parties and won crucial support from like-minded independent voters. At the beginning of 2011, Barack Obama faced a similar quandary: Should he abandon the Democratic Party's base by seeking support from newly empowered congressional Republicans (as Clinton did in 1995–1996), or draw a proverbial line in the sand and do partisan battle as leader of the Democratic Party on Capitol Hill?

THE PARTY IN CONGRESS

Although presidents have attempted to use their party as a way of bringing the executive and legislative branches together, Congress has been historically incapable of achieving a similar result, as regional diversity and special interests have overwhelmed appeals for party loyalty. This has not stopped key legislators from trying to use parties as action-centered instruments of government. Helping them is the fact that parties are important organizing mechanisms. For example, the side of the aisle on which one sits in Congress is determined by party affiliation. Likewise, committee chairs are often reserved for the senior party member of a particular committee, and the ranking member is a senior member of the minority party. Ideological appeals also help bind Democrats and Republicans together. And both parties have established congressional campaign committees that have assumed a growing role in the recruitment and election of members of Congress.

From the outset, congressional parties were an important "extra-constitutional" device that were inserted into the Framers' handiwork. For example, the Federalists, led by Alexander Hamilton, were strong supporters of the Jay Treaty, whereas their Democratic-Republican rivals, led by Thomas Jefferson, were unified in their opposition. As their policy disagreements escalated, party voting became the norm. From the 3rd Congress (1793–1795) to the 7th Congress (1801–1803), Federalist Party unity scores increased from 83.3 percent to 89.9 percent. Likewise, the Democratic-Republicans saw their bloc voting rise from 73.5 percent to 79.6 percent. Looking at this period, political scientist John F. Hoadley writes that party development passed through four distinct stages: (1) factionalism, (2) polarization, (3) expansion, and (4) institutionalization. In the first stage, factions developed and were centered on a variety of disparate issues and charismatic personalities. But these divisions were rarely organized and lasted only a short while. In the second stage, the factions stabilized into permanent groups that opposed each other on a broad range of issues. During the expansion phase, the public was drawn into the partisan arguments. Finally, in the institutionalization phase, a permanent linkage was made among the party organizations, party-in-the-electorate, and the party-in-government.[14]

Formalized party structures have developed over the centuries in Congress, as well as in 49 state legislatures (Nebraska has a non-partisan unicameral legislature). Both parties meet every two years at the beginning of each congressional session to select their leaders. There are two institutionalized leadership positions, one for each branch of the legislature. Article I of the Constitution states that the House "shall choose their Speaker."[15] The Speaker presides over that chamber, rules on points of order, announces results of votes, refers legislation to committees, names lawmakers to serve on the committees, and maintains order and decorum. In addition, the Speaker sets the House's agenda, controls the Rules Committee, chairs his or her party's committee assignment panel, and can bestow or withhold various tangible and intangible rewards to members of both parties. Both parties nominate candidates for the Speakership, but the majority party's candidate always prevails. It is extremely rare that a member will cross over and support the nominee of the other party. Such a rare event happened in 2009 when Alabama Democrat Parker Griffith became a Republican after telling a local newspaper that Democratic House Speaker Nancy Pelosi was "too divisive," and that if she did not like his opposition he would "provide her with a gift certificate to a mental health center."[16] In 2010, Parker lost his bid for reelection, having been defeated by another Republican in a GOP primary.

There are other important party leaders in Congress. The majority leader is the second in command of the majority party and works closely with the Speaker. The minority leader serves as the head of his or her party in the House. Minority leaders are the "Speakers-in-waiting" should their party become a majority. During the 111th Congress, House minority leader John Boehner was the "Speaker-in-waiting." With the Republicans gaining a majority of seats in the House chamber in the 2010 midterm elections, Boehner succeeded House Speaker Nancy Pelosi. Meanwhile, Pelosi decided to remain in the Congress as the Democratic leader. Should the Democrats regain their majority in 2012 elections, Pelosi would undoubtedly become the Speaker once more.

Following the Speaker are the majority and minority whips. Each party uses a variety of whips—ranging from head whip to deputy, at-large, regional, and assistant whips. The whips gather intelligence, encourage attendance at important votes and party events, count votes, persuade colleagues to support party measures, and forge lines of communication between the rank-and-file and party leaders. The foremost job of a whip is to encourage party discipline. Two other important party positions are (1) chair of the policy committees and (2) head of the campaign committees. The former is responsible for developing a policy plan for the coming session, and the latter for fundraising and distributing party funds during elections.

Table 8.1 Party Leadership Positions in the U.S. House and Senate, 112th Congress

House	Senate
Speaker: John Boehner	Vice President: Joseph R. Biden
Majority Leader: Eric Cantor	President Pro Tempore: Daniel K. Inouye
Majority Whip: Kevin McCarthy	Majority Leader: Harry Reid
Minority Leader: Nancy Pelosi	Assistant Majority Leader: Richard Durbin
Minority Whip: Steny Hoyer	Minority Leader: Mitch McConnell
	Republican Whip: Jon Kyl

In the U.S. Senate, the Constitution stipulates that the vice president serve as the presiding officer and, in case of a tie, cast the deciding vote. Other than on ceremonial occasions and when votes are expected to be very close, the vice president hardly ever sits in a Senate session. In the vice president's absence, the Constitution stipulates that a "president pro tempore" preside. Recently, a custom has developed whereby this officer is a member of the majority party with the longest continuous service. Today, that person is Democratic senator Daniel K. Inouye, a Hawaii Democrat who was elected to the Senate in 1962. As in the House, both parties in the Senate separately choose their leaders: The majority leader is the head of the majority party in the Senate; the minority leader leads the loyal opposition. Both persons are elected biennially by secret ballot. The remaining leadership posts in the Senate are much the same as in the House. There are whip organizations and chairs of policy committees and campaign committees. Table 8.1 notes the leadership of both parties in the 112th Congress, which began in January 2011.

DIVIDED PARTIES IN CONGRESS, 1937–1994

For most of the twentieth century, it was not *interparty* divisions, but *intraparty* divisions that required members of Congress to seek allies in order to pass legislation. The Democratic Party was especially divided. From 1937 until 1994, Congress was controlled by the Dixiecrat coalition—an alliance of conservative Southern Democrats (called Dixiecrats) and old-guard Republicans who opposed extending Franklin Roosevelt's New Deal, especially when it came to civil rights legislation and passing healthcare reform. Virginia

Democrat Howard Smith was a potent symbol of the Dixiecrat coalition. As chairman of the powerful House Rules Committee, Smith vetoed proposed legislation presented by Democratic presidents and congressional leaders, and he even opposed the elections of John F. Kennedy in 1960 and Lyndon B. Johnson in 1964. With Smith and the Dixiecrat-Republicans in opposition, John F. Kennedy (who had served in both the House and Senate) lamented, "The fact is that the Congress looks more powerful sitting here than it did when I was there in Congress. But that is because when you are in Congress you are one of 100 in the Senate or one of 435 in the House. So the power is divided. But from here I look at Congress, particularly the bloc action, and it is a substantial power."[17]

As Kennedy's frustrations with an intractable Congress demonstrate, only when there are grave national crises (such as the world wars, the Great Depression, or the September 11 terrorist attacks), or when foreign policies require congressional approval (as was the case during the cold war), or when there are periods of political abnormality (such as Lyndon Johnson's 1964 landslide and Ronald Reagan's 1980 Republican sweep, or the economic calamity of 2008–2009) are party-oriented presidents momentarily able to overcome the congressional tendency to delay and not act.

THE EMERGENCE OF RESPONSIBLE PARTY GOVERNMENT, 1994 TO THE PRESENT

By the mid-twentieth century, the inability of both parties to produce a truly party-oriented government frustrated political scientists and led them to search for ways of achieving greater party accountability. Those who believed parties should have the decisive role in making public policy advocated a doctrine commonly referred to as "responsible party government." Simply put, responsible party government occurs when the party in power manages the government and enacts the program spelled out in its platform. For its part, the opposition party develops alternative policies and makes its case to the voters. The public is asked to judge whether the party in power has done a good job and which party has the better program for the future.

The doctrine of responsible party government was best expressed in a 1950 report commissioned by the American Political Science Association (APSA) entitled *Toward a More Responsible Two-Party System*.[18] This book was the capstone of a multiyear effort by an

APSA-sanctioned Committee on Political Parties consisting of the leading party scholars of that time. After four years of deliberations, *Toward a More Responsible Two-Party System* operated from the following premise: "Throughout this report political parties are treated as indispensable instruments of government."[19] Thus, it followed that if the parties were in trouble, so was the nation's system of government. This is exactly the conclusion the committee reached—noting the doubts that surrounded Democratic president Harry S. Truman's ability to lead following the death of Franklin D. Roosevelt, the division of power created by the 1946 elections when Republicans assumed control of both houses of Congress, and the inability of either branch to agree on much-needed civil rights legislation. By the time the report was published in 1950, the APSA committee concluded that both parties had disintegrated to the point at which they could no longer effectively propose solutions to the problems facing the country. The report warned that unless the party system was overhauled, three disastrous consequences would follow: (1) the delegation of "excessive responsibility to the president," who would have to generate support for new public initiatives through personal efforts without the benefit of party; (2) continued disintegration of both major parties caused by their relative ineffectiveness; and (3) a presidential-congressional logjam that "might set in motion more extreme tendencies to the political left and the political right."[20]

In the decades following its publication, *Toward a More Responsible Two-Party System* became required reading for party scholars. Most extolled the report for its analysis of the problems parties faced, and they saw the report's warning of a weaker party system fulfilled in a more powerful but party-less presidency. To mark its fiftieth anniversary, the APSA held a major symposium at its 2000 meeting, and a new book was published in 2002 commemorating the report.[21] But celebrations aside, the APSA committee's work actually stifled a lively debate about the role parties should play in government begun at the turn of the twentieth century. Back then, scholars viewed the responsible party doctrine with considerable skepticism. As one wrote, "This theory [of responsible party government] appeared alluring enough to be adopted by some writers of prominence, and expanded in certain cases, with brilliancy of literary style. It has, however, one defect: it is not borne out by the facts."[22]

Perhaps no better party scholar demonstrated the inexorable movement of political scientists toward accepting the doctrine of responsible party government during the twentieth century than Woodrow Wilson. A prominent political scientist who once served as APSA president, Wilson told the Virginia Bar Association in 1897, "I, for my part, when I vote at a critical election, should like to be able to vote for a definite line of policy with regard to the great questions of the day—not for platforms, which Heaven knows, mean little enough—but for men known and tried in public service; with records open to be scrutinized with reference to these very matters; and pledged to do this or that particular thing; to take a definite course of action. As it is, I vote for nobody I can depend upon to do anything—no, not even if I were to vote for myself."[23] A decade later, Wilson saw party-centered government more favorably: "There is a sense in which our parties may be said to have been our real body politic. Not the authority of Congress, not the leadership of the President, but the discipline and zest of parties has held us together, has made it possible for us to form and to carry out national programs."[24]

The Frustration of Responsible Party Government, 1950–1994

The doctrine of responsible party government got a powerful grip on the academic community, even as events made the idea of a strong party-in-government less of a possibility at the time. During the 40-year Democratic reign in the House of Representatives (1954–1994), responsible party government had little meaning. Instead of relying on their party to win, Democrats used the tools of incumbency to preserve their offices. Congressional staffs, for example, became a new-style permanent campaign staff—answering mail, acting as ombudsmen, and serving as the "eyes and ears" of the legislator in the district. Money also helped Democrats win, as PAC directors steered their dollars to incumbents with a demonstrated ability to win.

But once in Congress, Democrats generally were free to ignore their party. Southerners had long abandoned appeals to party loyalty—as exemplified by the emergence of the Dixiecrat coalition. By the 1970s, Democrats began stripping their congressional leaders of the few remaining powers they had left. Following the Watergate-dominated elections of 1974, a crop of newly elected Democrats was determined to substitute party leadership for more openness. In a surprising move, these so-called Watergate babies deposed three incumbent committee chairs—a repudiation of the once ironclad seniority rule. Moreover, they adopted a Subcommittee Bill of Rights that reduced the power of both the Speaker and the committee chairs. These changes allowed committee Democrats to pick their chairs;

fixed the jurisdictions of subcommittees so that their ability to control certain subjects would not be given to another committee; gave each subcommittee a budget that it controlled; created more staff positions; and guaranteed that members of the full committee would have a right to at least one "choice" subcommittee assignment. These reforms stripped recalcitrant conservative Southern Dixiecrats, many of whom had accumulated enough seniority to become committee chairs, of their jealously guarded powers to frustrate the Democratic majority. But in so doing, they fragmented power among members who served on an ever-larger number of committees and spent their days literally running from one meeting to another.

By 1994, party leadership in Congress was at a low ebb. A series of relatively weak Democratic speakers were held hostage by stubborn committee chairs who were quite willing to resist demands for party loyalty. Bill Clinton, who had high hopes that unified Democratic Party control of the presidency and Congress would result in significant legislative accomplishments, found his hopes dashed when his healthcare initiative went down in flames. Even Clinton's much-touted economic recovery program—the basis for his 1992 election and his promise to focus on the economy "like a laser beam"—barely won House approval and was passed by the Senate only after Vice President Al Gore cast the decisive tie-breaking vote. Democrats limped into the 1994 midterm contests, hoping that history would prevail yet again and incumbents—meaning Democrats—would be reelected. It was not to be.

The Revival of Responsible Party Government, 1994–Present

The Republican takeover of Congress following the 1994 midterm elections was more than a mere shift from one party to another. The incoming 73 Republican freshmen differed significantly from their predecessors in both style and ideological persuasion. Stylistically, many saw themselves as "citizen politicians"—dispatched by their constituents to Washington, D.C., for a brief period before coming home. To further fortify themselves from becoming too comfortable in Washington, D.C., many Republican newcomers chose to live in their congressional offices—sleeping on their couches by night and showering in the House gymnasium by day. This practice differentiated them from their predecessors, whose families lived year-round in the nation's capital. During the 1960s, for example, House Minority

Leader Gerald R. Ford had a home in Alexandria, Virginia, where he resided with his wife, Betty, and their children. Once, President Lyndon B. Johnson called from the White House during a Thanksgiving recess and thought he had reached Ford in Michigan when, in fact, Ford was just a few miles away.[25]

But it was in their politics that the Republican freshmen were truly different. Motivated by conservative principles, the 1994 class was especially responsive to pleas to keep the faith when it came to implementing their Contract with America. As previously noted, the contract consisted of 10 poll-tested items that included balancing the federal budget, tough anticrime measures, a line-item veto for the president, welfare reform, and tax cuts targeted at families. Of 33 House roll calls taken in 1995 on contract-related items, House GOP members were *unanimous* on 16. For the entire series of roll calls, the median number of Republican dissents was *one*.[26] On average, 97 percent of the Republican freshmen voted in lockstep with their party, and no one fell below 90 percent.[27]

The contract gave Speaker Newt Gingrich an opportunity to assume powers that none of his Democratic predecessors dared imagine. He twice passed over Carlos Morehead, the ranking Republican on the Judiciary and Commerce committees, in favor of Gingrich loyalists Henry Hyde and Thomas Bliley. As Judiciary Chairman Hyde candidly admitted, "I'm really a sub-chairman .... I am a transmission belt for the leadership."[28] But Gingrich's most famous promotion was that of Robert Livingston, who was fifth in seniority to head the Appropriations Committee. Just to make sure that everyone knew who controlled this all-important committee, Gingrich required each Republican member to sign a "letter of fidelity" that gave the Speaker the final say over how much of the federal budget would be cut. In addition, Gingrich abolished three committees that had been liberal Democratic bastions: District of Columbia, Merchant Marine and Fisheries, and Post Office and Civil Service. Others were renamed to fit the new GOP-led conservative agenda. The Education and Labor Committee became Economic and Educational Opportunities, Government Operations became Government Reform and Oversight, and Public Works and Transportation became Transportation and Infrastructure. As one Republican put it, "The old names implied a desire to perpetuate and expand the size and scope of government. The new names were needed to put our imprimatur on Congress and indicate the direction in which we're taking the institution."[29]

Gingrich also gave his freshmen firebrands unusual access to the inner circles of power. In a highly irregular move, the so-called exclusive committees of the House—Rules, Ways and Means, and Appropriations—got new freshmen members over the objections of their Republican chairs. As one grateful recipient observed, "Newt really enjoys seeing some of us work because he sees the same rabble-rouser that he was a few years ago. Without Newt, the class wouldn't be such a dynamic class. Newt Gingrich asks: 'What do the freshmen think?' And he's giving us more than anyone else would have."[30]

Such largesse paid off handsomely, as Gingrich was able to keep his fellow Republicans in line. Indeed, the Republican takeover of Congress culminated a rise in party-centered voting that began during the 1980s. Many were captivated by Ronald Reagan, who led a large, activist, conservative following. During the 1990s, the so-called Reaganites were succeeded by religious-minded conservatives who had strong antiabortion, antigay, and antigun-control views. Following George W. Bush's election, Republicans were ready to follow Bush's lead—even if they had philosophical disagreements with the president. For example, House majority leader Tom DeLay expressed regrets after he cast a vote for Bush's 2001 No Child Left Behind Education bill, saying, "I came here to eliminate the Department of Education." DeLay explained that his "yea" vote was cast only because he wanted to support a Republican president: "I'm ashamed to say it was just blatant politics."[31] The same pattern occurred during much of Bush's tenure. On the eve of the 2004 election, Republicans cast aside their doubts about Medicare and government spending and voted for a prescription drug program that would be added to the entitlement and would benefit seniors.

Democrats, too, became more ideologically liberal. The continued exit of Southern conservatives from the party's congressional ranks, the introduction of social and cultural issues (such as abortion and gay rights), and their near-unanimous opposition to the Iraq War during George W. Bush's second term transformed congressional Democrats into a far more homogeneous group. House Speaker Nancy Pelosi exemplified the transition. First elected in 1987, Pelosi compiled a liberal voting record, one that reflected the beliefs of the residents of her San Francisco district.[32] In 2000, Pelosi received a perfect 100 percent rating from the liberally oriented Americans for Democratic Action.[33] By 2008, the ADA gave House Democrats an overall rating of 89 percent, while House Republicans scored an overall 22 percent rating. In the Senate, Democrats had a 90 percent positive score from the ADA; Republicans, 20 percent.[34]

Clearly, ideological purists from both parties have altered the way Congress conducts its business. Those who once subscribed to the late

Democratic House Speaker Sam Rayburn's wisdom that the best way to "get along" in Congress is to "go along" suddenly found themselves in the minority. House minority leader Bob Michel, an old-school Republican who was often chummy with his Democratic colleagues, first spotted the change. Of the 47 GOP newcomers elected in 1992, Michel concluded that "7 are thoughtful moderates, and the other 40 are pretty darn hardliners, some of them really hardline."[35] The Republican class of 1994 was even more zealous. Arizona freshman John Shadegg said his colleagues were not "interested in coming here to be reasonable and to settle for what they can get. They don't want to go along to get along."[36]

The heightened sense of partisanship in the halls of Congress persisted during the first two years of Barack Obama's presidency. Obama had come to prominence promising to end the partisan politics that had gripped Washington, D.C. But almost as soon as he was sworn in as president, partisanship reasserted itself with a vengeance. During the healthcare debate in 2009, Republican senator Jim DeMint offered an insight into GOP thinking, saying that if Obama were defeated on this issue, "It will be his Waterloo. We will break him."[37] Republicans unanimously opposed the Obama healthcare bill in the Senate, and only one Republican voted for it in the House. Likewise, when it came to supporting Obama's economic stimulus, no Republicans in either the House or Senate supported it. According to a study conducted by the Brookings Institution, the 111th Congress "is the most polarized in history. In both the House and Senate, the most conservative Democrat is more liberal than is the most liberal Republican."[38] Prospects are for an even more polarized 112th Congress, as only 23 of 54 conservative, so-called Blue Dog Democrats were reelected in 2010.[39]

Of course, there remains some diversity within the parties, particularly the Democrats, who tend to win in more ideologically and demographically diverse congressional districts. Thus, the House Democratic ranks contain established liberals like Barney Frank (Massachusetts) with a 90.7 liberal rating, and more conservative Democrats like Heath Shuler (North Carolina) whose composite liberal rating is 51.3.[40] In 2009, there were 39 moderate-to-conservative Democrats who bucked President Obama and House Speaker Nancy Pelosi and voted "no" on healthcare. These included Southerners (e.g., Shuler), Westerners (e.g., Stephanie Herseth-Sandlin, D-SD), and Midwesterners (e.g., Ike Skelton, D-MO).[41] A similar phenomenon occurs in the Senate, as there is a range of views within the Democratic caucus. Washington State's Patty Murray has a liberal score of 92.7, whereas Nebraska's Ben Nelson has a liberal rating of 49.8.[42] Thus, it was a considerable feat when Senate majority leader Harry Reid kept all 60 Senate Democrats in line to vote for healthcare reform on Christmas Eve 2009.

Republicans, too, have a modicum of internal diversity. Maine senators Susan Collins and Olympia Snowe have liberal scores of 49 and 50.8, respectively.[43] They sometimes find it hard to coexist with hardline conservatives such as Jim DeMint (R–SC) or Jon Kyl (R–AZ) whose liberal scores are 7.7 and 6.8, respectively.[44] Arlen Specter, a Republican who was elected to the Senate in 1980, surprised many by leaving the GOP and caucusing with the Democrats in 2009. Specter had a liberal rating of 53 in 2008, a score that was in line with Pennsylvania's electorate, who supported Democratic presidential candidates Al Gore, John Kerry, and Barack Obama, but left Specter a marked man in the Republican caucus.[45] Specter was defeated for reelection in 2010, when Pennsylvania congressman Joe Sestak beat him in the Democratic primary. (Sestak, in turn, was defeated by Republican Pat Toomey in a close contest to succeed Specter in the Senate.)

As the modicum of diversity within the Democratic and Republican ranks in Congress continues to diminish, the partisan warfare continues apace on Capitol Hill. Some find the political gamesmanship tiring. In 2010, Indiana Democrat Evan Bayh announced his retirement, arguing that the ongoing ideological polarization in the U.S. Senate had made that body dysfunctional: "For some time, I have had a growing conviction that Congress is not operating as it should." He continued, "There is too much partisanship and not enough progress—too much narrow ideology and not enough practical problem solving. Even at a time of enormous challenge, the people's business is not being done."[46]

THE RISE OF THE PUBLIC SPEAKERSHIP

One consequence of the visible partisan warfare in Washington, D.C., has been a more visible House Speakership. During the long reign of Democratic Party rule from 1954 to 1994, House Speakers ceded much of their power to committee chairs—many of them conservative Southern Democrats—who were the undisputed "kings of the hill." This suited most Speakers, as many of them were old-style operatives who worked behind closed doors. Sam Rayburn, one of the most powerful of the Democratic Speakers, had his famous "Board

of Education" where favored members would gather to discuss pending business and make deals over bourbon and branch water. Once,
when asked to appear on a Sunday talk show, Rayburn responded:

> I do appreciate your wanting me to be on *Meet the Press,* but I
> never go on programs such as yours .... The trouble about my
> going on one program is then I would have no excuse to say to
> the others that I could not go on their program. It is a chore that
> I have never relished and one that I doubt would be any good ....
> I would have to tell you what I tell all the others, and that is that
> I do not go on these programs.[47]

John McCormack and Carl Albert were far less powerful Speakers, yet, like Rayburn, they were ineffectual party spokespersons.
In 1969, McCormack was mentioned on the three network evening
television newscasts (CBS, NBC, and ABC) a mere 17 times.[48] Media
inquiries were so few that McCormack did not even bother hiring
a press secretary. Carl Albert got a press secretary, but still refrained
from assuming a public role. Thomas P. "Tip" O'Neill was much
more visible, but his heightened recognition was due to a unique
political situation: Republican control of the presidency and U.S.
Senate in 1980 had left O'Neill as the only viable Democratic Party
spokesperson.[49] Thus, in 1984, O'Neill was cited 168 times on the big
three network evening news programs.[50] His successor, Jim Wright,
sought O'Neill's visibility, but became much better known thanks
to Newt Gingrich's charge that Wright had violated congressional
ethics rules. Wright resigned and was succeeded by Democrat Tom
Foley. Although Foley appeared on the various Sunday talk shows,
he was eclipsed by other Democratic Party spokespersons—most
notably President Clinton.

All that changed with Newt Gingrich. In 1995, for the first time
in history, the House Speaker delivered a nationally televised address
to the American people. The following June, Gingrich shared a stage
with President Clinton in a small New Hampshire town to debate the
issues. Television, which had transformed the presidency, was working its magic on Congress. Gingrich became the first public Speaker
in memory, as he freely acknowledged, "Each generation produces
its own style of being effective. The most accurate statement of how
I see the Speakership [is] somebody who could somehow combine
grassroots organizations, mass media, and legislative detail into one
synergistic pattern."[51] Gingrich redesigned the Speaker's office to ac-
commodate his desire to "go public" by creating four media-oriented

staff positions: press secretary, deputy press secretary, press assistant, and communications coordinator. Unlike his predecessors, Gingrich had little appetite for the machinations of the House floor—preferring to leave those duties to his number-two man, then-majority leader Dick Armey.

The effects of the new public Speakership were immediate. During his first three months in power, Gingrich was mentioned in 114 stories that ran on the three network nightly news programs. NBC News congressional correspondent Lisa Myers gave Gingrich a thumbs-up review: "Newt is the star. Newt's setting the agenda." Refusing to seek the presidency in 1996, Gingrich declared, "I hardly need to run for president to get my message out."[52] (Having been out of power since 1998, Gingrich decided to seek the 2012 Republican presidential nomination. Without the Speakership, becoming a presidential candidate is a means for Gingrich to continue to have an impact on public policy debates.)

An old saying has it that "imitation is the sincerest form of flattery." Democrats paid attention to Gingrich's skilled use of the media during the early months of his Speakership and emulated his tactics, if not his style. Then-House minority whip David Bonior (D–MI)—a Gingrich nemesis—described his job this way: "My new role will not only be counting the votes by which we are going to lose. My role will be to emphasize the message which we are trying to convey to the American people."[53] Toward that end, Democrats established a communications team that coordinated appearances on the House floor by party members and ensured that each Democrat "stayed on message." Although Nancy Pelosi did few interviews as Speaker (much in the tradition of her Democratic predecessors), she excelled in wielding power behind the scenes—preferring to leave the messaging to others. Today, both congressional parties have message groups and communication strategy teams. During the 111th Congress, House Republican minority leader John Boehner justified the need for having large communications staffs, saying, "It's not what you're doing, but the perceptions that are so important."[54]

The Internet has become a particularly important tool for party leaders in Congress to get their message out. John Boehner has his own homepage, as does Nancy Pelosi. Each seeks to tell their side of the party story to a Web-connected audience. Increasingly, the Internet has become a forum for important Congress-related stories. There are numerous websites devoted to covering Capitol Hill, including Politico, Roll Call, The Hill, and National Journal. These same websites are also published in newspaper form. But, increasingly,

((((   ))))

PARTIES IN A NETWORKED AGE

The Republicans and the Internet in 2012

In response to the drubbing they took in 2008, Republicans are attempting to redefine themselves in relation to digital technology much the way the Democrats did in 2003. The fact that Democrats were up against the wall in the 2004 election cycle forced them to innovate and reach out beyond the usual avenues of communication. In the 2010 midterm elections, Republicans began to do the same. Heading into 2012, Republicans planned to maintain their digital momentum in opposing the reelection efforts of a media-savvy president. They hoped to be aided in this effort by the rise of a new conservative populism evident with the emergence of the Tea Party movement, and by conservative bloggers and tweeters.

Source: Cohen, Diana Tracy. Forthcoming. *Rightroots: Conservative Media and the New Republican Populism.* Boulder, CO: Paradigm Publishers.

Internet-only websites such as Talking Points Memo have reporters who cover politics, including Congress, while community sites like Daily Kos provide a steady stream of information from their readers.

CONGRESS AND THE "LITTLE ARTS OF POPULARITY"

The demise of the Dixiecrat-Republican coalition in Congress and its replacement with a highly charged partisanship has met with a general public revulsion. Sensing the public's disgust with the intense congressional partisanship, David Price, a respected North Carolina Democratic congressman, calls for a "subdued partisanship."[55] But the passions that rule today's congressional parties make "subdued partisanship" an almost impossible goal. It is not only the issues separating the two congressional parties that make bipartisanship more difficult to achieve, it is also the demeanor of both parties. Former Democratic House minority leader Dick Gephardt noted that "Democrats and Republicans don't even make eye contact when they pass one another in the halls of Congress, unless it's to exchange furious glares."[56] Similar complaints are heard on the Republican side. At a retreat of House Republicans in January 2010, President Obama made a surprise appearance (inviting the television cameras to accompany him), and heard complaints about how they were being treated by their Democratic colleagues. One came from Peter Roskam, a Republican congressman who once served with Obama in the Illinois state legislature. Their dialogue is instructive as to the tone and the limitations it places on bipartisan compromise in today's Congress:

> Roskam: [Y]ou've gotten this subtext of House Republicans that sincerely want to come and be a part of this national conversation toward solutions, but they've really been stiff-armed by Speaker Pelosi. Now, I know you're not in charge of that chamber, but there really is this dynamic of, frankly, being shut out. When John Boehner [House minority leader] and Eric Cantor [Republican whip] presented last February to you some substantive job creation, our stimulus alternative, the attack machine began to marginalize Eric—and we can all look at the articles—as "Mr. No," and there was this pretty dark story, ultimately, that wasn't productive and wasn't within this sort of framework that you're articulating today.
>
> Obama: [W]e've got to be careful about what we say about each other sometimes, because it boxes us in in ways that makes it difficult for us to work together, because our constituents start believing us. They don't know sometimes this is just politics what you guys—or folks on my side do sometimes.
>
> So just a tone of civility instead of slash and burn would be helpful. The problem we have sometimes is a media that responds only to slash-and-burn-style politics. You don't get a lot of credit if I say, "You know, I think [House Republican congressman] Paul Ryan is a pretty sincere guy and has a beautiful family." Nobody is going to run that in the newspapers.[57]

Still, rather than engaging in the hard task of governing, many congressional partisans find it more enticing to be sought-after guests on cable television programs such as MSNBC's *Hardball*, *The Last Word with Lawrence O'Donnell*, and *The Rachel Maddow Show*, Fox's *The O'Reilly Factor* and *Hannity*, and Comedy Central's *The Daily Show with Jon Stewart* and Stephen Colbert's *The Colbert Report*. These cable TV programs often promote entertainment values (i.e., the fight), rather than political enlightenment. This point was highlighted during the 2010 midterm campaign when the largest rally to assemble on the grounds of the Capitol was Comedy Central's "Rally to Restore

Sanity/Fear" featuring Jon Stewart and Stephen Colbert. While the gathering's central point was to highlight the public's disillusionment with partisan politics, it also had a strong entertainment quotient.

Writing in *The Federalist Papers,* Alexander Hamilton declared that the best legislators were those who vote their consciences and ignore pleas to do otherwise. Hamilton derided "the little arts of popularity"[58]—a dig at those who paid too much attention to the public opinion polls of their day—preferring strong congressional leaders who could muster support for unpopular positions when necessary. (Hamilton himself was instrumental in having the House support Jefferson's 1800 election as president over rival Aaron Burr.) On the other hand, Thomas Jefferson was much more sensitive to the need of lawmakers to pay attention to the folks back home—undoubtedly one reason why he was elected president and Hamilton was not. Given his predilection for viewing the country as a diverse collection of communities, Jefferson believed that legislators should act as delegates. In 1825, he wrote that the "salvation of the republic" rested on the regeneration and spread of devices like the New England town meeting.[59]

Hamilton's warning that legislators pay too much attention to "the little arts of popularity" still rings true. Because public opinion polls too often guide legislative behavior, and voters are increasingly polarized, the power of party leaders has grown. Cable television news serves as a means of mobilizing and polarizing public opinion—a phenomenon that has spilled over into the Congress where partisan leaders have more clout within their own parties. At the same time, these leaders have lost much of their ability to woo lawmakers from the other side over to their viewpoints on any given issue. Elected officials can sell their party's positions to their bases, yet have great difficulty enacting legislation, because they must keep all of their members together (a challenge) and woo members from the other party to their cause (an even greater challenge). Even some political scientists are rethinking the responsible party doctrine. The late Nelson Polsby was one: "The trouble began when we political scientists finally got our wish—'responsible' political parties instead of broad, nonideological coalitions. The idea was, of course, completely nuts from the start."[60] But, nuts or not, the prospects for more unified (hence responsible) parties remain bright. Hamiltonian nationalism has bred its own form of national politics on whose stage congressional party leaders assume a dominant role.

This rise of Hamiltonian nationalism and national congressional leaders who constantly bicker with one another has produced a backlash. At the aforementioned Rally to Restore Sanity/Fear, led by Comedy Central stars Jon Stewart and Stephen Colbert, Stewart ended the gathering on a somber note calling for a greater degree of bipartisanship:

> We hear every damn day about how fragile our country is—on the brink of catastrophe—torn by polarizing hate and how it's a shame that we can't work together to get things done, but the truth is we do. We work together to get things done every damn day!
>
> The only place we don't is here or on cable TV. But Americans don't live here or on cable TV. Where we live our values and principles form the foundation that sustains us while we get things done, not the barriers that prevent us from getting things done. Most Americans don't live their lives solely as Democrats, Republicans, liberals or conservatives. Americans live their lives more as people that are just a little bit late for something they have to do—often something that they do not want to do—but they do it. Impossible things every day that are only made possible by the little reasonable compromises that we all make.
>
> Look on the screen—this is where we are, this is who we are [points to a Jumbotron screen which shows traffic merging into a tunnel]. These cars—that's a schoolteacher who probably thinks his taxes are too high. He's going to work. There's another car—a woman with two small kids who can't really think about anything else right now. There's another car swinging I don't even know if you can see it—the lady's in the NRA. She loves Oprah. There's another car—an investment banker, gay, also likes Oprah. Another car's a Latino carpenter. Another car's a fundamentalist vacuum salesman. Atheist obstetrician. Mormon Jay-Z fan. But this is us. Every one of the cars that you see is filled with individuals of strong belief and principles they hold dear—often principles and beliefs in direct opposition to their fellow travelers.
>
> And yet these millions of cars must somehow find a way to squeeze one by one into a mile-long, 30-foot-wide tunnel carved underneath a mighty river. Carved, by the way, by people who I'm sure had their differences. And they do it. Concession by concession. You go, then I'll go. You go, then I'll go. You go, then I'll go. Oh my God, is that an NRA sticker on your car? Is that an Obama sticker on your car? Well, that's okay—you go and then I'll go.

And sure, at some point there will be a selfish jerk who zips up the shoulder and cuts in at the last minute, but that individual is rare and he is scorned and not hired as an analyst.

Because we know instinctively as a people that if we are to get through the darkness and back into the light we have to work together and the truth is, there will always be darkness. And sometimes the light at the end of the tunnel isn't the promised land.

Sometimes it's just New Jersey. But we do it anyway, together.[61]

Jon Stewart's plea for a return to political civility is likely to fall on deaf ears. The outcome of the 2010 midterm elections has created a shrinking political center within the halls of Congress. As the parties become even more polarized and nationalized, some believe that the prospects for a third party are enhanced. That prospect will be explored in the next chapter.

9

Third Parties in a
Networked Age

Washington, D.C., is not a great place to exhibit independence from the major political parties, making it a lonely place for Vermont U.S. senator James M. Jeffords in May 2001. A lifelong Republican, Jeffords—who had become distressed with the rightward tilt of his party—bolted the GOP and became an independent. Since the Senate is organized around Republicans and Democrats, the newly independent Jeffords could not simply stand alone, so he chose to caucus with Senate Democrats, who awarded Jeffords the chairmanship of the influential Environment and Public Works Committee. Jeffords's newfound independence had profound implications for the two parties, as his switch to the Democratic caucus gave Democrats control of the chamber. Republicans were furious. Most Republicans averted their eyes from Vermont's junior senator, refusing even to say hello or extend a handshake. The "Singing Senators" barbershop quartet that Jeffords had formed with other Republicans quickly disbanded. Even Jeffords's wife and children were distressed that he was abandoning his family's multigenerational loyalty to the Republican Party.

Six years later Jeffords left the Senate altogether, only to be replaced by another independent, Bernard Sanders, who had served as

Vermont's lone congressman since 1990. He also caucused with the Democrats, but in fact was not a Democrat at all. Sanders ran for his Senate seat as a "democratic socialist," not as a Democrat, explaining, "The reason why I am a democratic socialist is that I have a real problem with a society, the society in which we live today, in which the richest 1 percent of the population owns more wealth than the bottom 90 percent."[1]

When Sanders entered the Senate in 2007, he was joined by another independent, Joseph I. Lieberman of Connecticut. Lieberman, who had been the Democratic Party's vice-presidential nominee in 2000, was booted from his party in 2006 by Democratic primary voters angry with his vocal support for the Iraq War. In the wake of his primary defeat, Lieberman gathered enough signatures to win an independent line on the state ballot, and won his seat in the general election (thanks to strong support from independents and Republicans). Lieberman continued to caucus with Democrats, but he showed little loyalty to his former party. In 2008, Lieberman heartily campaigned for the Republican ticket of John McCain and Sarah Palin, only to be welcomed back to the Democratic caucus at the urging of president-elect Barack Obama. Even so, many Democrats were furious with Lieberman for his partisan transgressions and, like Republicans had done with Jeffords, avoided any contact with him.

Washington, D.C., is simply not a hospitable environment for independents or members of third parties, and not just because deviating from the norms of party loyalty can lead to social ostracism. Institutionally, everything is organized around the major parties. The caucus (or conference, as it is called by Republicans) is a gathering of every elected Democrat or Republican within their respective chamber. These organizations select the leaders of Congress—including the Speaker of the House, the majority and minority leaders, and whips. They also debate legislative policies, map out strategies on pending bills, provide valuable information to their members, and approve committee assignments. Without the aid of caucus leaders, new members can expect to be placed on undesirable committees that are of little importance back home. Noncaucus members accumulate no committee seniority—thereby dashing any hopes of one day becoming a committee or subcommittee chair.

Such partisan structures derived naturally from the stranglehold the major parties have long had over our political institutions and reflect the dominant role of the major parties in American political life. Nonetheless, third parties do form—some even endure—and at times third parties have had an important influence on our politics. It seems paradoxical that a political system so thoroughly dominated by two major parties would spawn minor parties. Yet, minor parties have been a consistent feature in the American political landscape. In this chapter, we'll explore why.

Third party or minor party (the terms can be used interchangeably) refers to entities that have formal organizational structures and procedures. Like major parties, minor parties write platforms, nominate candidates for office, and have formal party positions (e.g., a state party chair). They persist for long periods of time—far longer than one election. Splinter candidacies differ from minor parties in that they are "one-hit wonders" that happen when candidates with a following who are displeased with the major parties, or who are unable to win a nomination from one of them, decide to go it alone. Notable splinter presidential candidates have included J. Strom Thurmond in 1948, who deplored Harry S Truman's embrace of a pro–civil rights Democratic platform; George C. Wallace in 1968, who rejected Lyndon B. Johnson's support for civil rights; and John B. Anderson in 1980, who disagreed with the conservative policies of the Republican nominee Ronald Reagan. Each was either a prominent Democrat (Thurmond, Wallace) or a Republican (Anderson) prior to his independent bid for the White House.

THE THIRD-PARTY PARADOX

We have seen how the Democratic-Republican duopoly is an enduring feature of American political life. Minor parties, in contrast, have struggled for recognition and votes, yet they compete all the same. In the 2008 election, independent candidate Ralph Nader appeared on 45 state ballots; Constitution Party candidate Chuck Baldwin on 35; Green Party candidate Cynthia McKinney and Libertarian candidate Bob Barr on 30 apiece.[2] None of these candidates came even remotely close to being competitive. As political scientist Clinton Rossiter remarked some years ago, "The most momentous fact about the pattern of American politics is that we live under a persistent, obdurate, one might almost say tyrannical, two-party system. We have the Republicans and we have the Democrats, and we have almost no one else ... in the struggle for power."[3]

At the state and local levels, third-party competition makes some sense, as third-party candidates have had some success in statewide races. During the last 20 years, independents have won the governorships of Maine, Connecticut, Minnesota, and Rhode Island. In 1990, Republican Lowell Weicker left his party to form "A Connecticut Party" and was elected governor of that state, serving for one term. Four years later, independent Angus King, a former Democrat, was elected Maine's governor and served for two terms. In 1998, the Reform Party scored a stunning victory when former professional wrestler Jesse Ventura won the Minnesota governorship. In 2010, independent candidate Lincoln Chafee beat the Republican and Democratic candidates (who placed second and third, respectively) to win the governorship of Rhode Island.

At the national level, the story is different. When third-party candidates exert influence at the national level, it is usually in a spoiler role made available to them through the temporary fracturing of Republican or Democratic Party coalitions. In 1992, billionaire businessman Ross Perot ran for president as an independent. In the general election, Perot captured 19 percent of the vote—the largest percentage won by a third person since former Republican president Theodore Roosevelt ran as a third-party candidate in 1912. Four years later, Perot made a second foray into presidential politics as the candidate of the Reform Party. Although winning just 8 percent of the vote—less than half of what he received in 1992—Perot garnered the largest back-to-back votes ever given to a third-party candidate in the twentieth century. In 2000, Green Party presidential candidate Ralph Nader castigated Bill Clinton for not seriously pursuing campaign finance reform and becoming too closely associated with corporate interests. Nader won backing from progressives who were disenchanted with what they saw as the conservative direction the Democratic Party had taken under Clinton. Thanks to their support, Nader won 2.7 percent of the popular vote—enough to tip the closest presidential election in modern times to George W. Bush. Despite such notable showings, third parties confront many difficulties—including institutional barriers, the tides of history, and the constraints imposed by the U.S. political culture. In this chapter, we pose several questions:

- ♦ Why have third parties generally failed at the polls?
- ♦ Which parties have captured the public's attention, and why were they relatively successful?
- ♦ Has Internet politics altered the standing of third parties?
- ♦ How does our system's adherence to a two-party model square with the Jeffersonian and Hamiltonian views of democracy?

INSTITUTIONAL AND CULTURAL BARRIERS TO THIRD PARTIES

A number of institutional and cultural factors make it difficult for third parties to compete with Republicans and Democrats. In some instances, these barriers are intentional, placed there by the major parties for the express purpose of maintaining their dominance. In other cases, the barriers are rooted in American political culture and development. Institutional barriers include single-member electoral districts, the Electoral College, the executive-centered nature of American governance, ballot access restrictions, direct primaries, and campaign finance laws. Cultural barriers include an American tendency toward finding compromise and a decidedly centrist approach to politics, which has reinforced the dominance of two large political parties capable of finding supporters in the middle of the political spectrum.

Institutional Barriers to Third Parties

In some democracies—including Austria, Germany, Japan, and Israel—a voting system known as proportional representation is used to elect legislative candidates who, in turn, choose the leader of the government. This system has two important components that influence party formation. First, more than one elected official is sent to the national or provincial assembly from each legislative district. Second, the number of representatives elected is directly proportional to the votes that a party receives on election day. If, for example, the Socialist Party of Austria receives 20 percent of the ballots and a district has five members, then the Socialists can expect to send one member to parliament from that district. The key element that fosters minor party activity is that there are benefits even when the party does not win a plurality of votes. Extremist or rigidly ideological parties are encouraged to participate, because the multimember proportional representation system all but guarantees that they will win a few seats. This is in sharp contrast to the United States, which relies on a winner-take-all single-member district system for choosing most of its officeholders. No matter how hard a party might work, there is no payoff unless a candidate receives a plurality of votes on election day. Only one person is sent to the legislature.

To better illustrate the contrast between the multimember proportional representation system and the winner-take-all single-member district method, imagine a situation in which four parties are competing for a single seat. Let's say that Party A is at the far left of the ideological spectrum (the most liberal); Party B, left-of-center; Party C, right-of-center; and Party D, at the far right (the most conservative). In this hypothetical election, Party A wins 20 percent of the votes; Party B, 30 percent; Party C, 27 percent; and Party D, 23 percent. Under the proportional system, each party has roughly the same number of legislators in the national assembly, with a small edge going to Party B. Under the winner-take-all single-member district system, only Party B would send legislators to the capitol. The British, who use the winner-take-all method, liken such electoral outcomes to horse races and have characterized their system as being "first past the post."

In a winner-take-all single-member district system, there are strong incentives for political parties located near each other on the ideological spectrum to merge. Using the previous example, operatives from Party C might say to Party D, "You know, we don't agree on everything, but we think alike. If we joined forces, we could surely overtake Party B. After all, they netted only 30 percent of the vote in the last election, whereas together we grabbed 50 percent." Under these rules, Party C's operatives know that it does not matter whether there are 4, 14, or 40 parties vying for support. When the laws dictate a winner-take-all single-member district system, there is no payoff for coming in second.

Another institutional barrier limiting minor party success in the United States is the Electoral College. Recall that the Electoral College was designed by the Framers of the Constitution to nominate and elect a nonpartisan president (see Chapter 4). Two aspects of the Electoral College hinder minor party success. First, each state is granted a number of electors equal to its total federal representatives in Congress (both House and Senate members combined). Although the Constitution is silent on how each state should apportion these electors, most employ a winner-take-all scheme whereby the candidate who receives a plurality of votes receives all of that state's electors.[4] Second, under the Electoral College rules, the winning presidential candidate must receive an absolute majority of the electoral votes cast—currently 270 out of 538. (In 2008, Barack Obama received 365 electoral votes to John McCain's 173.) If no candidate wins an electoral majority, the House of Representatives chooses the president by having each state's delegation cast one vote. This happened only once in the disputed presidential election of 1824, when the House chose John Quincy Adams (see Chapter 2). Today, it is hard to imagine that a body composed entirely of Democrats and Republicans would select a third-party candidate—especially if that person did not garner more than 50 percent of the popular vote.

The way the Electoral College punishes third-party candidates is illustrative of the problems confronting alternatives to the major parties in a single-member district system. In 1912, Theodore Roosevelt was unable to wrest the GOP nomination from William Howard Taft, so he left the GOP to form the Progressive (Bull Moose) Party. The former president finished second with 27 percent of the popular vote. But in the Electoral College, Roosevelt captured just 17 percent of the electoral votes cast. Ross Perot met a similar fate in 1992. His 19 percent of the popular vote was the third largest in U.S. history—behind two former presidents, Theodore Roosevelt and Millard Fillmore—but because his supporters were spread uniformly across the country and not concentrated in particular states, Perot was unable to garner a single electoral vote.[5]

Besides the Electoral College, another reason for the persistence of the two-party system is that the U.S. polity is executive centered. Voters expect their executives—be they mayors, governors, or presidents—to exercise vast powers. When a great deal of power is given to one person, and citizens accept this arrangement as legitimate, there are strong incentives for elites to form broad-based parties capable of winning an executive position. For their part, voters do not want to "waste their vote" on a third-party candidate who is unlikely to win because there is so much at stake. The "I don't want to waste my vote" phenomenon was very much in evidence as Election Day approached in 2000. As he was boarding a plane for another campaign rally, third-party candidate Ralph Nader encountered a supporter who told him, "You're trying to improve the country, and they call you a spoiler."[6] Given the prevalence of such attitudes, and the willingness of Democratic and Republican leaders to exploit them, the two-party system has flourished.

Regulations to limit ballot access further restrict minor party development. Getting a new party on the ballot and keeping it there poses extraordinarily difficult legal challenges. The major parties do not have this problem, as they have automatic ballot access by virtue of their prior success. For example, some states stipulate that a party whose gubernatorial candidate wins 10 percent of the vote is automatically listed on the next election ballot. Because Democrats and Republicans almost always garner that many votes, they have virtually automatic ballot access.

Another strong institutional force limiting minor party success is the direct primary. In most other political systems where nominations are controlled by party elites, intraparty dissidents often leave to form their own parties. In the United States, the direct primary system has the effect of channeling dissent into the two major parties.[7] Frustrated voters can support a maverick candidate in a primary—or become candidates themselves.

The presidential campaign finance system poses another institutional barrier to minor party success. The Federal Election Campaign Act (FECA) stipulates that a presidential candidate is eligible for public funds, provided that the party's nominee receives a given percentage of votes in the previous election. For "major parties," a 25 percent threshold is required. If this goal is met, then the nominee is entitled to full funding ($84.1 million in 2008).[8] For minor party candidates, the threshold is only 5 percent, but the amount they receive from the federal government is far less than what their Democratic or Republican counterparts get. Ross Perot, who won 19 percent of the vote in 1992, was given $29 million in public funds in 1996—less than half of what Bill Clinton and Bob Dole received. Ralph Nader, who won 2.7 percent of the popular vote as the 2000 Green Party candidate, was not eligible for federal funds in 2004. This is a prime example of how those who write the rules (Democrats and Republicans) will not want to change them to benefit someone else.

Even though money is a chief obstacle confronting minor party candidates, it is not the only one. In 1996, the Commission on Presidential Debates (a private organization) ruled that Ross Perot was not a serious contender, and banned him from the televised debates featuring major party nominees Bill Clinton and Bob Dole. Perot argued that he could not win unless he was allowed to debate the other candidates. But the commission, which was composed of Democrats and Republicans, lent an unsympathetic ear to Perot's complaint. Much the same thing happened in 2000, when the Commission on Presidential Debates ruled Green Party candidate Ralph Nader ineligible. The commission even denied Nader a seat in the audience for the first George W. Bush–Al Gore face-off, causing Nader to loudly complain about unfair treatment. Overall, these legal and structural mechanisms stack the deck against minor parties.

Cultural Barriers to Third Parties

Institutional constraints like single-member districts, the Electoral College, direct primary laws, and ballot access restrictions perpetuate the existence of the two-party model in the United States. Cultural barriers present an additional barrier to third-party development. A nation's political culture encompasses the fundamental values and beliefs that influence society within which political behavior and government policies are bound. It is the umbrella under which political activities take place and where public questions are resolved. Several core values of American political culture help maintain a two-party system, including adherence to peaceful resolutions of conflicts, acceptance of compromise and incremental change, and a strong endorsement of the nation's governing framework.

Americans peacefully accepted the constitutional arrangements that the Framers instituted in 1787, and, in 1801, peacefully accepted the transfer of power from the Federalists to the Democratic-Republicans—a transfer of power that remains a rarity in today's world. From these origins, Americans came to expect that power would be peacefully passed between rival parties following legitimately held elections, which has had a moderating influence on public opinion that serves as a point of pride for many Americans. It is one reason why Americans extol their governing system, built around two-party competition, as the best ever devised.

For example, during the depths of the Great Depression, pollsters asked, "Which one of the following most nearly represents your opinion of the American form of government? (a) Our form of government based on the Constitution is as near perfect as it can be and no important changes should be made in it; (b) the Constitution has served its purpose well, but it has not kept up with the times and should be thoroughly revised to make it fit present day needs; or (c) the systems of private capitalism and democracy are breaking down and we might as well accept the fact that sooner or later we will have to have a new form of government." Sixty-four percent said our political system is "as near perfect as it can be"—including 58 percent who were classified as being "poor."[9]

American attitudes are also decidedly centrist. Louis Hartz, a political theorist best known for his commentary on the uniqueness of the U.S. political culture, maintains that there is a national consensus centered on individual freedoms. "It is a remarkable force," Hartz writes, "this fixed, dogmatic liberalism of a liberal way of life. It is the secret root from which have sprung many of the most puzzling aspects of American cultural phenomena."[10] Englishman G. K. Chesterton wrote in 1920 that the United States was founded on a "creed." He elaborated, "That creed is set forth with dogmatic and even theological lucidity in the Declaration of Independence; perhaps the only piece of practical politics that is also theoretical politics and also great literature."[11] This creed allows little tolerance for extremes.

Lewis Cass, the 1848 Democratic nominee for president, once told a Tammany Hall audience that he was "opposed to all the isms of the day ... to communism and socialism, and Mormonism; to polygamy and concubinage, and to all the humbugs that are now rising among us."[12] Abraham Lincoln warned that if the Declaration of Independence were amended to read that "all men are created equal, except Negroes, and foreigners, and Catholics," then "I should prefer emigrating to some country where they make no pretense of loving liberty—to Russia, for instance, where despotism can be taken pure, and without the base alloy of hypocrisy."[13] Karl Marx acknowledged communism's failure in the United States, blaming it on "the tenacity of the Yankees," citing their "theoretical backwardness" and their "Anglo-Saxon contempt for all theory."[14]

Additionally, historical constraints have reinforced the American cultural predisposition toward two-party dominance. Consider the words of political scientist V. O. Key on the connections between the formative years for political parties and the contemporary party system: "Human institutions have an impressive capacity to perpetuate themselves or at least to preserve their form. The circumstances that happened to mold the American party system into a dual form at its inception must bear a degree of responsibility for its present existence."[15]

As noted in Chapters 1 and 2, the narrowness of U.S. political arguments has been attributed to its two most important party founders, Alexander Hamilton and Thomas Jefferson. The struggle between Hamiltonian nationalism and Jeffersonian localism that has been waged continuously throughout American history creates a sense of déjà vu—issues change, but not the essential nature of the conflict about the proper place for the federal government. Journalist Walter Lippmann put it this way: "To be partisan ... as between Jefferson and Hamilton is like arguing whether men or women are more necessary to the procreation of the race. Neither can live alone. Alone—that is, without the other—each is excessive and soon intolerable."[16]

SIGNIFICANT THIRD PARTIES
IN U.S. HISTORY

Although history has not been kind to minor parties, several have changed the direction of political debate and influenced the outcomes of elections. From the Anti-Masons of the 1820s through Ralph

Nader's Green Party candidacy in 2000, the history of American two-party competition has been periodically influenced by the emergence of third parties that were too weak to win elections but influential enough to shape them.

The Anti-Mason Party

The first significant minor party emerged shortly after the Era of Good Feelings ended in 1824. For decades prior to the Revolution, nearly every large community had a Masonic Lodge, or what was called a Freemason organization. These secretive clubs were composed of middle- and upper-class white Protestants, often the leading business-men of their communities who were interested in the issues of the day and had a strong belief in moral self-improvement. Prominent Masons included George Washington, Henry Clay, and Andrew Jackson. According to historian Phyllis F. Field, "In a nation with high rates of geographic mobility, Masonry provided a convenient way for nomadic American middle-class men to integrate themselves quickly into a new community and feel at home there."[17]

But the elitism and secret Masonic rites created a public backlash—especially among religious fundamentalists. Following the mysterious disappearance of New York Freemason William Morgan in 1826, after he threatened to reveal the secret rituals of the group, the anti-Mason movement was born. Anti-Masons maintained that the secretive cliques were conspiring against the working class and, through their bizarre rituals such as frequent cross burnings, were a threat to Christianity. Within four years of their humble beginnings in 1826, the anti-Masons became a powerful political force. In 1831, they held a presidential nominating convention—a novel idea for its day—and chose as their candidate former attorney general William Wirt.

Wirt proved to be an ineffectual campaigner, and the Anti-Mason Party finished a distant third in the 1832 presidential election with 100,000 votes (8 percent) behind Democrat Andrew Jackson and Whig Party candidate Henry Clay. However, Wirt finished first in Vermont, winning that state's seven electoral votes—the first time a third-party candidate had garnered any support in the Electoral College. The Anti-Masons fared better in state contests, winning the governorships of Vermont and Pennsylvania, and several congres-sional and state legislative seats in New York, Vermont, Pennsylva-nia, Rhode Island, and Connecticut. Their most significant policy achievement was the passage of a national law outlawing extrajudicial oaths of office.

By the mid-1830s, the Anti-Mason Party began to fade. Part of its demise was due to the fact that President Andrew Jackson endorsed policies that gave political leverage to working-class voters. More than anything else, the Anti-Mason Party disappeared because the Freemason movement was out of step with the democratic impulses of the 1830s. There was less public concern about elitism in the years after Jackson's election and his brand of Jacksonian Democracy.

The Free-Soil Party

Several antislavery groups nipped at the edges of the political system prior to the 1840s. The most notable of these were the Barnburners, the Conscience Whigs, and the Liberty Party. Controlled by extremists and religious fanatics whose ideas about ending the interstate slave trade were considered radical—even in a time of rising opposition to slavery—these groups were relatively short-lived.

The Free-Soil Party had better luck. The impetus for this party's founding in 1848 was the debate over the Wilmot Proviso, which limited the extension of slavery into the new western territories. Operating on a platform of "free soil, free speech, free labor, and free men," the Free-Soil Party combined opposition to slavery with a desire for cheap western land. As the Free-Soil Party gained followers, it became more pragmatic than its abolitionist predecessors. It advocated policies that would allow blacks to vote and attend school. At the same time, Free-Soilers bowed to existing racial prejudices by arguing that the Wilmot Proviso would keep blacks in the South.[18] Free-Soilers did not endorse the abolition of slavery, nor did they denounce either the Fugitive Slave Act or the three-fifths clause of the U.S. Constitution (which counted blacks as "three-fifths" of a person for the purpose of determining how they would be represented in the House of Representatives). Other planks that broadened the Free-Soil Party's appeal included cheaper postage rates, reduced federal spending, tariff reform, the election of all civil officers, and free homesteading in the west.[19]

In 1848, the Free-Soil Party held a convention in Buffalo, New York, with nearly 20,000 delegates and spectators in attendance. Hopes were high when they nominated former president Martin Van Buren for president and Charles Francis Adams, son of John Quincy Adams and grandson of John Adams, for vice president. Despite the ticket's high name recognition, Van Buren and Adams won just 10 percent of the popular vote and failed to carry a single state. Congressional results were equally disappointing, as the party won a mere 12 seats. Shortly after the 1848 election, the Free-Soil Party disappeared.

Most Free-Soilers returned to the parties they previously supported, albeit with a renewed determination to change their parties' respective stands on slavery-related issues. This movement back to the major parties caused considerable strife that led to the current two-party alignment. Republicans replaced the Whigs, and Democrats became the party of the South.

The American (Know-Nothing) Party

For many Americans living urban areas, immigration was a primary concern prior to the Civil War. A vast number of working-class, native-born Protestants were deeply troubled by the heavy influx of Irish Catholics beginning in the early 1840s. Jobs, cultural differences, and the transformation of the United States into an ethnic polyglot became contentious political issues. In 1854, the American Party emerged in response to these anxieties. Originally organized around two groups known as the Supreme Order of the Star Spangled Banner and the National Council of the United States of America, adherents were dubbed the Know-Nothings after a reporter asked a member about their secret meetings only to be told that he "knew nothing." The party's core philosophy was simple: "Americans should rule America .... Foreigners have no right to dictate our laws, and therefore have no just ground to complain if Americans see proper to exclude them from offices of trust."[20] The Know-Nothing platform included planks mandating that immigrants live in the United States for 21 years before being allowed to vote; that they never hold public office; and that their children should have no rights unless they were educated in public schools. Taking aim at Catholics and their allegiance to the pope, the Know-Nothings declared, "No person should be selected for political station (whether of native or foreign birth), who recognizes any alliance or obligation of any description to foreign prince, potentate or power."[21]

The popularity of the Know-Nothings is one of the darker tales in U.S. history. In 1854, the party achieved extraordinary success by capturing scores of congressional and state legislative seats, mostly in the Northeast. In Massachusetts, where immigrants were pouring in at a rate of 100,000 per year, the Know-Nothings won an astounding 347 of 350 state house seats and all of the state senate, congressional, and statewide contests, including the governorship. In New York, they elected 40 members of the state legislature and took control of the governorship. The party also won the governorships of Rhode Island, New Hampshire, and Connecticut.

In 1856, the Know-Nothings became caught up in the politics of slavery. At the party's convention in Philadelphia, Northern delegates wanted to nominate a presidential candidate who opposed the extension of slavery into the new western territories. Southerners blocked the move, and Northern delegates bolted out of the convention hall. The remaining Southern delegates nominated former president Millard Fillmore as their candidate for president and Andrew Jackson Dodelson of Tennessee for vice president. The Fillmore-Dodelson ticket captured 875,000 votes, or 21 percent of the popular vote and 8 Electoral College votes (from the state of Maryland). After two stunning showings at the polls, the Know-Nothings faded rapidly. Passage of the 1854 Kansas-Nebraska Act accentuated the slavery issue and created deep sectional divisions. The Republicans—a Northern, antislavery party—burst on the scene, and most Northern Know-Nothings joined their ranks. In the South, the Know-Nothings were absorbed by the former Whigs. By 1860, the Know-Nothings were no more.

The Greenback and Populist (People's) Parties

During the early 1870s, the nation entered hard times and Midwestern farmers suffered from plummeting crop prices. Railroads were the only means by which to ship Midwestern farm goods to major markets in the East, and privately owned companies charged exorbitant rates. Adding to the farmers' plight was a deflation of the currency, which made it difficult for them to pay their high bills.

The first efforts to organize agricultural interests culminated in the formation of hundreds of local organizations called farmers' alliances, or granges. Mixing political and social activities, the granges united farmers into a cohesive voting bloc. Many who belonged to the granges were supportive of a third party, and after the economic panic of 1873 the Greenback Party was created. The Greenback Party proposed an inflated currency based on cheap paper money known as "greenbacks" that were first introduced during the Civil War.[22] Their argument was simple: By making the greenback legal tender, there would be enough money in circulation to ease the burden of indebted farmers and laborers. The Greenback Party was also known as the Greenback-Labor Party.

In 1878, Greenback congressional candidates won more than 1 million votes and fourteen U.S. House races. Two years later they nominated General James Weaver of Iowa as their presidential candidate. By that time, however, the national economy had improved and the Greenback Party lost its initial appeal. Weaver won just 300,000 votes, and the Greenbacks sent just 8 members to Congress. In 1884, the Greenbacks found their presidential support almost cut in half.

Overproduction and increased world competition led to another agricultural crisis in the early 1890s. The remaining Greenbacks merged with a new party called the Populists, or People's Party, in 1891. Unlike the Greenbacks, the Populists' demands were more radical and far-reaching: "We meet in the midst of a nation brought to the verge of moral, political, and material ruin .... From the womb of governmental injustice, we breed the two great classes—tramps and millionaires."[23] Among other things, the Populist platform proposed public regulation of railroads and telegraphs; free coinage of silver and gold (as a means to increase currency in circulation); creation of postal savings banks; prohibition of alien ownership of land; a graduated federal income tax; direct election of U.S. senators; and a reduction of the workday to eight hours. The Populists readily won adherents in the Midwest, West, and even the South. One historian summarized the new party's appeal this way: "The Populist Party was the embodiment of an attitude, a way of looking at life that had been prevalent for almost 20 years, and a general position taken against concentrated economic power."[24]

The Populists selected former Greenback James Weaver as their 1892 presidential nominee. Weaver won just 8 percent of the popular vote (about a million votes) and 22 Electoral College votes. Nearly all of his support came from western states. In effect, the Populists split the Republican vote, giving Democrat Grover Cleveland a chance to capture the presidency. Democrats also won control of both houses of Congress—a rarity in this Republican-dominated era. Populist strength grew in 1894, when they won nearly 1.5 million votes and elected six U.S. senators and seven House members, all from the West.

Then, in 1896, something unusual happened: Both the Populists and the Democrats nominated William Jennings Bryan for president. Bryan endorsed many Populist planks—most notably, the elimination of the gold standard. At the Democratic National Convention, Bryan gave one of the most famous speeches in the history of U.S. oratory, the so-called "Cross of Gold" speech. After the Democratic Convention, the Populists—also moved by Bryan's "Cross of Gold" speech—chose him for president.[25] Although Bryan lost, many of the Populist Party's proposals were accepted by both parties and incorporated into law during the twentieth century.

The Progressives: 1912–1924, 1948, and Today

In Chapter 3, we outlined the rationale behind the Progressive movement, its numerous successes against machine-dominated locales, and
its eventual coalescence into a third party in 1912 behind former President Theodore Roosevelt. Calling for a "new nationalism," Roosevelt
bolted the Republican Convention to form the Progressive (or Bull
Moose) Party, running on a platform that promised stricter regulation of corporations; downward revision of tariffs; popular election
of U.S. senators; women's suffrage; and support for the referendum,
ballot initiatives, and recall. With 27 percent of the popular vote and
88 Electoral College votes, Roosevelt finished in second place behind
Democrat Woodrow Wilson. William Howard Taft, the Republican
nominee, finished third—the first time that had happened to a GOP
presidential candidate since the party's inception.

Certainly, the high point of the Progressive movement was
Roosevelt's strong showing in 1912. Thereafter, President Woodrow
Wilson pursued a Progressive agenda—including passage of new an-
titrust laws, banking regulations, and scores of business reforms. But
the Progressive Party did not die completely, especially in states with
strong populist traditions. In 1924, Robert La Follette—a former U.S.
representative, U.S. senator, and governor of Wisconsin—became the
Progressive Party's presidential nominee. La Follette was an articulate
champion of labor reform, business regulation, a graduated income
tax, and a constitutional amendment providing for direct election
of judges to the federal courts. His party's platform proposed public
ownership of the nation's water power, strict control and conservation
of all natural resources, farmers' cooperatives, and legislation to make
credit available to farmers and small businessmen. La Follette captured
17 percent of the popular vote (4.8 million ballots), but won only 13
Electoral College votes (all from his home state of Wisconsin). With
his death in 1925, La Follette's brand of progressivism died as well.
Though his children and grandchildren became active in politics and
continued to push the Progressive agenda, they did not attract much
attention beyond the Wisconsin borders.

In 1948, the Progressive Party reemerged. That year, a left-wing
group led by former vice president Henry A. Wallace bolted from
the Democratic Party. At issue was President Harry S. Truman's "get
tough" policy toward the Soviet Union, which Wallace strongly
opposed. The Progressive Party accused President Truman of being
vociferously anticommunist, which they said stemmed from "the
dictates of monopoly and the military" and resulted in "preparing

for war in the name of peace."[26] To the utopian-minded Progressives, peace was "the prerequisite of survival": "There is no American principle of public interest, and there is no Russian principle of public interest, which would have to be sacrificed to end the Cold War and open up the Century of Peace which the Century of the Common Man demands."[27] Given these views, the Progressive Party called for a wholesale reversal in how the U.S. government dealt with domestic communism. The party favored eliminating the House Un-American Activities Committee, claiming it had vilified and prosecuted citizens "in total disregard of the Bill of Rights." It also rejected any ban of the U.S. Communist Party or the required registration of its members, likening such legislation to the Alien and Sedition Acts.

In July 1948, the Progressive Citizens of America selected Wallace as its presidential candidate. As the Progressive Party standard-bearer, Henry Wallace drew large crowds—including many young liberals, blue-collar workers, and African Americans. His liberal listeners worried Truman, who attempted to link Wallace with the U.S. Communist Party. At campaign stops, Truman vowed, "I do not want and I will not accept the political support of Henry Wallace and his communists."[28] Wallace's public statements made Truman's task an easy one. A Gallup poll taken shortly before the Progressive convention found 51 percent agreed that the Progressive Party was communist dominated.[29]

Despite Wallace's political shortcomings, he influenced the election result. When the ballots were counted, Wallace received 1,157,172 votes (slightly more than 2 percent). This was enough to throw three states to GOP presidential nominee Thomas E. Dewey: New York, Maryland, and Michigan. If Wallace had done somewhat better in California and had not been kept off the Illinois ballot, the 1948 contest might have been decided in the House of Representatives.

Progressive ideas have been a recurring force in U.S. politics, although progressivism has assumed different meanings in different eras. Originally, its focus was centered in the religious belief that the human condition could be infinitely improved. By the end of the nineteenth century, progressivism meant ridding the political system of corrupt influences. At the turn of the twentieth century, Progressives wanted greater participation by average citizens in governmental affairs, and they believed government could be improved by bringing scientific methods to bear on public problems. In the late twentieth century, a new progressivism emerged as a collection of liberal ideas centered on greater government involvement to cure society's ills. In 1991, the Progressive Caucus was created in the House of Representatives.

Today, it has 75 members (all of them Democrats), making it the largest group within the 185-member Democratic caucus.[30] Its core principles are "(1) fighting for economic justice and security for all; (2) protecting and preserving our civil rights and civil liberties; (3) promoting global peace and security; and (4) advancing environmental protection and energy independence."[31]

States' Rights Party (1948) and the American Independent Party (1968)

After the Civil War, the roots of the Democratic Party became deeply planted in the South. During the 1930s, Franklin D. Roosevelt transformed the Democratic Party from a minority into a majority by including labor, middle- and lower-class urban residents, Catholics, African Americans, and Jews in its ranks—along with the ever-loyal Southerners. Relations between progressive Northern Democrats and conservative Southern Democrats became a "marriage of convenience." Northern Democrats controlled the White House, thanks to their Southern partners, and Southern Democrats chaired important congressional committees—thanks to their party's majority status and adherence to the seniority rule.

By the late 1940s, the marriage between Northern and Southern Democrats was in trouble. Civil rights split the two factions apart in 1948. That year, the Democratic Convention adopted a strong pro-civil rights plank. Many Southern delegates walked out and reconvened in Birmingham, Alabama. The gathering adopted the name States' Rights Party and quickly became known as the Dixiecrat Party, given its overwhelming Southern base of support. The convention reiterated a plank extracted from the 1840 Democratic Party platform: "Congress has no power under the Constitution to interfere with or control the domestic institutions of the several states, and . . . such states are the sole and proper judges of everything appertaining to their own affairs not prohibited by the Constitution."[32] This so-called states' rights argument was designed to keep the existing racial segregation intact.

The delegates nominated J. Strom Thurmond, then governor of South Carolina, as their presidential candidate. On election day, Thurmond garnered 1.1 million votes (2.4 percent) and won 38 Electoral College votes from five Southern states. The party closed shop after the election, and Thurmond went on to have a successful political career. In 1954, Thurmond won a write-in Senate campaign after the state Democratic Party rejected him.[33] Ten years later, Thurmond formally switched his party registration from Democratic to Republican. In 2002, he retired from the U.S. Senate as a Republican at age 100, and he died a year later on June 26, 2003.

The final blow to the post–Civil War Democratic coalition came in 1968. Once again, the breakdown centered upon efforts to broaden legal protections for African Americans. The American Independent Party was established in 1968 as the personal organization of Alabama governor George C. Wallace. Wallace was elected governor in 1962 as a Democrat and ardent segregationist. A year later, Wallace entered the national spotlight when the federal government ordered the integration of public colleges. In a televised display of defiance, Wallace and his state troopers blocked access to the University of Alabama to two incoming African American students before eventually stepping aside.

After an unsuccessful (but impressive) primary campaign against Lyndon B. Johnson in 1964, Wallace abandoned the Democratic Party in 1968 to form his own party, which followed his get-tough, law-and-order, segregationist beliefs. With old-time populist themes and a powerful gift for oratory, Wallace won nearly 10 million ballots—13.5 percent of the total votes cast. His 46 electoral votes from 5 Southern states were more than Republican nominee Barry Goldwater received in 1964. Much of Wallace's Southern strength came from former Democrats who used the Wallace candidacy as a way station before entering the Republican Party. In 1972, Richard Nixon won the vast majority of the 1968 Wallace backers, and during the 1980s Wallace voters began supporting Republicans for other offices such as governor, members of Congress, and the state legislature. Wallace, meanwhile, reentered Democratic presidential politics in 1972, only to be shot and permanently paralyzed at a rally in Laurel, Maryland. Although he later won the Alabama governorship as a Democrat, Wallace's days in presidential politics were over. His American Independent Party and its offshoot, the American Party, continued to nominate candidates for a while before disappearing altogether.

The Reform Party

The difference between minor parties and splinter candidacies is clearly evident when comparing Ross Perot's 1992 run for the presidency with his second try four years later. In his first effort, Perot did not field candidates for other offices, affirming his independence from all officeholders and parties. Using his hefty pocketbook to finance his campaign, Perot ran on a platform that stressed the importance of a balanced budget during a time of economic difficulty and the need to enact major campaign finance reforms. His foremost strength was his charisma and can-do attitude. After winning an impressive 19 percent of the vote, Perot remained active by organizing a new political party centered on the issues of a balanced budget and campaign finance reform. The Reform Party was born, and by 1996 it qualified to run a slate of candidates in all 50 states. It had a national organization, developed formal rules, and even held a convention to nominate its presidential candidate, who, not surprisingly, was Perot. This time, however, Perot accepted federal funds, thus saving him from once again having to finance his own campaign. Perot received only 8 percent of the vote, a signal that the days of the Reform Party were numbered.

Although the party received $12.6 million from the federal government for the 2000 general election based upon Ross Perot's 1996 showing, the money made the party a target for candidates far removed from its original emphasis on eliminating federal deficit spending. Patrick J. Buchanan, who unsuccessfully sought the Republican presidential nomination in 1992, attempted to become the Reform Party nominee. He competed against John Hagelin, who had been the 1996 Natural Law Party's candidate for president. The contest split what was left of the Perot movement in two. In a convention marred by fisticuffs, both Buchanan and Hagelin claimed to have enough support to clinch the Reform Party's presidential nomination. Ultimately, the Federal Election Commission decided that Buchanan was the legitimate nominee and awarded him the $12.6 million. Disgusted at the turn of events, Perot refused to back Buchanan and gave his endorsement to George W. Bush. Meanwhile, Minnesota governor Jesse Ventura, who had been the Reform Party's greatest success story, decided to leave the party, calling it "hopelessly dysfunctional."[34] For his part, Buchanan fared poorly, winning fewer than 1 million votes out of more than 100 million cast. The Reform Party promptly faded into obscurity.

The Green Party

During Bill Clinton's tenure as president, some Democrats became restive, seeing Clinton as a self-styled "new kind of Democrat" who eschewed the party's old New Deal liberalism. Many liberals complained that with the presidency in Democratic hands, they had little to show for it. In 1996, the Green Party echoed these sentiments and selected Ralph Nader as its presidential candidate. Nader did not actively run for president; rather, he let his name appear on the ballot and made no campaign appearances. Even so, Nader's presence cost Clinton the state of Colorado.

Things were different in 2000. With Republicans in control of Congress, Bill Clinton was compelled to strike deals with them, telling confidants, "Strategically I want to remove all divisive issues for a conservative [Republican presidential] candidate, so all the issues are on progressive terrain."[35] But Nader and the Greens complained that far from being progressive, Clinton and the Republicans had sided with corporate interests. Nader decided to confront the Clinton–Gore administration in 2000, charging that its obsession with deficit reduction and not using the powers of government more forcefully—especially when it came to protecting the environment—had transformed the Democrats into a "me-too" party that emulated the Republicans. To Nader and the Greens, the failure to enact campaign finance reform was proof-positive of how strongly corporations controlled what happened inside the federal government.[36]

Nader won 2.73 percent of the votes for president, making him a "spoiler" in the race. The 97,488 votes Nader received in Florida made a difference, given that George W. Bush's statewide margin was 537 votes out of nearly 6 million cast. Nader had a similar effect in New Hampshire, where he received 22,198 votes, enough to cost Al Gore a victory in the state where Bush edged Gore by just 7,211 votes. If Nader had not been in the race, it is very likely that Democrat Al Gore would have won a majority of electoral votes and would have been the nation's forty-third president.[37]

Democrats were well aware of their missed opportunity to win the White House in 2000, and they made sure that their supporters were not tempted to vote for Ralph Nader in 2004. That year, Nader ran once more, but received less than 1 percent of the votes cast. Democratic nominee John Kerry argued that defeating George W. Bush was far more important than casting a protest vote for Nader. By 2008, Nader abandoned the Green Party and ran as an independent, garnering 739,278 votes—the most of any of the third-party candidates, but still just one-half of 1 percent of the total votes cast. When asked by pollsters in 2008 whether they would even consider voting for Nader, an overwhelming 77 percent said no.[38] Largely ignored by the media, Nader had became little more than a gadfly in presidential politics.

CONTEMPORARY THIRD PARTIES

Despite their uneven electoral history, third parties remain a presence in the contemporary political landscape, as growing voter frustration with Republicans and Democrats has led many people to embrace the idea of alternative parties, at least in theory. Third parties have also responded to the technological transformations we have seen elsewhere influencing the party system, and in some cases have established a presence for themselves on the Internet. As we chart the recent explosion of minor parties, we will explore changing voter attitudes toward minor party candidates and examine how social networking capabilities have bolstered the visibility of otherwise obscure third-party operations.

An Explosion of Minor Parties

Despite the numerous barriers to third-party formation, there has been an explosion of minor parties in the United States. A recent study of almost 600 minor-party candidates reveals interesting details about their motivation for taking an independent political path.[39] The vast majority belonged to one of the major parties before striking out on their own. In fact, 14 percent had actually belonged to both parties at one time in the past. Most cited the failure of two-party politics—claiming that the Democrats and Republicans were ineffective, elitist, committed to the status quo, and corrupt. However, although they were disillusioned with the two parties, nearly all believed in the party system. Demographically, most minor party candidates were well educated and affluent: 77 percent had personal incomes over $40,000 per year, and 33 percent made over $60,000 annually.

Perhaps the most significant finding is that like their nineteenth- and twentieth-century predecessors, today's third parties emerge out of the sense that neither major party is addressing the concerns of ordinary voters. Abolitionist parties developed because of slavery, the Populists and Greenbacks because of economic issues, the Progressives because of corruption, and the segregationist parties in response to pending civil rights legislation. Today, third parties have been rising because consumers of party politics are increasingly discouraged by the status quo.

Nowhere is this more evident than in the Tea Party movement, which is attempting to move the Republican Party in a more conservative populist direction. Tea Party followers are extremely concerned about the size of the federal deficit, support tax reductions, and oppose an expanding U.S. government, especially during the Obama administration. But the Tea Party lacks a formal party structure, preferring instead to influence Republican primaries by supporting candidates who empathize with their cause and providing them with

Mainstream Media Coverage of the Tea Party

"Liberal media bias" is an ongoing charge leveled by conservatives in general and the Republican Party in particular. Counter to this claim, the nonpartisan media monitoring group Fairness and Accuracy in Reporting (FAIR) has documented that throughout 2010, significant progressive protests and gatherings were superseded by media focus on the much smaller Tea Party in the run-up to the midterm Congressional elections. As just one example, the 15,000–20,000 attendees of the U.S. Social Forum gathering in Detroit received only 1.5 percent of the coverage granted to the 600 attendees of the February 2010 Tea Party Convention in Nashville, Tennessee.

Source: Street, Paul, and Anthony DiMaggio. 2011. *Crashing the Tea Party: Mass Media and the Campaign to Remake American Politics.* Boulder, CO: Paradigm Publishers.

considerable financial support. A survey of 650 Tea Party organizations conducted by the *Washington Post* found most had fewer than 50 members.[40] Matt Ney, a Tea Party activist, described his Tea Party group's focus: "We're not wanting to be a third party. We're not wanting to endorse individual candidates ever. What we're trying to do is be activists by pushing a conservative idea."[41] But should the Republican Party fail to heed the wishes of its Tea Party followers, the movement may join the ranks of other third-party efforts with the same likely result: an inability to succeed in electoral politics while potentially influencing one (or both) major parties.

More Positive Voter Attitudes Toward Minor Parties

Throughout history, political parties have fallen in and out of favor with voters. When a 1938 Roper poll asked voters what parties they would like to see competing in the next presidential race, a plurality answered only a Republican and a Democrat.[42] Today, the idea of having some choice other than the Democrats or Republicans is popular. A 2010 CNN/Opinion Research poll found 64 percent favored having a third party run candidates for president, Congress, and state offices.[43] Moreover, 59 percent wanted a third party, even if it meant that "the winner of some elections would be a candidate who disagrees with you on most issues that matter to you."[44] This sentiment is not surprising, given the persistent voter anger toward the two major parties. A 2010 Gallup poll found voters were disillusioned with the major parties: Only 35 percent thought the Democratic and Republican parties "do an adequate job of representing the American people," while 58 percent believed a third party was needed.[45] Of course, history and the institutional and cultural obstacles to third-party formation suggest it will be difficult for a viable third party to emerge and satisfy these wishes.

Minor Parties and the Internet

Although dissatisfaction with both the Democrats and the Republicans is a primary cause for increased third-party activism, technology is also giving third parties a boost. Minor party activists are better able to communicate with voters and each other than in the past, as the Internet has vastly simplified the job of creating, maintaining, and broadening their reach. The type of person who might be interested in third-party activities is likely to own a personal computer and have access to the Internet.

Table 9.1 lists the website addresses of several third parties, some of which are particularly adept at integrating social media. The Green Party homepage includes a blog permitting interaction with other Green Party supporters, a link to the Green Party Facebook page, and a tool for learning about local Green Party activities. On the opposite end of the ideological spectrum, the Libertarian Party has a sophisticated website that links to its sites on Twitter, Facebook, and Meetup, as well as to Libertarian state party organizations.

JEFFERSON, HAMILTON, AND THE FUTURE OF THIRD PARTIES IN AMERICA

Scores of institutional barriers—including the winner-take-all electoral system, the Electoral College, barriers to ballot access, and a host of historical and cultural forces—push the U.S. polity toward a two-party model. Yet minor parties have played a critical role at key moments before fading into the history books. Thus, to ignore minor parties is to overlook a key factor in the evolution of the American party system.

Table 9.1 U.S. Third-Party Locations on the World Wide Web, 2010

Party	World Wide Web Address
America First Party	www.americafirstparty.org
American Party	www.theamericanparty.org
American Conservative Party	www.theamericanconservatives.org
American Independent Party	www.selfgovernment.us
American Moderate Party	www.americanmoderateparty.org
American Reform Party	www.americanreform.org
Communist Party USA	www.cpusa.org
Confederate National Party	www.confederateamericanpride.com
Constitution Party	www.constitutionparty.com
Creator's Rights Party	www.tcrp.us
Green Party of the United States	www.gp.org
Labor Party	www.thelaborparty.org
Libertarian Party	www.lp.org
Modern Whig Party	www.modernwhig.org
Natural Law Party	www.natural-law.org
Peace and Freedom Party	www.peaceandfreedom.org
Prohibition Party	prohibition.org
Reform Party of the United States of America	www.reformparty.org
Socialist Party USA	www.sp-usa.org
United States Marijuana Party	www.usmjparty.org
Workers Party USA	www.workersparty.org
Working Families Party	www.workingfamiliesparty.org

One way to understand the paradox of institutions that repeatedly emerge but never win national elections is to return to the fundamental split between Hamiltonian nationalism and Jeffersonian localism. American political parties rest on a Hamiltonian foundation—meaning that party elites at the state and national levels control the inner workings of their respective parties. For these folks, community-based party organizations and grassroots activism are directed toward winning elections. Policy innovation is usually sluggish, as party operatives retreat to proven themes that win at the polls. Yet the desire for a Jeffersonian-style party system centered around deep-seated policy concerns is a powerful and recurring counterforce. Minor parties burst on the scene when a sizable segment of the electorate feels that the Hamiltonian-style parties are not adequately addressing important issues. Third parties become a manifestation of voter desire for a policy-driven politics. Invariably, the two-party Hamiltonian-style party system reacts and reasserts itself by addressing the concerns that precipitated the third-party split.

Several scholars have explored the idea that minor parties help shape the party system in a way that major parties cannot. Theodore J. Lowi, a former president of the American Political Science Association, writes, "New ideas and issues develop or redevelop parties, but parties, particularly established ones, rarely develop ideas or present new issues on their own .... Once a system of parties is established, the range and scope of policy discussion is set, until and unless some disturbance arises from other quarters."[46] The "disturbance" Lowi speaks of is the development of aggressive third parties. Lowi notes there have been four historical eras when Democrats and Republicans have been especially innovative: (1) 1856–1860; (2) 1890–1900; (3) 1912–1914; and (4) 1933–1935. In these years, party leaders became more susceptible to mass opinion as a result of third-party competition. Once the policy innovations were achieved, however, third parties withered away. Using the Hamilton-Jefferson model, third parties have periodically shaken the system and have temporally shifted it toward Jeffersonian localism.

How will third parties fare in the today's networked age? Certainly, the social networking capability of the Internet has made it easier for minor party leaders to connect with potential supporters at a greatly reduced cost. In this respect, the minor parties may find it easier to do business in the twenty-first century than during the past 100 years. It is possible that if more minor party candidates overcome the odds, more voters will act upon their pro-third-party proclivities, setting aside the concern that they are wasting their votes by supporting third-party candidates. And as we have seen, although the success of third-party candidates has been limited, more are jumping into the fray.

Nonetheless, the institutional and cultural obstacles to a viable multiparty system remain daunting. Over the past three decades, we have witnessed a centralization and professionalization of electoral politics with a profound shift toward Hamiltonian nationalism. Candidates realize that the best way to win elections is to amass huge war chests, and the level of funding needed to become competitive is beyond the reach of most third parties. Given the increased professionalization of U.S. politics, it is likely that minor parties will continue to exert their greatest influence at the margins, even if such marginal influences are at times profound.

Conclusion

Hamilton's Moment of Zen

W e started this book by noting how Alexander Hamilton and Thomas Jefferson passionately disagreed about the proper course for governing their new nation, leading them to confront each other during George Washington's cabinet meetings. By 1800, each had established a political party and carried the battle of ideas from behind closed doors into the electoral arena. The origins of the U.S. party system can be traced to their heated debate. Yet the two men remained civil, honorable adversaries. After all, they worked closely on a deal placing the nation's capital on the banks of the Potomac River as Jefferson hoped, and Hamilton won Jefferson's backing for a tax and spending plan designed to boost the fortunes of the business class. In fact, Jefferson so admired Hamilton that he had a bust of his opponent placed at the front hall of his home, Monticello; the bust faced one of Jefferson, reflecting Jefferson's acknowledgment that both were opposites in life.

If we could resurrect these two important figures from our nation's past, they would certainly marvel at the changes that have taken place. They never could have envisioned the omnipotence of the federal government, the relative equality afforded to African Americans and women (including the right of both groups to vote), the rise of nearly instantaneous communications, and the high-tech nature of contemporary campaigns. Nonetheless, some things would be surprisingly familiar—especially the broad outlines of the federal government that each helped fashion more than 200 years ago, and the public's enduring commitment to the ideas of liberty, individualism, hard work, self-reliance, and self-governance. Alexis de Tocqueville's observation that the public desire for "standing alone," and believing that the future lies in one's individual efforts, continues to be a centerpiece of American political thought.[1]

The contrasting impulses between Hamilton's desire for a strong national government and Jefferson's preference for localism and individual self-reliance are evident in today's public thought. As has been true throughout our history, contemporary Americans are caught in a paradox: They want the federal government to act when it must, but prefer government to stay out of those things best left to individuals and businesses. Today, confidence in government is at a low ebb. According to a 2010 survey, only 33 percent either have "a lot" or "some" confidence in the federal government; 31 percent answer "*none*."[2] This distrust of government is matched by a whopping 57 percent who believe "government is doing too many things better left to businesses and individuals."[3] On the other hand, the same poll found 61 percent who want government to *do more* when it comes to developing new clean energy sources; 60 percent want *more government* involvement in improving public schools; 60 percent want *more government* action to make college affordable; 57 percent believe government should *do more* to reduce poverty; and 51 percent want *more government* initiatives to ensure access to affordable healthcare (the latter statistic coming *after* congressional passage of President Obama's healthcare reform bill).[4] Even after the Republicans seized control of the House of Representatives following the 2010 midterm elections, only 41 percent wanted the Obama program repealed, whereas 54 percent wanted to wait and see how the program works or thought it should be left alone.[5]

Whether Democrats or Republicans control either the presidency or Congress, more government is expected in the years ahead. One sign of the times: By a 42 percent to 18 percent margin, Americans believe the federal government will become even more important in improving the lives of the American people (36 percent expect no change).[6] Hamilton would be pleased.

When it comes to the extra-constitutional device known as political parties, Hamilton's triumph is even more complete. Just as the federal government has become more powerful, so, too, has the U.S. party system with its hierarchal structure and professional politicians overseeing aggressive national party organizations. Hamiltonian nationalism has created a largely top-down party system managed by elites, which has emerged at the expense of Jefferson's idea of a community-based politics. Recall that Jeffersonian localism is based on the idea that, given its size and diversity, the United States can only be viewed as a series of relatively independent communities. In Jefferson's view, power is vested at the local level and great trust is placed in the hands of ordinary citizens. Party politics is best undertaken by amateurs, whose virtue and commitment are to ideas benefitting the local citizenry. Jeffersonian localism places a premium on policy coherence and intraparty democracy. It is a bottom-up political system wherein individuals are at the center of a politics of ideas designed to reorient the government in a particular direction.

Today, Jefferson's approach is best expressed by progressive netroots activists who toil online to replace a top-heavy, professional Democratic and Republican Party with a more mass-based apparatus centered in Internet communities. Yet, even their view of localism is something Jefferson would have trouble fathoming: virtual networks of people dispersed throughout physical communities across the country and even around the world. Today, the very meaning of the word "local" has been challenged by new technologies that create community without proximity, even as the appeal of Jefferson's ideas lives on.

This recent dominance of Hamiltonian nationalism over Jeffersonian localism has come after two centuries of struggle. Throughout this period, the two surviving major parties, Democrats and Republicans, each took a turn as guardians of the Hamiltonian or Jeffersonian approach. During the Civil War and Industrial Revolution, the newly formed Republican Party became closely identified with Hamiltonian nationalism, as it sought to give the federal government the necessary tools to fight the Civil War, end slavery, and transform an agricultural society into an industrial one. Democrats, largely dominated by their southern wing, spoke of states' rights as code for continuing the separation between blacks and whites. Franklin Roosevelt's New Deal, Harry Truman's Fair Deal, John Kennedy's New Frontier, Lyndon Johnson's Great Society, and Barack Obama's New Foundation aligned the Democratic Party with the Hamiltonian idea that the national government must overcome the Great Depression and be strong enough to lead the nation through World War II, the cold war, the fight for civil rights, and to contain the Great Recession that ended the first decade of the twenty-first century. From the 1930s to the 1960s, Americans believed in the simple proposition that big government worked. When pollster George Gallup asked in

1936, "Which theory of government do you favor: concentration of power in the federal government or concentration of power in the state government?" respondents chose the federal government by a 56 percent to 44 percent margin.[7]

In the intervening years those attitudes have changed, with many more expressing a profound mistrust of centralized government, suggesting a swing toward Jeffersonian localism. This mistrust was aided by conspicuous failures of government, including a lost war in Vietnam; the twin economic evils of high inflation and unemployment during the 1970s; stalemated wars in Iraq and Afghanistan at the end of the Bush administration; and a widespread belief that the federal bailouts of the banking and automotive industries at the beginning of the Obama administration benefitted the few, not the many.

And yet, there has been a vast Hamiltonian-like expansion of government in both foreign and domestic affairs. Declaring a state of emergency on September 11, 2001, George W. Bush authorized $40 billion in emergency spending, with $20 billion earmarked for restoring New York City, and an additional $15 billion to bail out faltering airlines. At the beginning of 2003, federal workers in a new Transportation Security Administration began screening passengers in the nation's airports. Even more important, Congress and the president approved the creation of a Department of Homeland Security, the largest and most ambitious cabinet-level reorganization since the Defense Department was created in 1947. Grover Norquist, president of the conservative-minded group Americans for Tax Reform, worried aloud, "Wars are nasty things. They make governments grow."[8] The same might be said about moments of economic insecurity. To address the 2008 financial crisis, the Bush administration asked Congress for permission to insure or buy hundreds of billions of troubled financial assets from teetering financial institutions. The Obama administration followed suit with a $787 billion stimulus program designed to put people back to work and jump-start the economy. Later, the federal government devoted billions to bailing out the U.S. automobile industry. While Americans debated the efficacy of these programs, there remained a prevailing consensus that in these times of crisis the federal government must "do something."

Looking at the American party system from the perspective of Hamiltonian nationalism versus Jeffersonian localism, Hamilton's triumph is even more complete. During the heyday of party politics, stretching from the Jacksonian Democracy of the 1830s to the Industrial Revolution of the early 1900s, Jeffersonian localism dominated. Party politics was local politics. Partisan affiliation was infused in the workplace and social circles and influenced how people viewed the issues and candidates of the day. Parties were key mechanisms for integrating whole groups of immigrants into the culture and mores of civic life—and were celebrated by political scientists for the job they did. In the first line of his 1942 book *Party Government*, E. E. Schattschneider solemnly declared, "Modern democracy is unthinkable save in terms of parties."[9]

As this text has documented, party machines of the late nineteenth and early twentieth centuries were not models for democracy. Progressives wanted to clean up the machines, but their reforms transformed political parties into regulated public utilities controlled by federal, state, and local laws. In effect, the Progressives legalized the two-party system of Democrats versus Republicans, thereby making it difficult (but not impossible) for grassroots minor parties to become viable players. By attacking the party machines and focusing on how politics could be better managed, Progressive reformers further isolated people from politics—even as they threw open the formerly closed doors to smoke-filled party back rooms.

The nationalization of party politics during the New Deal era solidified Hamilton's triumph. As government shifted to the national sphere, so did the party system. National party organizations began providing more cutting-edge services and lots of money to needy candidates, and political parties became professional, centralized organizations. Against this backdrop of strong, centralized parties, a number of important normative questions developed about the role parties should play, including:

◆ Are parties a desirable feature in a democratic system, or do they detract from allowing the will of the people to prevail?

◆ Should parties be more concerned with winning elections or implementing policies, and can both objectives be realized?

◆ Is American-style democracy best served by having nationally centered party organizations where elites can dominate, or by a diverse Jeffersonian-like system of community-level organizations dominated by amateurs? Or, is it possible to have some combination of both in today's networked age, with the rise of virtual communities?

◆ Should elected officials use party affiliation as a guide to voting, or should they be independent operators hired to represent their local constituencies?

◆ Is intraparty democracy necessary, or is it a hindrance to electoral efficiency?

♦ Why is the United States one of the few democracies that relies on a two-party model, and is this something we might wish—or be able—to change?
♦ What role should parties play in the presidential nominating process, and can they help presidents to govern?
♦ Should parties be afforded a special place in the campaign finance system, or should they be treated in a way similar to any other group or individual?
♦ Have court decisions and state and national regulations reshaped parties to the benefit or detriment of the party system?
♦ How might we conceptualize the complex, changing relationship between party organizations and voters?

Answers to these and other questions are needed as we push forward into the second decade of the new millennium. There is an old maxim that still holds true: How our democracy is doing is directly related to how our political parties are faring. Collectively, our polity's answers to the democratic questions we raise will have a direct impact on our political parties.

PARTY POLITICS IN THE TWENTY-FIRST CENTURY

Notwithstanding the dangers of predicting trends in politics, especially in an era of rapid technological change, we close this book with a few informed judgments about what may lie ahead. We have collapsed our projections into three areas: organizational developments, voter trends and legislative politics, and the role of minor parties.

Organizational Developments

It is likely that party organizations will continue to grow in power and influence. Party operatives realize that the only way to remain players in electoral politics is to raise money aggressively, provide cutting-edge services to candidates, and stay abreast of technological changes made possible by today's networked age. This accentuates the importance of centralized, Hamiltonian-style professional party organizations. In light of the *Citizens United* decision by the U.S. Supreme Court, party organizations are likely to grow as they accumulate and dispense ever-larger sums of campaign dollars. This growth from the top will make national party officeholders—including the chairs of the Democratic and Republican national committees—vital players in politics at all levels. The national parties and their respective organizations will not only have an expanding role to play in presidential and congressional elections, but their influence in state and local politics is also likely to expand.

The one significant exception to this trend is the community-centered, volunteer-oriented activity one finds in portions of the political blogosphere. The so-called netroots have become important in gauging the national mood (especially among activists), and they have an outsized role to play in partisan politics. But even these on-line activists seek not to weaken party organizations as much as to democratize them both in form and function.

Voter Trends and Legislative Politics

Throughout U.S. history, there have been times when voters have moved away from parties only to be reconnected to them through an economic crisis or war. In each instance, realigning elections reestablished the party connection. Some have suggested that party-brand loyalty may again swell under similar conditions. And there are signs that the bases of the Democratic and Republican parties have solidified during the past decade. The result is that the major party candidates have depended upon overwhelming support from their partisans. Republican nominees George W. Bush and John McCain won the backing of 91 percent, 93 percent, and 90 percent of their fellow Republicans in 2000, 2004, and 2008, respectively. Democratic candidates Al Gore, John Kerry, and Barack Obama won equally sizable backing from their partisans in 2000, 2004, and 2008: 86 percent for Gore, and 89 percent for Kerry and Obama apiece.[10] This partisan divide continues to persist. In 2010, 91 percent of Democrats supported their party's congressional candidate; 94 percent of Republicans did the same.[11]

Increased partisanship has resulted in a heightening of incivility both in the public dialogue and within the halls of Congress. When President Obama went before the Congress to argue for his health-care reform plan, his address was interrupted by South Carolina Republican Representative Joe Wilson, who shouted the words, "You lie!" Wilson's outburst made him something of a folk hero among Republicans, and he was reelected in 2010. On the other side of the aisle, Florida Democratic Representative Alan Grayson (defeated for reelection in 2010) took to the House floor to accuse the GOP of wanting to kill Americans by opposing Obama's healthcare reforms.

Immediately after the 2010 midterm elections were concluded, Republican Senate minority leader Mitch McConnell declared that his "top political priority should be to deny President Obama a second term in office."[12] In each case, heightened rhetoric resulted in increased campaign contributions from responsive partisans. After Minnesota congresswoman Michelle Bachmann accused President Obama of having "anti-American views" she took in nearly $1 million in campaign contributions. In 2010, Bachmann raised $13.5 million, making her the top fundraiser in the U.S. House. When former congressman Grayson declared that a 2009 Republican healthcare plan told seniors to "die quickly," he raised $1 million from his supporters. Ron Bonjean, a Republican political consultant, notes: "If you're in the money game and you say something controversial, you'll have support from a very energetic core."[13] Certainly, the advent of a 24-hour cable news cycle and the rise of social media intensifies incendiary remarks and makes bipartisanship an ever-elusive goal.

All of this is in stark contrast to a time not so long ago when Democrats and Republicans were willing to work together. One small example: It was Republican Bob Dole who sponsored legislation to name the Health and Human Services building in Washington, D.C., after the late Hubert H. Humphrey, who was the Democratic presidential nominee in 1968. Such acts of comity, fairly common in the post–World War II era, now appear quaint. In a 2010 commencement address, President Obama bemoaned the prevailing media culture and the tendency of Americans both inside and outside of government to listen only to those voices with whom they agree:

> Today's 24/7 echo chamber amplifies the most inflammatory
> sound bites louder and faster than ever before. And it's also,
> however, given us unprecedented choice. Whereas most
> Americans used to get their news from the same three networks
> over dinner, or a few influential papers on Sunday morning, we
> now have the option to get our information from any number of
> blogs or websites or cable news shows. And this can have both a
> good and bad development for democracy. For if we choose only
> to expose ourselves to opinions and viewpoints that are in line
> with our own, studies suggest that we become more polarized,
> more set in our ways. That will only reinforce and even deepen
> the political divides in this country.
>
> [I]f you're somebody who only reads the editorial page of
> the *New York Times,* try glancing at the page of the *Wall Street
> Journal* once in a while. If you're a fan of Glenn Beck or Rush

Limbaugh, try reading a few columns on the Huffington Post website. It may make your blood boil; your mind may not be changed. But the practice of listening to opposing views is essential for effective citizenship. It is essential for democracy.[14]

Despite Obama's plea for a new civility, there is every indication that U.S. politics will continue to be characterized by a vast partisan divide—an electoral chasm that manifests itself in public opinion polls, presidential and congressional elections, and an impenetrable partisanship in the hallowed halls of Congress.

Minor Parties

In the current hyperpartisan atmosphere, voters may be poised for new choices, and they may find outlets in minor party candidates. Information technology has afforded minor parties a greater opportunity than ever before to communicate with a large pool of voters at minimal cost. Thus, the contemporary third parties mentioned in Chapter 9 will continue to have an active presence in cyberspace. Although we do not foresee an end to the two-party model, stress points in the political system caused by growing polarization may increase the appeal of alternative voices.

The Tea Party certainly captures the public's willingness to hear new voices. However, there are signs that the Tea Party may already be declining in strength as a movement. By mid-2011, only 26 percent of registered voters considered themselves to be Tea Party supporters; an overwhelming 62 percent did not.[15] Moreover, for the first time since its inception, a plurality held unfavorable views of the Tea Party movement. According to an April 2011 poll, 47 percent had an unfavorable impression of the Tea Party; just 33 percent were favorably disposed.[16] Not surprisingly, only 8 percent of respondents in a June 2011 survey wanted the 2012 Republican presidential nominee to be part of the Tea Party; 27 percent did not want the nominee to be from the Tea Party; and 61 percent said it did not matter to them.[17]

A PARTY OF GRIEVANCE VERSUS A PARTY OF GOVERNMENT

One decade into the new millennium, Americans are beset with a public life that is marked by the failure of parties to effectively run the government. In 2010, 52 percent of voters in the midterm elections held an *unfavorable* view of the Democratic Party. This view is not surprising given the historic losses suffered by Democrats—the worst defeat for the party since 1946. But, equally surprising, were the very negative views voters had of the victorious Republicans: 53 percent held an *unfavorable* view of the GOP.[18] Even as the parties grow in strength and importance, we react negatively to the political polarization that is reflective of their newfound strength. This issue is particularly acute for Republicans who face a choice in 2012: either select a presidential candidate whose overtly partisan views satisfy their political base, or nominate someone who can broadly appeal to notoriously antipartisan independents. While Republicans would preferably like to accomplish both goals, their partisan base may make that impossible. This explains some of the difficulty Republicans have had in getting their presidential field launched. By mid-2011, the list of would-be Republican presidential candidates was not yet settled, and dissatisfaction with the party's list of prospective presidential nominees was rampant. Just 45 percent of voters who would cast a ballot in the 2012 Republican presidential primaries said they were satisfied with their choices; 45 percent were not.[19] Democrats do not have to face this issue in 2012, as the lack of intraparty opposition to Barack Obama's renomination makes this point moot.

Although we may hold the parties in low regard, we still expect them to get things done. Perhaps more than in the distant past, when Jeffersonian localism was ascendant, Americans continue to look to the party-in-government to keep them financially secure and physically safe, to carry out the desires of the Framers "to form a more perfect Union, establish Justice, insure domestic Tranquility, provide for the common defense, promote the general Welfare, and secure the Blessings of Liberty." Undoubtedly, public opinion of Democrats and Republicans is diminished when the parties are perceived as failing to deliver, as the public has blamed both parties for insufficiently addressing the economic damage caused by the Great Recession. But that does not mean we stop seeking results within the confines of a two-party system that has been the hallmark of U.S. politics for generations.

Thus, we are presented with a paradox: A new century when the two parties are stronger than ever is also an age when the party system deeply disappoints. If the past is a good predictor, we are likely to see the parties struggle to respond to public pressure and manage to adapt, albeit imperfectly, to demands for more effective performance. This is what they have always done. And, while it is possible that our networked age will eventually herald a return to the amateur politics of a redefined localism, for the time being the parties hold the upper hand as large, mass-based institutions, for we live in a time of nationalized politics. Hamilton might be unnerved by how poorly these institutions are currently received, but even Jefferson would have to concede that, for the time being, Hamilton is winning the debate.

Notes

ACKNOWLEDGMENTS NOTE

1. Office of the Press Secretary, "Remarks by the President at a Memorial Service for the Victims of the Shooting in Tucson, Arizona," McKale Memorial Center, University of Arizona, Tucson, Arizona, January 12, 2011.

INTRODUCTION NOTES

1. See Dick Wirthlin with Wynton C. Hall, *The Greatest Communicator: What Ronald Reagan Taught Me about Politics, Leadership, and Life* (Hoboken, NJ: John Wiley and Sons, 2004), pp. 78–79.

2. David S. Broder, *The Party's Over: The Failure of Politics in America* (New York: Harper and Row, 1972), p. xvi.

3. Everett C. Ladd, "Realignment? No. Dealignment? Yes," *Public Opinion,* Volume 3, Number 5, October/November 1980, p. 55.

4. Wilson Carey McWilliams, "The Meaning of the Election," in Gerald M. Pomper, ed., *The Election of 1980* (Chatham, NJ: Chatham House Publishers, 1981), p. 170.

5. Richard Wirthlin quoted in "Face Off: A Conversation with the Presidents' Pollsters—Patrick Caddell and Richard Wirthlin," *Public Opinion,* Volume 3, Number 6, December/January 1981, p. 64.

6. Quoted in John Kenneth White, *The Fractured Electorate: Political Parties and Social Change in Southern New England* (Hanover, NH: University Press of New England, 1983), p. 79.

7. Quoted in Dudley Clendinen, "The Medium and Mondale," *New York Times,* November 9, 1984, p. A1.

8. See Theodore J. Lowi, *The Personal President: Power Invested, Promise Unfulfilled* (Ithaca, NY: Cornell University Press, 1985).

9. American Political Science Association, *Toward a More Responsible Two-Party System* (New York: Rinehart, 1950), p. 93.

10. Quoted in Jonathan Alter, *The Promise: President Obama: Year One* (New York: Simon & Schuster, 2010), p. 36.

11. Quoted in Dan Balz and Haynes Johnson, *The Battle for America, 2008: The Story of an Extraordinary Election* (New York: Penguin Group, 2009), p. 369.

12. See Richard Wolffe, *Renegade: The Making of a President* (New York: Crown Publishers, 2009), p. 1, and Balz and Johnson, *The Battle for America, 2008,* p. 371.

13. Ibid., p. 11.

14. Quoted in Evan Thomas and the staff of *Newsweek, A Long Time Coming: The Inspiring, Combative 2008 Campaign and the Historic Election of Barack Obama* (New York: Public Affairs, 2009), p. 179.

15. John McCain, Concession Speech, Phoenix, Arizona, November 4, 2008.

16. Barack Obama, Victory Speech, Chicago, Illinois, November 5, 2008.

17. Quoted in Alter, *The Promise,* p. 40.

18. Ibid., p. 41.

19. Ibid., p. 38.

20. Edison Media Research and Mitofsky International, exit polls, November 4, 2008.

21. Hugh Sidey, "A Conversation with Reagan," *Time,* September 3, 1984.

22. See http://www.opensecrets.org/pres08/summary .php?cid=N00009638. Accessed June 16, 2009.

23. "Behind the Scenes: Campaign '08 Strategists Talk Candidly," *On the Record: A Publication of the Annenberg Public Policy Center of the University of Pennsylvania,* May 2009, Volume 2, Number 2, p. 9.

CHAPTER ONE NOTES

1. George Washington, "Farewell Address," September 17, 1796. Reprinted as Senate Document Number 3, 102nd Cong., 1st sess., 1991.

2. Abraham Lincoln, "Address to the Young Men's Lyceum of Springfield, Illinois," in *Abraham Lincoln: Speeches and Writings, 1832–1858* (New York: Library of America), pp. 32–33.

3. Quoted in James MacGregor Burns, *Cobblestone Leadership: Majority Rule, Minority Power* (Norman: University of Oklahoma Press, 1990), p. 5.

4. Ibid.

5. John F. Kennedy, *Profiles in Courage* (New York: Harper, 1956).

6. Caroline Kennedy, ed., *Profiles in Courage for Our Time* (New York: Hyperion, 2002).

7. *USA Today*/Gallup Poll, October 28–31, 2010. Text of question: "Thinking ahead to your vote in the election for Congress this November, what will make the biggest difference in how you vote for Congress in your district— national issues, local or state issues, the candidate's character and experience, or the candidate's political party?" National issues, 37 percent; local or state issues, 25 percent; character/experience, 22 percent; political party, 11 percent; other (volunteered), 2 percent; no opinion, 3 percent.

8. James Madison, "Federalist 10," in Edward Meade Earle, ed., *The Federalist* (New York: Modern Library, 1937), p. 77.

9. Ibid., p. 59.

10. Ibid., p. 61.

11. Quoted in James Thomas Flexner, *Washington: The Indispensable Man* (New York: New American Library, 1974), p. 263.

12. Washington, "Farewell Address."

13. Quoted in David McCullough, *John Adams* (New York: Simon & Schuster, 2001), p. 422.

14. Quoted in A. James Reichley, *The Life of the Parties: A History of American Political Parties* (New York: Free Press, 1992), p. 29.

15. David Herbert Donald, *Lincoln* (New York: Touchstone Books, 1995), p. 537.

16. See Richard Morin and E. J. Dionne Jr., "Majority of Voters Say Parties Have Lost Touch," *Washington Post,* July 8, 1992, p. 1.

17. Democracy Corps, poll, January 22–25, 2006. Text of question: "Which one of the following best describes what the corruption in Washington is all about? Bad apples in both parties enriching themselves in Washington, big corporations exerting too much influence in Washington, corrupt lobbyists influencing and bribing individual members of Congress, one party with so much power in Washington that it becomes arrogant and overreaches?" Bad apples in both parties enriching themselves in Washington, 39 percent; big corporations exerting too much influence in Washington, 23 percent; corrupt lobbyists influencing and bribing individual members of Congress, 19 percent; one party with so much power in Washington that it becomes arrogant and overreaches, 16 percent; none of the above (volunteered), 1 percent; don't know/no answer, 2 percent.

18. Barack Obama, Keynote Address to the 2004 Democratic National Convention, Boston, July 27, 2004.

19. President Ford Committee, "Ford Campaign Strategy Plan," August 1976. Courtesy of Gerald R. Ford Library.

20. George W. Bush, Acceptance Speech, Republican National Convention, Philadelphia, Pennsylvania, August 3, 2000.

21. See Al Gore, Acceptance Speech, Democratic National Convention, Los Angeles, California, August 17, 2000.

22. Quoted in Leon D. Epstein, *Political Parties in the American Mold* (Madison: University of Wisconsin Press, 1986), p. 18.

23. Amicus curiae brief filed by the Committee for Party Renewal in *Colorado Republican Federal Campaign Committee v. Federal Election Commission,* February 1996, p. 3. John K. White, personal copy.

24. Committee for Party Renewal, "Statement of Principles," September 1977. John K. White, personal copy.

25. V. O. Key Jr., *Politics, Parties, and Pressure Groups* (New York: Crowell, 1958), p. 23.

26. See Everett Carll Ladd with Charles D. Hadley, *Transformations of the American Party System* (New York: Norton, 1975), p. 1.

27. The PIE, PO, PIG model was first developed by Ralph M. Goldman in 1951. See Ralph M. Goldman, *Party Chairmen and Party Faction, 1789–1900* (PhD diss., University of Chicago, 1951), introduction; and Ralph M. Goldman, *The National Party Chairmen and Committees: Factionalism at the Top* (New York: M. E. Sharpe, 1990).

28. Daniel Bell, *The Coming of Post-Industrial Society* (New York: Basic Books, 1973).

29. Bureau of Labor Statistics, "Usual Weekly Earnings of Wage and Salary Workers Second Quarter, 2011," news release, July 19, 2011. See http://data.bls .gov/search/query/results?cx=013738036195919377644:6ih0hfrgl50&cof=FORI D:10&filter=0&sa=Search&q=blue+collar#913. Accessed September 5, 2011.

30. See "Even More E-Mail?," *Opinion Wire*, October 18, 2001.

31. Interview with Mitch Stewart, Organizing for America, Democratic National Committee, Washington, D.C., May 27, 2010.

32. Joseph A. Schlesinger, *Political Parties and the Winning of Office* (Ann Arbor: University of Michigan, 1991).

33. Leon D. Epstein, *Political Parties in Western Democracies* (New Brunswick, NJ: Transaction Books, 1980).

34. John H. Aldrich, *Why Parties?* (Chicago: University of Chicago Press, 1995).

35. "Thoughts on the Cause of the Present Discontents" (1770), in Paul Langford, ed., *The Writings and Speeches of Edmund Burke* (Oxford: Clarendon Press, 1981), p. 317.

36. Jay M. Shafritz, *The Dorsey Dictionary of American Government and Politics* (Chicago: Dorsey Press, 1988).

37. Alexis de Tocqueville, *Democracy in America*, Richard D. Heffner, ed. (New York: New American Library, 1956), p. 90.

38. George W. Bush, Address to Congress, Washington, D.C., September 20, 2001.

39. Seymour Martin Lipset, *American Exceptionalism: A Double-Edged Sword* (New York: Norton, 1996).

40. Daniel Boorstin, *The Genius of American Politics* (Chicago: University of Chicago Press, 1953), p. 14.

41. See William Nisbet Chambers, "Party Development and the American Mainstream," in William Nisbet Chambers and Walter Dean Burnham, eds., *The American Party Systems* (New York: Oxford University Press, 1975), p. 6.

42. Quoted in Reichley, *The Life of the Parties*, p. 40.

43. See Morton J. Frisch, ed., *Selected Writings and Speeches of Alexander Hamilton* (Washington, DC: American Enterprise Institute, 1985), p. 316.

44. Quoted in Ted Morgan, *FDR: A Biography* (New York: Simon & Schuster, 1985), p. 38.

45. Quoted in Richard Reeves, *The Reagan Detour* (New York: Simon & Schuster, 1985), p. 19.

46. Quoted in Robert F. Kennedy, *To Seek a Newer World* (New York: Doubleday, 1967), p. 56.

47. Quoted in A. James Reichley, "Party Politics in a Federal Polity," in John Kenneth White and Jerome M. Mileur, eds., *Challenges to Party Government* (Carbondale: Southern Illinois University Press, 1992), p. 43.

48. Barack Obama, Commencement Address, University of Michigan, Ann Arbor, May 1, 2010.

49. 1936 Republican National Platform, as reprinted in the *New York Times,* June 12, 1936, p. 1.

50. Alfred M. Landon, "Text of Governor Landon's Milwaukee Address on Social Security," Milwaukee, Wisconsin, September 27, 1936; Available at http://199.173.224.3/history/alfspeech.html.

51. Republican Party, *A Pledge to America: A New Governing Agenda Built on the Priorities of Our Nation, the Principles We Stand For, and America's Founding Values* (Washington, DC: Republican Party, 2010), p. 2.

52. Ibid., p. 16.

CHAPTER TWO NOTES

1. E. E. Schattschneider, *Party Government* (New York: Rinehart, 1942), p. 1.

2. Harris poll, November 29, 2010. See Harris Interactive, at http://www.harrisinteractive.com/Insights/HarrisVault.aspx.

3. Howard Bement, ed., *Burke's Speech on Conciliation with America* (Norwood, MA: Ambrose and Company, 1922), pp. 45, 54–55, 61.

4. Quoted in David McCullough, *John Adams* (New York: Simon & Schuster, 2001), p. 422.

5. "Essays of Brutus, October 18, 1787," in Robert Ketcham, ed., *The Anti-Federalist Papers and the Constitutional Convention Debates* (New York: Signet Classic, 2003), p. 277.

6. Alexander Hamilton, James Madison, and John Jay, "Federalist 57," in Edward Mead Earle, ed., *The Federalist* (New York: Modern Library, 1937), p. 370.

7. Quoted in A. James Reichley, *The Life of the Parties: A History of American Political Parties* (New York: Free Press, 1992), p. 42.

8. Quoted in McCullough, *John Adams,* p. 422.

9. Cited in Thomas E. Patterson, *The American Democracy* (New York: McGraw-Hill, 1990), p. 350.

10. Quoted in James Thomas Flexner, *Washington: The Indispensable Man* (New York: New American Library, 1974), p. 276.

11. Quoted in Reichley, *The Life of the Parties,* p. 52.

12. Ibid., p. 64.

13. Quoted in Joseph J. Ellis, *Founding Brothers: The Revolutionary Generation* (New York: Vintage Books, 2000), p. 204.

14. *Marbury v. Madison,* 1 Cr. 137 (1803).

15. See A. James Reichley, "Party Politics in a Federal Polity," in John Kenneth White and Jerome M. Mileur, eds., *Challenges to Party Government* (Carbondale: Southern Illinois University Press, 1992), p. 44. The originator of the phrase was New York governor William Marcy, a close Van Buren ally.

16. Quoted in Reichley, *The Life of the Parties,* p. 120.

17. Quoted in Elinor C. Hartshorn, "Know-Nothings," in L. Sandy Maisel, ed., *Political Parties and Elections in the United States: An Encyclopedia* (New York: Garland, 1991), p. 549.

18. Quoted in William E. Gienapp, "Formation of the Republican Party," in Maisel, *Political Parties and Elections in the United States,* p. 399.

19. Quoted in James Albert Woodburn, *Political Parties and Party Problems in the United States* (New York: Putnam, 1903), pp. 416–417.

20. "Happy Birthday, Mr. Jefferson," posted by Hogan on RedState, April 13, 2010.

21. "Jefferson, Madison, Hamilton: Left-wing Radicals," posted by Doc Dorango on Daily Kos, December 22, 2010.

CHAPTER THREE NOTES

1. Charles Dickens, *American Notes* (London: Chapman & Hall, 1842), p. 149, as cited in Howard L. Reiter, *Parties and Elections in Corporate America,* 2nd ed. (New York: Longman, 1993), p. 6.

2. American National Election Study Cumulative Data File, 1952–2000. Information collected online at http://www.umich.edu/~nes/ nesguide/ nesguide.htm.

3. CBS News, poll, November 7–10, 2008. Text of question: "Did anyone call you or talk to you in person on behalf of either major presidential campaign about coming out to vote? (If yes,) From which campaign?" Yes, Obama campaign, 14 percent; Yes, McCain campaign, 5 percent; Yes, both campaigns, 14 percent; No, neither campaign, 65 percent; Don't know/no answer, 2 percent.

4. "Progressive Platform, 1912," in Kirk H. Porter and Donald Bruce Johnson, *National Party Platforms, 1840–1968* (Urbana: University of Illinois Press, 1970), p. 173.

5. Frances Fox Piven and Richard A. Cloward, *Why Americans Still Don't Vote, and Why Politicians Want It That Way* (Boston: Beacon Press, 2000), p. 89.

6. Franklin D. Roosevelt, Address to the Commonwealth Club, 1932. Quoted in Sidney M. Milkis, "Programmatic Liberalism and Party," in John Kenneth White and Jerome M. Mileur, eds., *Challenges to Party Government* (Carbondale: Southern Illinois University Press, 1992), p. 111.

7. Barry M. Goldwater, "Acceptance Speech," Republican National Convention, San Francisco, California, July 16, 1964.

8. Edwin Diamond and Stephen Bates, *The Spot: The Rise of Political Advertising on Television* (Cambridge, MA: MIT Press, 1988).

9. See Joe McGinniss, *The Selling of the President, 1968* (New York: Trident, 1969).

10. Philip A. Klinkner, *The Losing Parties: Out-Party National Committees, 1956–1993* (New Haven, CT: Yale University Press, 1994), p. 39.

11. Ibid., p. 144.

12. A. James Reichley, *The Life of the Parties: A History of American Political Parties* (New York: Free Press, 1992), p. 356.

13. John F. Bibby, "Party Renewal in the National Republican Party," in Gerald M. Pomper, ed., *Party Renewal in America: Theory and Practice* (New York: Praeger, 1980), p. 113.

14. Anne Campbell quoted in Klinkner, *The Losing Parties,* p. 157.

15. See Paul S. Herrnson, *Party Campaigning in the 1980s* (Cambridge, MA: Harvard University Press, 1988), p. 37.

16. See http://www.opensecrets.org/parties/totals.php?cmte=NRCC&cycle=2010 and http://www.opensecrets.org/parties/totals.php?cycle=2010&cmte=NRSC. Accessed October 25, 2010.

17. Quoted in Reichley, *The Life of the Parties,* p. 365.

18. See http://www.opensecrets.org/parties/totals.php?cmte=DSCC&cycle=2010 and http://www.opensecrets.org/parties/totals.php?cmte=DCCC&cycle=2010. Accessed October 25, 2010.

19. See, for instance, Thomas Patterson, *Out of Order* (New York: Knopf, 1993).

20. Matthew R. Kerbel, *Netroots: Online Progressives and the Transformation of American Politics* (Boulder, CO: Paradigm Publishers, 2009).

CHAPTER FOUR NOTES

1. Quoted in Fred Blumenthal, "How to Prepare for the Presidency," *Parade Magazine,* 1962. Reprinted in *The World Book Encyclopedia* (Chicago: Field Enterprises Educational Corporation, 1965), pp. 678–679.

2. Quoted in James Wooten, *Dasher: The Roots and the Rising of Jimmy Carter* (New York: Summit Books, 1978), p. 40.

3. Clinton Rossiter, *The American Presidency* (New York: New American Library, 1956), p. 250.

4. CBS News, poll, May 30–June 3, 2008.

5. See David Maraniss, *First in His Class: A Biography of Bill Clinton* (New York: Simon & Schuster, 1995), pp. 280–281. To which Carr replied, "Oh you are, are you?"

6. Ibid., p. 437.

7. The exceptions are Spiro Agnew, Nelson Rockefeller, Dan Quayle, and Dick Cheney. Quayle was a presidential candidate in 2000.

8. Quoted in John Kenneth White, "YES—Vice-Presidential Candidates Should Be Selected from the Also-Ran Category," in Gary L. Rose, ed., *Controversial Issues in Presidential Selection* (Albany: State University of New York Press, 1994), p. 80.

9. Quoted in John Heilemann and Mark Halperin, *Game Change: Obama and the Clintons, McCain and Palin, and the Race of a Lifetime* (New York: HarperCollins, 2010), p. 63.

10. Ibid., p. 94.

11. Ibid.

12. Ibid., p. 108.

13. Alexander Hamilton, "Federalist 68," in Edward Meade Earle, ed., *The Federalist* (New York: Modern Library, 1937), p. 50.

14. ABC News/*Washington Post,* poll, December 14–15, 2000.

15. In 2008, Barack Obama won the congressional district in Nebraska that included Omaha, and therefore received one electoral vote from the state that John McCain carried.

16. For more on some of these proposals see Paul Schumaker, "Analyzing the Electoral College and Its Alternatives," in Paul D. Schumaker and Burdett A. Loomis, *Choosing a President: The Electoral College and Beyond* (New York: Chatham House Publishers, 2002), especially pp. 10–30.

17. Barack Obama, Weekly Radio Address, January 23, 2010, Washington, D.C.

18. See ABC News/*Washington Post,* poll, March 25–27, 2001, and Center for Survey Research and Analysis, University of Connecticut, poll, May 16–June 6, 2001.

19. *Citizens United v. Federal Election Commission,* 558 U.S. 50 (2010).

20. See http://www.opensecrets.org. Accessed March 18, 2010.

21. See Stephen J. Wayne, "When Democracy Works: The 2008 Presidential Nominations," in William J. Crotty, *Winning the Presidency 2008* (Boulder, CO: Paradigm Publishers, 2009), pp. 57–60.

22. Quoted in James MacGregor Burns, *The Power to Lead* (New York: Simon & Schuster, 1984), p. 220.

23. Quoted in James W. Ceaser, *Presidential Selection: Theory and Development* (Princeton, NJ: Princeton University Press, 1979), p. 147.

24. Quoted in A. James Reichley, *The Life of the Parties: A History of American Political Parties* (New York: Free Press, 1992), p. 92.

25. George W. Bush wanted the 2004 Republican National Convention held in New York City and as close to September 11 (the date of the terrorist attacks) as possible in order to stress his national security credentials.

26. Reichley, *The Life of the Parties,* pp. 133–134.

27. Ibid., p. 134.

28. Quoted in E. E. Schattschneider, *The Semi-Sovereign People: A Realist's View of Democracy in America* (Hinsdale, IL: Dryden Press, 1975 reprint), p. 84.

29. Quoted in "Democrats End Two-Thirds Rule," *New York Times,* June 25, 1936, p. 1. It is interesting to note that Daniels equates the convention with the nation.

30. Lyndon B. Johnson, Address to the Nation, Washington, D.C., March 31, 1968.

31. Theodore H. White, *The Making of the President, 1968* (New York: Atheneum, 1969), p. 376.

32. George McGovern, *Grassroots: The Autobiography of George McGovern* (New York: Random House, 1977), p. 130. Eugene McCarthy became a candidate in November 1967; Robert Kennedy entered in mid-March, 1968; Lyndon Johnson withdrew from the race on March 31; Hubert Humphrey became an official candidate in late April (after most of the primary deadlines had passed). The charge that Humphrey was an unrepresentative candidate of the Democratic Party rank and file remains a contested issue. Humphrey

easily led McCarthy in the Gallup polls as the party's choice for the presidential nomination and was competitive in a three-way contest involving Eugene McCarthy, Robert Kennedy, and Humphrey. For more information, see Richard Scammon and Ben J. Wattenberg, *The Real Majority* (New York: Coward-McCann, 1970).

33. *Mandate for Reform: A Report of the Commission on Party Structure and Delegate Selection to the Democratic National Committee* (Washington, DC: Democratic National Committee, April 1970).

34. McGovern, *Grassroots*, p. 137.

35. *Cousins v. Wigoda*, 419 U.S. 477 (1975).

36. McGovern, *Grassroots*, p. 48.

37. Republicans have also been spared major changes in their delegate selection process because, unlike the Democrats, they avoided squabbles among presidential contenders involving party rules. This was possible because Republicans won most White House contests held between 1968 and 1988. Only once in this period did the rules figure in a GOP contest: In 1976, Ronald Reagan promulgated Rule 14C, which would have required prospective candidates to name their vice presidential candidates in advance of their own selection by the convention. Reagan lost this battle and the nomination to Gerald Ford, and Rule 14C was relegated to the cobwebs of history.

38. McGovern, *Grassroots*, p. 153.

39. Cited in Nelson W. Polsby, *Consequences of Party Reform* (New York: Oxford University Press, 1983), p. 114.

40. Tom Wicker, "A Party of Access?" *New York Times*, November 25, 1984, p. E17.

41. NBC News/*Wall Street Journal*, poll, April 25–28, 2008. Text of question: "In addition to primaries and caucuses, the Democratic selection rules for the presidential nominee include the votes of elected officeholders or party officials who are often called superdelegates. If one of the candidates loses among delegates selected by voters but still wins the nomination by winning among superdelegates, would you consider that nominee legitimate, would you consider that nominee not legitimate, or do you not have an opinion either way?" Would consider nominee legitimate, 31 percent; would consider nominee not legitimate, 37 percent; no opinion either way, 27 percent; not sure, 5 percent.

42. CBS News/*New York Times*, poll, February 20–24, 2008. Text of question: "The 4,048 delegates to the (2008) Democratic Convention include 795 superdelegates. Superdelegates, a distinction the party created in 1982, include some elected officials like governors and members of Congress as well as some unelected people who have other ties to the Democratic Party. Should they decide based on the votes the candidates have received overall, or the votes the candidates received in their state?" Based on overall votes, 62 percent; votes received in their state, 36 percent; don't know/no answer, 2 percent.

43. Ibid.

44. CBS News/*New York Times*, poll, February 20–24, 2008. Text of question: "The 4,048 delegates to the (2008) Democratic Convention include 795 superdelegates. Superdelegates, a distinction the party created in 1982, include some elected officials like governors and members of Congress as well as some unelected people who have other ties to the Democratic Party. Which of these comes closest to your thinking about how the superdelegates should

decide who to vote for at the party's convention in August? The superdelegates should vote for whichever candidate received the most votes in the primaries and caucuses. The superdelegates should vote for whomever they want. The superdelegates should vote for the candidate they think has the best change to win (the presidential election) in November?" Vote for the candidates with most votes, 52 percent; vote for whomever they want, 25 percent; vote for the candidate with the best chance to win, 20 percent; don't know/no answer, 3 percent.

45. Ibid.

46. Opinion Research Corporation/CNN, poll, March 14–16, 2008. Text of question: "As you may know, nearly 800 delegates to the (2008) Democratic Convention are party leaders and elected officials known as superdelegates. These superdelegates are not chosen in primaries or caucuses and are able to support any (presidential) candidate they want. In general, do you think it is a good idea or a bad idea for the Democratic Party to have superdelegates at the national convention?" Good idea, 42 percent; bad idea, 50 percent; mixed (volunteered), 5 percent; no opinion, 3 percent.

47. Democratic National Committee, *Report of the Democratic Change Commission,* December 2009. See http://my.democrats.org/page/content/changecommissionreport. Accessed June 20, 2010.

48. The states that could hold contests before the first Tuesday in March are Iowa, New Hampshire, South Carolina, and Nevada. No state could hold either a caucus or a primary before February 1, 2012. See Susan Milligan, "2012 Primary Plans Would Keep New Hampshire First," *Boston Globe,* June 8, 2010. See http://www.boston.com/news/nation/washington/articles/2010/06/08/1012_primary_plans. Accessed June 8, 2010. See also Philip Elliot, "Democrats 2012 Election Calendar: Iowa, New Hampshire, and Nevada Lead the Way," *Huffington Post,* July 9, 2010. See http://www.huffingtonpost.com/2010/07/09/democrats-2012-election-c_n_641300.html. Accessed July 10, 2010.

49. See http://www.washingtonpost.com/wp-dyn/content/article/2010/08/06/AR2010080604069.html. Accessed October 25, 2010. The proposed changes in the Republican presidential selection process would take effect only if and when Democrats adopt a convention calendar that also restricts states other than Iowa, New Hampshire, Nevada, and South Carolina from having their primaries and caucuses before March 1, 2012.

50. Richard Reeves, *President Kennedy: Profile of Power* (New York: Simon & Schuster, 1993), p. 14.

51. Walter F. Morse, "Political Convention," *World Book Encyclopedia,* vol. 15 (Chicago: Field Enterprises Educational Corporation, 1964), pp. 553–554.

CHAPTER FIVE NOTES

1. See James MacGregor Burns, *Roosevelt: The Lion and the Fox* (New York: Harcourt, Brace, 1956), pp. 452–454.

2. Theodore H. White, *The Making of the President, 1960* (New York: Signet Books, 1961), p. 30.

3. See Julie Nixon Eisenhower, *Pat Nixon: The Untold Story* (New York: Simon & Schuster, 1986), pp. 246–247.

4. Quoted in Jake Tapper, *Down and Dirty: The Plot to Steal the Presidency* (Boston: Little, Brown 2001), p. 41.

5. Ibid., p.37.

6. Edison Media and Mitofsky International, exit poll, November 8, 2008.

7. Quoted in Michael E. McGerr, *The Decline of Popular Politics: The American North, 1865–1928* (New York: Oxford University Press, 1986), p.13.

8. Paul F. Lazarsfeld, Bernard R. Berelson, and Hazel Gaudet, *The People's Choice* (New York: Columbia University Press, 1940).

9. Bernard R. Berelson, Paul F. Lazarsfeld, and William N. McPhee, *Voting* (Chicago: University of Chicago Press, 1948).

10. Gallup poll, October 9–14, 1952. Text of question: "Which presidential candidate—Stevenson or Eisenhower—do you think could handle the Korean situation best?" Eisenhower, 65 percent; Stevenson, 19 percent; no difference (volunteered), 8 percent; no opinion, 8 percent.

11. Angus Campbell, Philip E. Converse, Warren E. Miller, and Donald E. Stokes, *The American Voter* (New York: Wiley, 1960).

12. Ibid., p. 148.

13. Edison Media Research and Mitofsky International, exit poll, November 8, 2008.

14. John Zogby, *The Way We'll Be: The Zogby Report on the Transformation of the American Dream* (New York: Random House, 2008), pp. 91–119.

15. Quinnipiac University Poll, March 22–23, 2010. Text of question: "From what you've heard or read, do you mostly approve or mostly disapprove of the changes to the health care system just passed by Congress?" Mostly approve, 40 percent; mostly disapprove, 49 percent; unsure, 11 percent. Republicans: approve, 9 percent; disapprove, 82 percent; unsure, 9 percent. Democrats: approve, 71 percent; disapprove, 18 percent; unsure, 11 percent. Independents: approve, 36 percent; disapprove, 53 percent; unsure, 11 percent.

16. Gerald M. Pomper, "Toward a More Responsible Two-Party System? What, Again?" *Journal of Politics* 33 (1971): p. 936.

17. Norman H. Nie, Sidney Verba, and John R. Petrocik, *The Changing American Voter* (Cambridge, MA: Harvard University Press, 1976).

18. Anthony Downs, *An Economic Theory of Democracy* (New York: Harper, 1957).

19. NBC News/*Wall Street Journal,* poll, June 17–21, 2010. Text of question: "Generally speaking, do you think of yourself as a Democrat, a Republican, an Independent, or something else? (If Democrat/Republican, ask:) Would you call yourself a strong Democrat/Republican or a not very strong Democrat/Republican? (If Independent, ask:) Do you think of yourself as closer to the Republican Party, closer to the Democratic Party, or do you think of yourself as strictly Independent?" Strong Democrat, 19 percent; not very strong Democrat, 14 percent; independent/lean Democrat, 12 percent; strictly independent, 14 percent; independent/lean Republican, 10 percent; not very strong Republican, 10 percent; strong Republican, 16 percent; other (volunteered), 4 percent; not sure, 1 percent.

20. Herbert F. Weisberg, "A Multidimensional Conceptualization of Party Identification," in Richard G. Niemi and Herbert F. Weisberg, *Controversies in Voting Behavior,* 2d ed. (Washington, DC: Congressional Quarterly Press, 1984).

21. In 1994, the last time this question was asked, the results were as follows: Democrats: 0–10 degrees, 4 percent; 11–20 degrees, 6 percent; 21–30 degrees, 10 percent; 31–40 degrees, 10 percent; 41–49 degrees, 0 percent; 50 degrees, 20 percent; 51–60 degrees, 16 percent; 61–70 degrees, 16 percent; 71–80 degrees, 2 percent; 81–90 degrees, 10 percent; 91–100 degrees, 5 percent; don't know /can't judge, 1 percent. Republicans: 0–10 degrees, 3 percent; 11–20 degrees, 4 percent; 21–30 degrees, 6 percent; 31–40 degrees, 9 percent; 41–49 degrees, 1 percent; 50 degrees, 1 percent; 51–60 degrees, 18 percent; 61–70 degrees, 16 percent; 71–80 degrees, 2 percent; 81–90 degrees, 12 percent; 91–100 degrees, 4 percent; don't know/can't judge, 2 percent. See Center for Political Studies, poll, November 9, 1994–January 9, 1995.

22. Quoted in Alan Brinkley, *The End of Reform: New Deal Liberalism and War* (New York: Knopf, 1995), p. 16.

23. "Moving Right Along? Campaign '84's Lessons for 1988: An Interview with Peter Hart and Richard Wirthlin," *Public Opinion* (December/January 1985): p. 8.

24. Gallup poll, August 3–8, 1951. Text of question: "Suppose a young person just turned 21, asked you what the Republican party (Democratic party) stands for today—what would you tell them?" The number one Republican response, 16 percent, was "for the privileged few, moneyed interests." The number one Democratic response, 19 percent, was "for the working man, for the public benefit, for the common man."

25. V. O. Key Jr., "A Theory of Critical Elections," *Journal of Politics* 17 (February 1955): pp. 3–18.

26. V. O. Key Jr., "Secular Realignment and the Party System," *Journal of Politics* 21 (May 1959): p. 199.

27. Walter Dean Burnham, *Critical Elections and the Mainsprings of American Politics* (New York: Norton, 1970), p. 10.

28. Kevin P. Phillips, *The Emerging Republican Majority* (New Rochelle, NY: Arlington House, 1969), p. 25.

29. See, for example, Dan Balz, "Team Bush: The Iron Triangle," *Washington Post,* July 23, 1999, p. C1.

30. John B. Judis and Ruy Teixeira, *The Emerging Democratic Majority* (New York: Scribner, 2002).

31. See John Kenneth White, *Barack Obama's America: How New Conceptions of Race, Family, and Religion Ended the Reagan Era* (Ann Arbor: University of Michigan Press, 2009).

32. Democrats gained 75 House seats in 1948. Truman made Congress an issue by running against what he called the "Do Nothing" 80th Congress.

33. Yankelovich, Skelly, and White, survey, September 20–22, 1983. Text of question: "Do you feel that the Democratic party or the Republican party can do a better job of handling ... or don't you think there is any real difference between them?" The "no difference" results were as follows: reducing crime, 58 percent; stopping the spread of communism, 52 percent; dealing effectively with the U.S.S.R., 48 percent; providing quality education, 47 percent; reducing the risk of nuclear war, 46 percent; providing health care, 46 percent; reducing waste and inefficiency in government, 45 percent; protecting the environment, 45 percent.

34. Everett C. Ladd, "Like Waiting for Godot: The Uselessness of Realignment for Understanding Change in Contemporary American Politics," *Polity* XXII, no. 3 (Spring 1990): p. 512.

35. Ibid., p. 518.

36. See David R. Mayhew, *Electoral Realignments: A Critique of an American Genre* (New Haven, CT: Yale University Press, 2002), passim.

37. Key, "A Theory of Critical Elections," pp. 16–17.

38. See John Kenneth White, "Partisanship in the 1984 Presidential Election: The Rolling Republican Realignment," paper prepared for the 1985 Annual Meeting of the Southwestern Political Science Association, March 20–23, 1985, Houston, Texas.

39. Ronald Reagan, Inaugural Address, Washington, D.C., January 20, 1981.

40. Walter Dean Burnham, "Realignment Lives: The 1994 Earthquake and Its Implications," in Colin Campbell and Bert A. Rockman, eds., *The Clinton Presidency: First Appraisals* (Chatham, NJ: Chatham House, 1996), p. 370.

41. For more on this see John Kenneth White, *The Values Divide: American Politics and Culture in Transition* (Washington, DC: Congressional Quarterly Press, 2003).

42. Harold D. Lasswell, *Politics: Who Gets What, When, How* (New York: Meridian Books, 1958).

CHAPTER SIX NOTES

1. Mary Clare Jalonick, "The Best Sites of the 2000 Campaign," *Campaigns and Elections* (January 2001): pp. 70–74.

2. Chuck Raasch, "Political Parties Deploy Web Erratically, Study Says," Gannett News Service, April 11, 2002.

3. Ibid.

4. Remarks by Governor Howard Dean to the Democratic National Committee Winter Meeting, Washington, D.C., February 21, 2003.

5. Joe Trippi, *The Revolution Will Not Be Televised: Democracy, the Internet, and the Overthrow of Everything* (New York: Harper Paperbacks, revised 2008).

6. Ibid.

7. Matthew R. Kerbel and Joel David Bloom, "Blog for America and Civic Involvement," *Harvard International Journal of Press/Politics* Volume 10, Number 4 (2005): pp. 3–27.

8. Trippi, *The Revolution*.

9. Matthew R. Kerbel, *Netroots: Online Progressives and the Transformation of American Politics* (Boulder, CO: Paradigm Publishers, 2009), p. 135.

10. Trippi, *The Revolution*.

11. Ibid., p. 100.

12. Kerbel, *Netroots*, pp. 138–139.

13. Joe Antonio Vargas, "Obama's Wide Web," Washingtonpost.com, August 20, 2008.

14. Cited in Sean Quinn, "On the Road: Toledo, OH," Fivethirtyeight.com, October 14, 2008.

15. Chris Bowers and Matthew Stoller, "Emergence of the Progressive Blogosphere: A New Force in American Politics." Newpolitics.net, August 10, 2005.

16. Ibid.

17. Ibid.

18. Jessica Clark and Tracy Van Slyke, *Beyond the Echo Chamber: Reshaping Politics Through Networked Progressive Media* (New York: The New Press, 2010).

19. Ibid.

20. Markos Moulitsas, "Better Democrats," Daily Kos, December 14, 2007, emphasis in original.

21. Joan McCarter, "AR-Sen and Wall Street Reform: The Value of a Good Primary Challenge," Daily Kos, May 13, 2010.

22. Ibid.

23. Matthew R. Kerbel, "The Dog That Didn't Bark: Obama, Netroots Progressives, and Healthcare Reform." Presented at the 2010 Dilemmas of Democracy Conference, Loyola Marymount University, Los Angeles, March 2010.

24. Christina Bellantoni, "OFA Metrics Nine Months In." Talking Points Memo, November 11, 2009.

25. Ibid.

26. Christopher Snow Hopkins, et al., "Twelve Tea Party Players To Watch," NationalJournal.com, February 4, 2010.

27. Chris Cillizza, "Utah Senator Bob Bennett Loses Convention Fight," Washingtonpost.com, May 8, 2010.

28. Brendan Farrington, "Crist, Obama Hug Haunting Florida Governor in Senate Primary," Huffington Post, http://www.huffingtonpost.com/2009/10/25/crist-obama-hug-haunting-_n_332963.html, October 25, 2009.

29. Tom Brown, "Florida's Crist Launches Independent Senate Bid," Reuters, April 29, 2010.

30. Steve Kornacki, "Rand Paul Wins Kentucky Senate Primary," Salon.com, May 18, 2010.

31. David Weigel, "Conservatives Rework Rhetoric After High-Profile New York Loss," *The Colorado Independent,* November 4, 2009.

32. John Tomasic, "Musgrave to GOP: 'Don't Just Assume We're Yours.'" *The Colorado Independent,* November 4, 2009.

CHAPTER SEVEN NOTES

1. Barack Obama, State of the Union Address, Washington, D.C., January 27, 2010.

2. Pew Research Center for the People and the Press, poll, March 11–21, 2010. Text of question: "As I read a few criticisms people have made of elected officials in Washington, please tell me if you think each is a major problem, a minor problem, or not a problem .... They are influenced by special interest money." Major problem, 82 percent; minor problem, 11 percent; not a problem, 2 percent; don't know/refused, 4 percent.

3. The First Amendment to the U.S. Constitution states, "Congress shall make no law respecting an establishment of religion, or prohibiting the free

exercise thereof; or abridging the freedom of speech, or of the press; or the right of the people peaceably to assemble, and to petition the Government for a redress of grievances."

4. Herbert E. Alexander, *Financing Politics: Money, Elections, and Political Reform*, 3d ed. (Washington, DC: Congressional Quarterly Press, 1984), pp. 5–6.

5. Robert J. Dinkin, *Campaigning in America: A History of Election Practices* (Westport, CT: Greenwood Press, 1989), p. 8.

6. Center for Responsive Politics, *A Brief History of Money in Politics* (Washington, DC: Center for Responsive Politics), p. 3.

7. As cited in Dinkin, *Campaigning in America*, p. 13.

8. Center for Responsive Politics, *A Brief History of Money in Politics*, p. 3.

9. As cited in Center for Responsive Politics, *A Brief History of Money in Politics*, p. 3.

10. See Kenneth Jost, "Campaign Finance Debates," *CQ Researcher* 20: 457–480. Retrieved July 7, 2010, from *CQ Researcher Online*, http://library .cqpress.com.proxycu.wrlc.org/cqresearcher/cqresrre2010052800.

11. For an interesting discussion of the role of money in the 1896 election, see Keith Ian Polakoff, *Political Parties in American History* (New York: Wiley, 1981), pp. 259–266.

12. The union leader mentioned here was Samuel Gompers, founder and first president of the American Federation of Labor; the senator was Boies Penrose. This quotation is cited in Center for Responsive Politics, *A Brief History of Money in Politics*, p. 5. See also George Thayer, *Who Shakes the Money Tree? American Campaign Practices from 1789 to the Present* (New York: Simon & Schuster, 1974).

13. The study was conducted by Louise Overacker. See Frank J. Sorauf, *Money in American Elections*, Scott, Foresman/Little, Brown College Division, 1988, pp. 16–25.

14. See http://www.opensecrets.org/pres08/index.php. Accessed July 31, 2010.

15. The actual cost in 2008 was $5,285,680,883. See http://uselectionatlas .org/. Accessed July 31, 2010.

16. "Non-Party Spending Doubled in 2010, But Did Not Dictate the Results," press release, Campaign Finance Institute, November 5, 2010. See http://www.cfinst.org/pdf/federal/PostElec2010_Table3_.pdf. Accessed November 8, 2010.

17. Alexander, *Financing Politics*, p. 12.

18. See Kenneth Vogel, "Axelrod Mulls Huge Pay Cut," *Politico*, November 12, 2008. See http://dyn.politico.com/printstory.cfm?uuid=92F57BD1-18FE-70B2-A8C16DDB1C51D95A. Accessed July 26, 2010.

19. PACs are defined in the law as organizations that receive contributions from 50 or more individuals and contribute money to at least 10 candidates for federal office.

20. See Louis Sandy Maisel and Mark D. Brewer, *Parties and Elections in America*, Lanham, MD: Rowman & Littlefield, 2007, p. 178.

21. Ibid., p. 180.

22. Ibid., p. 183.

23. Ibid.

24. See Brody Mullins and Alicia Mundy, "Corporate Political Giving Swings Toward the GOP," *Wall Street Journal*, September 21, 2010. See http://

online.wsj.com/article/SB10001424052748703989304575503933125159928
.html. Accessed November 8, 2010.

25. New England Survey Research Associates, poll, August 16–26, 2007.
Text of question: "Now please tell me whether you agree or disagree with the
following statements: The government should be able to place restrictions on the
amount of money a private individual can contribute to someone else's election
campaign?" Strongly agree, 48 percent; mildly agree, 16 percent; mildly disagree,
11 percent; strongly disagree, 22 percent; don't know/refused, 3 percent.

26. Greenberg Quinlan Rosner Research, poll, April 29–May 3, 2010.
Text of question: "Recently, the Supreme Court ruled on a case brought
by the group Citizens United that changed campaign finance laws and will
allow corporations, unions, and other groups to use general treasury funds on
elections. Before the decision, the law restricted money corporations and unions
could spend directly on political advertising. The Supreme Court overturned
this previous law and ruled that corporations and unions have the right to spend
money to support or oppose specific candidates. Do you agree or disagree with
this decision? If agree/disagree, ask: Is that strongly or somewhat?" Strongly
agree, 11 percent; somewhat agree, 17 percent; somewhat disagree, 18 percent;
strongly disagree, 47 percent; don't know/refused, 6 percent.

27. Pew Research Center for the People and the Press, poll conducted by
Princeton Survey Research Associates International, November 6–9, 2008. The
sample was 1,500 voters who voted in the 2008 presidential election.

28. See Jost, "Campaign Finance Debates."

29. Under the spoils system, it was common for public employees to kick
back a portion of their salary to the party machine. This practice remained
commonplace at the local level.

30. Cited in *Citizens United v. Federal Election Commission*, 558 U.S. 50, at
p. 42 (2010).

31. See Jost, "Campaign Finance Debates."

32. Ibid. The Federal Corrupt Practices Act of 1925 applied only to
congressional candidates. It said nothing about presidential campaigns.

33. Cited in *Citizens United v. Federal Election Commission*, 558 U.S. 50, at
p. 27 (2010).

34. Sorauf, *Money in American Elections*, pp. 32–33.

35. Currently, the check-off is $3.

36. Sorauf, *Money in American Elections*, p. 36.

37. Cited in Mary W. Cohn, ed., *Congressional Campaign Finances: History,
Facts, and Controversy* (Washington, DC: Congressional Quarterly, 1992), p. 42.

38. As cited in Alexander, *Financing Politics*, p. 38.

39. *Buckley v. Valeo*, 424 U.S. 1 (1976).

40. The Supreme Court also ruled that only the president, not Congress,
could appoint members of the Federal Elections Commission.

41. *Buckley v. Valeo*, 424 U.S. 1 (1976).

42. Maisel and Brewer, *Parties and Elections in America*, p. 150.

43. Ralph Nader, *Crashing the Party: Taking On the Corporate Government in an
Age of Surrender* (New York: St. Martin's Press, 2002), p. 289.

44. See David E. Rosenbaum, "Campaign Finance: Behind Debate,
Jockeying for Advantage," *New York Times*, February 14, 2002, p. A34.

45. Issue advocacy advertisements do not expressly tell voters to vote for or against a particular candidate. Rather, they imply such a position by featuring a candidate's position on an important issue. Thus, an issue advocacy advertisement can say, "Candidate Jones supports a balanced budget amendment." Or, "Candidate Smith opposes a balanced budget amendment."

46. See *Colorado Republican Federal Campaign Committee, v. FEC*, 518 U.S. 604 (1996). The Court ruled that as long as the issue advocacy advertisement did not say the words "elect," "vote for," "defeat," or "vote against," they were permitted. Many believed that the Court's decision erased the wall between issue advocacy and expressed advocacy (i.e., vote for Candidate X) that had been constructed in several previous court cases (including *Buckley v. Valeo*).

47. Trevor Potter, "New Law Follows Supreme Court Rulings," *BNA Money and Politics Report,* April 22, 2002. See also Brookings Institution, http://www.brook.edu/dybdocroot/GS/CF/debate/challenge.htm.

48. Quoted in Maisel and Brewer, *Parties and Elections in America,* p. 164.

49. Ibid.

50. See Adam Liptak, "Court Under Roberts Is Most Conservative in Decades," *New York Times,* July 24, 2010, p. 1.

51. *Federal Election Commission v. Wisconsin Right to Life, Inc.* 551 U.S. 449 (2007).

52. Year 2000 Republican presidential candidate Steve Forbes also refused to accept federal matching funds.

53. For more on this see Joe Trippi, "Down from the Mountain," speech, February 9, 2004.

54. See http://www.opensecrets.org. Accessed March 18, 2010.

55. Ibid.

56. See Maisel and Brewer, *Parties and Elections in America,* p. 187.

57. Ibid., p. 188.

58. Ibid.

59. Quoted in Jost, "Campaign Finance Debates."

60. See Justice Stevens's dissent in *Citizens United v. FEC.*

61. The five justices in the majority were Anthony Kennedy, John Roberts, Clarence Thomas, Antonin Scalia, and Samuel Alito. The four dissenters were John Paul Stevens, Ruth Bader Ginsberg, Sonya Sotomayor, and Stephen Breyer.

62. McCain-Feingold restricted television advertisements that were capable of reaching 50,000 persons in the 30- or 60-day period prior to a primary or a general election. These advertisements were banned if there was "no reasonable interpretation other than as an appeal to vote for or against a specific candidate."

63. *Citizens United v. FEC,* 558 U.S. 50, at p. 37 (2010).

64. Ibid., p. 1.

65. Ibid., p. 57.

66. Ibid., p. 49.

67. Ibid., p. 55.

68. Ibid., p. 6.

69. Ibid., p. 76.

70. Ibid., p. 21.

71. Ibid.

72. Ibid., p. 56.

73. Ibid., p. 57.

74. Ibid., p. 60.

75. Ibid., p. 90.

76. Quoted in Liptak, "Court Under Roberts Is Most Conservative in Decades," p. A1.

77. Quoted in Jost, "Campaign Finance Debates."

78. Ibid.

79. Ibid.

80. Jost, "Campaign Finance Debates."

81. See Holly Bailey, "2010 Campaigns Cost $4 Billion, and Other Fun Midterm Facts," November 5, 2010. http://news.yahoo.com/s/yblog_upshot/20101105/el_yblog_upshot/2010-was-a-4-billion-campaign-and-other-fun-facts-about-tuesdays-midterm-elections. Accessed November 8, 2010.

82. See Sharyl Attkisson, "Republican 'SuperPAC' American Crossroads Raised $24 Million in Seven Months, Report Shows," CBS News, October 21, 2010. See http://www.cbsnews.com/8301-503544_162-20020313-503544.html. Accessed November 8, 2010.

83. See "Political Parties: Overview, 2010 Spending found at http://www.opensecrets.org/parties/index.php. Accessed November 8, 2010. See also Bailey, "2010 Campaigns Cost $4 Billion, and Other Fun Midterm Facts."

CHAPTER EIGHT NOTES

1. Newt Gingrich, *Lessons Learned the Hard Way* (New York: HarperCollins, 1998), pp. 1, 2.

2. The 10 items in the Contract with America were as follows: (1) The Fiscal Responsibility Act proposed a constitutional amendment requiring the president to submit, and the Congress to pass, a balanced federal budget for each fiscal year and would give the president a line-item veto over specific budgetary provisions in a bill passed by Congress; (2) the Taking Back Our Streets Act limited federal and state habeas corpus appeals, mandated minimum sentences for and victim restitution from those convicted of gun-related crimes, replaced recently passed crime-prevention programs with block grants for local law-enforcement programs, relaxed rules for admission of evidence at criminal trials, and would speed deportation procedures for aliens convicted of serious crimes; (3) the Personal Responsibility Act limited eligibility for the federal Aid to Families with Dependent Children (AFDC) program, denied AFDC benefits to teenage mothers, imposed work requirements for those receiving AFDC benefits, and transferred much of the responsibility for social welfare programs to the states; (4) the Family Reinforcement Act granted tax credits for adoption and for care of elderly dependents and increased penalties for sexual offenses against children; (5) the American Dream Restoration Act granted tax credits for families with children, reduced taxes on some married couples, and expanded uses for Individual Retirement Accounts (IRAs); (6) the National Security Restoration Act restricted participation of U.S. forces in

U.N. peacekeeping activities, subjected all funding for and participation in U.N. peacekeeping activities to congressional approval, and reinstated development of the "Star Wars" antiballistic missile defense system and other such systems; (7) the Senior Citizens Equity Act doubled the income level beyond which Social Security benefits are reduced, reduced taxes on upper-income recipients of Social Security, and created tax benefits for the purchase of private long-term healthcare insurance; (8) the Job Creation and Wage Enhancement Act cut the capital gains tax, increased the estate tax exemption, and imposed additional requirements for and restrictions on federal regulation; (9) the Common Sense Legal Reforms Act required the loser to pay the legal expenses of the winner in lawsuits filed in federal courts, reformed product liability laws, and limited lawsuits by shareholders against companies whose stock they hold; and (10) the Citizen Legislature Act proposed a constitutional amendment to limit tenure of senators and representatives to a maximum of 12 years. See House Republican Conference, *Legislative Digest,* September 27, 1994.

3. Quoted in Linda Killian, *The Freshmen: What Happened to the Republican Revolution?* (Boulder, CO: Westview Press, 1998), p. 7.

4. Alexander Hamilton, "Federalist 68," in Alexander Hamilton, James Madison, and John Jay, *The Federalist Papers* (New York: Mentor Books, 1961), p. 414.

5. See Charles O. Jones, *The Trusteeship Presidency: Jimmy Carter and the United States Congress* (Baton Rouge: Louisiana State University Press, 1988).

6. Cited in Adam Cohen, *Nothing to Fear: FDR's Inner Circle and the Hundred Days That Created Modern America* (New York: Penguin Books, 2009), p. 40.

7. Quoted in Jonathan Alter, *The Defining Moment: FDR's Hundred Days and the Triumph of Hope* (New York: Simon & Schuster, 2006), p. 251.

8. Republican control of the Senate was short-circuited when Vermont senator Jim Jeffords left the GOP to become an independent and affiliated himself with the Democrats. For more on this, see Chapter 9.

9. Quoted in John Heilemann and Mark Halperin, *Game Change: Obama and the Clintons, McCain and Palin, and the Race of a Lifetime* (New York: HarperCollins, 2010), p. 200.

10. Capitol Journal, "In Crisis, Opportunity for Obama," *Wall Street Journal,* November 21, 2008. See http://online.wsj.com/article/SB122721278056345271.html. Accessed November 8, 2010.

11. Woodrow Wilson, Inaugural Address, Washington, D.C., March 4, 1913.

12. Quoted in Stanley Kelley Jr., *Interpreting Elections* (Princeton, NJ: Princeton University Press, 1983), p. 127.

13. See especially Richard Reeves, *President Nixon: Alone in the White House* (New York: Simon & Schuster, 2001).

14. See John F. Hoadley, "The Emergence of Political Parties in Congress, 1789–1803," *American Political Science Review* Volume 74 (1980): pp. 761, 768–769.

15. Interestingly, the provision does not require that this person be an actual member of the House, although all Speakers have been members.

16. Quoted in Jos Kraushaar, "Griffith Faults Pelosi for Switch," *Politico,* December 22, 2009.

17. Quoted in Dale Vinyard, *The Presidency* (New York: Scribner's, 1971), p. 107.

18. Committee on Political Parties, *Toward a More Responsible Two-Party System* (New York: Rinehart, 1950).

19. Ibid., p. 15.

20. Ibid., pp. 92, 94, 95.

21. See John C. Green and Paul S. Herrnson, eds., *Responsible Partisanship? The Evolution of American Parties Since 1950* (Lawrence: University of Kansas Press, 2002).

22. M. I. Ostrogorski, *Democracy and the Party System* (New York: Macmillan, 1910), p. 380.

23. Woodrow Wilson, "Leaderless Government," an address before the Virginia Bar Association, August 4, 1897, in *Public Papers,* vol. 1, pp. 336–359. Quoted in Austin Ranney, *The Doctrine of Responsible Party Government: Its Origins and Present State* (Urbana: University of Illinois Press, 1954), p. 33.

24. Quoted in David E. Price, *Bringing Back the Parties* (Washington, DC: Congressional Quarterly Press, 1984), p. 103.

25. See Michael R. Beschloss, *Taking Charge: The Johnson White House Tapes, 1963–1964* (New York: Simon & Schuster, 1997), p. 64.

26. Gerald M. Pomper, "Parliamentary Government in the United States?" in John C. Green and Daniel M. Shea, eds., *The State of the Parties: The Changing Role of Contemporary American Parties* (Lanham, MD: Rowman & Littlefield, 1999), p. 260.

27. See John H. Aldrich and David W. Rohde, "The Transition to Republican Rule in the House: Implications for Theories of Congressional Politics," *Political Science Quarterly* 112 (Winter 1997–1998), p. 563. In fewer than 100 days, 8 of the contract's 10 items had been approved by the House, thanks to nearly unanimous support from the GOP freshmen. Only two measures failed: term limits, thanks to the opposition of Judiciary Committee chairman Henry Hyde; and a provision prohibiting the Pentagon from using funds for U.N. peacekeeping operations.

28. Quoted in John E. Owens, "The Return of Party Government in the U.S. House of Representatives," *American Political Science Review* 27 (April 1997), p. 245.

29. Nicol C. Rae, *Conservative Reformers: The Republican Freshmen and the Lessons of the 104th Congress* (Armonk, NY: Sharpe, 1998), p. 69.

30. Ibid., pp. 70–71.

31. Quoted in "Washington Wire," *Wall Street Journal,* July 27, 2001, p. A1.

32. Pelosi won a special election in 1987 to fill the seat left by the late Sala Burton.

33. See Michael Barone with Richard E. Cohen and Grant Ujifusa, *The Almanac of American Politics, 2002* (Washington, DC: National Journal, 2001), p. 182.

34. See "2008 Congressional Voting Record," *ADA Today* volume 64, number 1, Spring 2009. Also available at http://www.adaction.org/media/votingrecords/2008.pdf. Accessed February 18, 2009.

35. Quoted in Aldrich and Rohde, "The Transition to Republican Rule in the House," p. 561.

36. Ibid., p. 562.

37. Ben Smith, "Health Reform Foes Plan Obama's Waterloo," *Politico*, July 17, 2009.

38. See William A. Galston, "Can a Polarized American Party System Be 'Healthy'?" *Brookings Institute Issues in Governance Studies*, April 2010, p. 4. See http://www.brookings.edu/papers/2010/04_polarization_galston.aspx. Accessed April 29, 2010.

39. NPR Staff, "Midterm Losses Bite Blue-Dog Democrats," November 6, 2010. See http://www.scpr.org/news/2010/11/06/midterm-losses-bite-blue-dog-democrats/. Accessed November 8, 2010.

40. *National Journal*, "House Rankings: How House Members Scored on Liberal-Conservative Scales in Three Issue Categories and Overall," February 28, 2009. See http://www.nationaljournal.com/njmagazine/cs_20090228_9659.php. Accessed February 10, 2010.

41. Herseth-Sandlin and Skelton were defeated for reelection in 2010.

42. *National Journal*, "Senate Rankings: How Senators Scored on Three Liberal Conservative Categories Overall," February 28, 2009. See http://www.nationaljournal.com/njmagazine/cs_20090228_4726.php. Accessed February 10, 2010.

43. Ibid.

44. Ibid.

45. Ibid.

46. Quoted in Adam Nagourney, "Democrats Reel as Senator Says No to Third Term," *New York Times*, February 15, 2010.

47. Quoted in Douglas B. Harris, "The Rise of the Public Speakership," *Political Science Quarterly* (Summer 1998), p. 198.

48. Ibid., p. 195.

49. See especially John A. Farrell, *Tip O'Neill and the Democratic Century* (Boston: Little, Brown, 2001).

50. Ibid.

51. Ibid., p. 195.

52. Ibid., pp. 193, 196, 202, 210.

53. Ibid., p. 203.

54. Ibid., p. 210.

55. John Kenneth White, interview with David Price, Washington, D.C., October 25, 2000.

56. Richard Gephardt, *An Even Better Place: America in the 21st Century*, (New York: Public Affairs, 1999), p. 18.

57. Obama Remarks at House Republican Retreat, Baltimore, Maryland, January 29, 2010. See Washingtonpost.com at http://projects.washingtonpost.com/obama-speeches/speech/173/.

58. Hamilton, "Federalist 68," p. 414.

59. Quoted in Robert F. Kennedy, *To Seek a Newer World* (New York: Doubleday, 1967), p. 56.

60. Quoted in Joe Klein, "The Town That Ate Itself," *New Yorker*, November 23, 1998, p. 80.

61. Jon Stewart, Speech on the Washington, D.C. mall, October 30, 2010. See http://www.examiner.com/celebrity-in-national/rally-to-restore-sanity-jon-stewart-s-closing-speech-full-text. Accessed November 8, 2010.

CHAPTER NINE NOTES

1. Quoted in Michael Barone with Richard E. Cohen and Grant Ujifusa, *The Almanac of American Politics, 2002* (Washington, DC: National Journal, 2001), p. 1548.

2. See Leslie Wayne, "The Caucus: A Third Party Forum," *New York Times,* October 16, 2008.

3. Clinton Rossiter, *Parties and Politics in America* (Ithaca, NY: Cornell University Press, 1960), p. 3.

4. Only Maine and Nebraska do not employ a winner-take-all electoral vote system, preferring to allot their electoral votes according to which candidate wins a particular congressional district. In 2008, Barack Obama received one electoral vote from Nebraska because he carried the congressional district that included the city of Omaha. This was the first time since 1968 when Nebraska and Maine enacted their method of allocating electoral votes that either state split their electoral votes.

5. In 1856, Fillmore was the presidential candidate of the Know-Nothing Party, receiving 22 percent of the popular vote.

6. Quoted in Ralph Nader, *Crashing the Party: Taking on the Corporate Government in an Age of Surrender* (New York: St. Martin's Press, 2002), p. 280.

7. This argument is made in John F. Bibby and L. Sandy Maisel, *Two Parties—Or More? The American Party System* (Boulder, CO: Westview Press, 1998), p. 58.

8. John McCain took the $84.1 million in 2008. See http://www.fec.gov/press/press2008/20080908cert.shtml. However, Barack Obama became the first major party nominee not to accept federal funding, as Obama was able to raise a total of $747.8 million for his entire campaign. Many believe that Obama's refusal to accept federal funds means that the Federal Election Campaign Act is essentially null and void, especially those provisions providing public funding for the general election.

9. Survey conducted by the Roper Organization, December 1939. The results were taken among "whites only." There were no dollar definitions as to what constitutes "poor" in this survey.

10. Louis Hartz, *The Liberal Tradition in America: An Interpretation of American Political Thought Since the Revolution* (New York: Harcourt Brace, 1955), p. 7.

11. Quoted in Everett Carll Ladd, *The American Ideology: An Exploration of the Origins, Meaning, and Role of American Political Ideas* (Storrs, CT: Roper Center for Public Opinion Research, 1994), p. 32.

12. Quoted in John Gerring, "A Chapter in the History of American Party Ideology: The Nineteenth Century Democratic Party, 1828–1892." Paper presented at the Northeastern Political Science Association, Newark, N.J., November 11–13, 1993, pp. 36–37. Cass made these remarks on September 2, 1852.

13. See Roy P. Basler, ed., *The Collected Works of Abraham Lincoln* (New Brunswick, NJ: Rutgers University Press, 1953), p. 323.

14. Cited in Seymour Martin Lipset, "Why No Socialism in the United States," in Seweryn Bailer and Sophia Sluzar, eds., *Radicalism in the Contemporary Age* (Boulder, CO: Westview Press, 1977), p. 40.

15. Quoted in Daniel M. Shea, ed., *Mass Politics: The Politics of Popular Culture* (New York: St. Martin's Press, 1999), p. 207.

16. Quoted in James Reston, "Liberty and Authority," *New York Times,* June 29, 1986, p. E23.

17. Phyllis F. Field, "Masons," in L. Sandy Maisel, ed., *Political Parties and Elections in the United States: An Encyclopedia* (New York: Garland, 1991), pp. 641–642.

18. Robert J. Spitzer, "Free-Soil Party," in Maisel, *Political Parties and Elections,* pp. 409–410.

19. Edward W. Chester, *A Guide to Political Platforms* (New York: Archon Books, 1977), p. 58.

20. See Elinor C. Hartshorn, "Know-Nothings," in Maisel, *Political Parties and Elections,* pp. 549–550.

21. See Chester, *A Guide to Political Platforms,* p. 70.

22. Earl R. Kruschke, *Encyclopedia of Third Parties in the United States* (Santa Barbara, CA: ABC-Clio, 1991), p. 71.

23. Quoted in Chester, *A Guide to Political Platforms,* pp. 121–135.

24. Frederick J. Augustyn Jr., "Populists (People's) Party," in Maisel, *Political Parties and Elections,* pp. 849–850.

25. But in a strange twist, the Populists refused to endorse the Democratic vice presidential candidate, Arthur Sewall, a banker from Maine.

26. "Progressive Party Platform, 1948," in Kirk H. Porter and Donald Brace Johnson, eds., *National Party Platforms: 1840–1968* (Urbana: University of Illinois Press, 1970), p. 437.

27. Ibid., p. 439.

28. Quoted in A. James Reichley, *The Life of the Parties: A History of American Political Parties* (New York: Free Press, 1992), p. 297.

29. Gallup poll, June 16–23, 1948. Text of question: "Do you think that the Henry Wallace third party is run by Communists?"

30. See The Party of No, "House Democratic Caucus in 2011, Smaller, but More Liberal," Dailycaller.com. See http://thepartyofknow.com/2010/11/04/daily-callerhouse-democratic-caucus-in-2011-smaller-but-more-liberal/. Accessed November 15, 2010.

31. See http://cpc.grijalva.house.gov/index.cfm?SectionID=2&ParentID=0&SectionTypeID=2&SectionTree=2. Accessed June 8, 2010.

32. Kruschke, *Encyclopedia of Third Parties in the United States,* p. 183.

33. Thurmond's record stood until 2010, when Lisa Murkowski won reelection to her U.S. Senate seat from Alaska on a write-in campaign. Murkowski had been defeated in the Republican primary after former governor Sarah Palin endorsed Murkowski's challenger, Joe Miller.

34. Quoted in "Ventura Leaves Reform Party." *PBS Online NewsHour.* See http://www.pbs.org/newshour/election2000/states/minnesota/ventura.html. December 10, 2002.

35. Quoted in Michael Waldman, *Potus Speaks: Finding the Words That Defined the Clinton Presidency* (New York: Simon & Schuster, 2000), p. 181.

36. See Nader, *Crashing the Party*, p. 289.

37. Gore won 266 electoral votes to Bush's 271 electoral votes (one more than needed for a majority). One elector in Washington, D.C., did not vote for Gore in order to protest to D.C.'s lack of statehood.

38. Fox News/Opinion Dynamics, poll, March 18–19, 2008. Text of question: "Do you think you would seriously consider voting for third-party candidate Ralph Nader over one of the major party candidates (for president) in November? Yes, 14 percent; no, 77 percent; don't know, 9 percent.

39. Ibid.

40. Amy Gardner, "Gauging the Scope of the Tea Party Movement in America," *Washington Post*, October 24, 2010, p. A1.

41. Ibid.

42. Roper Organization, poll, May 1938. Text of question: "Which parties would you like to see competing in the next presidential race .... Republican and Democrat only .... Republican and Democrat and minor parties as before .... Republican, Democrat, and a new strong third party .... Two new parties with all conservatives voting together and all liberals voting together?" Republican and Democrat, 44 percent; Republican and Democrat and minor parties as before, 21 percent; Republican, Democrat, and a new strong third party, 13 percent; two new parties with all conservatives voting together and all liberals voting together, 6 percent; don't know, 15 percent.

43. CNN/Opinion Research Corporation, poll, February 12–15, 2010. Text of question: "Would you favor or oppose having a third political party that would run candidates for president, Congress, and state offices against the Republican and Democratic candidates?" Favor, 64 percent; oppose, 34 percent; no opinion, 2 percent.

44. CNN/Opinion Research Corporation, poll, February 12–15, 2010. Text of question: "Suppose that having a third political party would mean that the winner of some elections would be a candidate who disagrees with you on most issues that matter to you. Would you favor or oppose having a third political party under those circumstances?" Favor a third political party under those circumstances, 59 percent; oppose a third political party under those circumstances, 41 percent.

45. See Jeffrey M. Jones, "Americans Renew Call for Third Party," Gallup poll, press release, September 17, 2010.

46. Theodore J. Lowi, "Toward a Responsible Three-Party System," in John C. Green and Daniel J. Coffey, *The State of the Parties: The Changing Role of Contemporary Party Organizations*, Lanham, MD: Rowman & Littlefield, 2011, p. 47.

CONCLUSION NOTES

1. Alexis de Tocqueville, *Democracy in America*, Richard D. Heffner, ed. (New York: New American Library, 1956), p. 194.

2. Survey by Peter D. Hart Research Associates, May 10–22, 2010. Reported in Guy Molyneux and Ruy Teixeira, with John Whaley, *Better, Not Smaller: What Americans Want from Their Federal Government* (Washington, DC: Center for American Progress, July 2010), p. 3. See http://www.americanprogress.org/issues/2010/07/pdf/what_americans_want.pdf. Accessed August 19, 2010.

3. Ibid., p. 14.

4. Ibid., p. 17.

5. Selzer and Company, poll, March 4–7, 2011. Text of question: "Turning to the healthcare bill passed last year, what is your opinion of the bill?" It should be repealed, 41 percent; see how it works, 42 percent; should be left alone, 12 percent; not sure, 5 percent.

6. Molyneux and Teixeira with Whaley, *Better, Not Smaller,* p. 18.

7. George Gallup, survey, 1936. Text of question: "Which theory of government do you favor: concentration of power in the federal government or concentration of power in the state government?" Federal government, 56 percent; state government, 44 percent.

8. Ibid.

9. E. E. Schattschneider, *Party Government* (New York: Rinehart, 1942), p. 1.

10. See Voter News Service, exit poll, November 7, 2000, Edison Media Research and Mitofsky International, exit poll, November 2, 2004, and Edison Media Research and Mitofsky International, exit poll, November 4, 2008.

11. Edison Media Research and Mitofsky International, exit poll, November 2, 2010.

12. See Mitch McConnell, Address to the Heritage Foundation, Washington, D.C., November 4, 2010. See http://republican.senate.gov/public/index.cfm?FuseAction=Blogs.View&Blog_Id=5094359f-c864-4679-a9e7-2b54ba08e472. Accessed November 17, 2010.

13. Quoted in Dan Eggen and T. W. Farnum, "Michelle Bachmann, Others Raise Millions for Political Campaigns with 'Money Blurts,'" *Washington Post,* June 20, 2011, p. A1.

14. Barack Obama, Commencement Address, University of Michigan, Ann Arbor, Michigan, May 1, 2010.

15. NBC News/*Wall Street Journal,* poll, May 5–7, 2011. Text of question: "Do you consider yourself a supporter of the Tea Party movement?" Yes, 26 percent; no, 62 percent; depends, 2 percent; not sure, 10 percent.

16. Gallup poll, April 20–23, 2011. Text of question: "Next, we'd like to get your overall opinion of some people in the news. As I read each name, please say if you have a favorable or unfavorable opinion of these people—or if you have never heard of them. How about the Tea Party movement?" Favorable, 33 percent; unfavorable, 47 percent; never heard of, 7 percent; no opinion, 13 percent.

17. CBS News, poll, June 3–7, 2011. Text of question: "Would you prefer the 2012 Republican nominee for president be someone who is part of the Tea Party movement, or someone who is not part of the Tea Party movement, or would this not matter?" Part of the Tea Party, 8 percent; not part of the Tea Party, 27 percent; doesn't matter, 61 percent; don't know/no answer, 4 percent.

18. Edison Media Research and Mitofsky International, exit poll, November 2, 2010.

19. NBC News/*Wall Street Journal,* poll, June 9–13, 2011. Text of question: "Are you satisfied or dissatisfied with your choices for the Republican presidential nomination?" Satisfied, 45 percent; dissatisfied, 45 percent; not sure, 10 percent. Asked of registered voters who say they are likely to vote in a Republican presidential primary.

Index

About the Authors

John Kenneth White is a professor of politics at the Catholic University of America. He is the author of several books on political parties and the presidency. His latest is titled *Barack Obama's America: How New Conceptions of Race, Family, and Religion Ended the Reagan Era* (University of Michigan Press 2009).

Matthew R. Kerbel is professor of political science at Villanova University. Among his eight books on mass media, the presidency, and the political process is his latest work, *Netroots: Online Progressives and the Transformation of American Politics* (Paradigm 2009).